Hollywood's
New Yorker

THE SUNY SERIES

HORIZONS OF CINEMA

MURRAY POMERANCE | EDITOR

Hollywood's New Yorker

The Making of Martin Scorsese

Marc Raymond

Cover image: Martin Scorsese on the set of *Shutter Island* (Paramount Pictures, 2010). Courtesy Photofest.

Published by State University of New York Press, Albany

Permissions

Part of Chapter One previously appeared as "Politics, Authorship and History: The Production, Reception and Marginalization of Street Scenes 1970," *Film History* 22, no. 2 (June 2010): 3–47.

Part of Chapter Five previously appeared as "Too Smart, Too Soon: The King of Comedy and American Independent Cinema Sensibility," *Film Criticism* 34, no. 1 (Fall 2009): 17–35.

For information, contact State University of New York Press, Albany, NY
www.sunypress.edu

Production by Eileen Nizer
Marketing by Anne M. Valentine

Library of Congress Cataloging-in-Publication Data

Raymond, Marc, 1975–
    Hollywood's New Yorker : the making of Martin Scorsese / Marc Raymond.
        p. cm. — (SUNY series, horizons of cinema)
    Includes bibliographical references.
    ISBN 978-1-4384-4571-7 (hc : alk. paper)— 978-1-4384-4572-4 (pb : alk. paper)
    1. Scorsese, Martin—Criticism and interpretation.   I. Title.

PN1998.3.S39R39 2013
791.4302'33092—dc23   2012014295

10 9 8 7 6 5 4 3 2 1

Contents

Illustrations

Acknowledgments

I would like to thank the staff at SUNY press for all their work in producing the book. In particular, James Peltz and Jen Stelling were very helpful in answering questions and guiding me through the process, and Murray Pomerance offered both his enthusiasm for the project and his sharp critical eye.

This project began at Carleton University in Ottawa, and I need to thank all the professors and staff within the Film Studies and Cultural Mediations departments. Mark Langer was a great mentor throughout, and Chris Faulkner contributed very useful comments on the text. The Film Studies program gave me the opportunity to teach a course on Scorsese that allowed me to work out the material, and I deeply appreciated all of the students in that class for their hard work and participation. Finally, my colleague and friend Nick Nguyen spent countless hours discussing this subject matter with me, and I am grateful for his interest in the topic and for sharing his opinions and ideas so selflessly.

I've been lucky to have numerous close friends, in both Canada and South Korea, who have helped me through the process: Dave Musgrave, Andrew and Angie Wilkes, James Missen, Mounir and Isobel Khoury, Trevor Cory, Patrick Artz, and many others I do not have space to mention. I need to thank both of my parents for their love and support, and, most of all, my wonderful wife Lisa for staying with me through this long journey.

Finally, in the course of writing this book I lost four close family members: my two uncles, Raymond Hare and Thomas Raymond, and my two grandmothers, Matilda Hare and Margaret Raymond. They are and will continue to be missed.

Introduction

Martin Scorsese and Film Culture

IN MARCH 2007 THREE VETERAN filmmakers of the New Hollywood, Francis Ford Coppola, George Lucas, and Steven Spielberg, came to the stage of the Academy Awards to present the award for Best Director. The moment this occurred, it became obvious to anyone in the know who the announced winner would be. Martin Scorsese was the prohibitive favorite, a veteran of American cinema who had been nominated five times previously without a victory. Like the three presenters, Scorsese was a director associated with the New Hollywood of the 1970s. Furthermore, he was widely regarded as the greatest of that generation and as arguably the best of all living American filmmakers. It became clear that the Oscar ceremony was carefully staged theater. Typically, the previous year's winner presents the award. In this case, it would have been Ang Lee, the winner in 2005 for *Brokeback Mountain*. The Academy decided to break with this tradition and have Coppola, Lucas, and Spielberg announce the winner.

Scorsese was thus finally inducted into the Hollywood "inside" with his fellow New Hollywood directors. Scorsese's acceptance speech tellingly made reference to the importance of film preservation and protecting Hollywood's great tradition. Scorsese was both placing himself in this tradition while referencing his own work as a cultural historian. Even as he was accepting this symbol of middlebrow respectability, Scorsese attempted to remind his audience that his true passion was not his own filmmaking but the whole of film culture. As much as possible, Scorsese worked to mitigate the move to the mainstream of Hollywood production, a move signaled shortly before his Oscar win by his signing of a major production deal with Paramount studio, the first such production deal Scorsese had in several years.

1

This long-awaited victory for Scorsese had little to do with either the quality of his film *The Departed* (2006) or with cultural prestige, especially within film culture as a whole. Paradoxically, it represented a risk of cultural status. Why this is the case is one of the many curiosities about American cinema that this book explores. As far back as Scorsese's first studio film, *Alice Doesn't Live Here Anymore* (1974), the question has been asked: Has Martin Scorsese gone Hollywood? The answer to this question is much more complex than initially thought because the idea of Hollywood is a complicated one, especially in the contemporary environment. Many variations of the term now exist: Classical Hollywood, Old Hollywood, New Hollywood, Post-Classical Hollywood, and even Independent Hollywood. In addition, Hollywood is now theorized in many ways within the film studies discipline. If Hollywood was simply a place, there could be a simpler answer to the question: Martin Scorsese went to Hollywood in 1970, and he became a studio filmmaker in 1974. Since then, he has made most of his work, especially the films on which his critical reputation rests, for the major studios. But Hollywood is more than a place. It symbolizes something much more, and what it symbolizes is neither simply embraced nor rejected by Scorsese. Rather, it is a concept and idea that Scorsese has had to negotiate.

This study examines the work of Scorsese and, with few exceptions, covers Scorsese's career in chronological order and is structured by Scorsese as an object of study. In this way, it is similar to most of the literature written about Scorsese thus far. However, it differs in almost every other way. Unlike other studies, a textual analysis of the style and themes of Scorsese's feature films is not emphasized. Scorsese the auteur is less significant to this work than his place in the field of cultural production, and Scorsese as a filmmaker is less important than Scorsese as a cultural figure. Because of the vast amount of cultural activities in which he has been involved, examining the relationship among all of Scorsese's various projects and how this has formed the figure known as "Scorsese" today is more productive. This analysis not only explains the various meanings that have developed around the idea of Scorsese, but also how these associations developed over the course of his career. My main argument is that extratextual factors, rather than the films themselves, have led to his prestigious position as an artist. And because Scorsese is an American director working for the major studios, of utmost importance is how he has negotiated with Hollywood and all of the contradictory connotations of that term.

This book deals with two broad areas. The first is the general reception of Scorsese and his work over the past few decades. I am specifically interested in examining how Scorsese's reputation has influenced the ways in which his relationship to cultural institutions has been mediated. This includes not only the commercial sector, such as Hollywood, but also cultural institutions such as the university and film archives. The second broader concern is with applying a different methodological approach to Scorsese in order to produce a broader understanding of his place within American culture. In particular, we need to move beyond the formal, critical approaches to his feature films that have dominated even the scholarly work undertaken so far. While these approaches have produced certain knowledge about Scorsese, they have also largely ignored many other questions that arise when the focus is shifted away from exclusively textual analysis. By using alternative models, particularly sociological models of aesthetic taste, a greater understanding of Scorsese's entire cultural output, including his feature films, can be reached.

Within film studies and many other fields of culture, the aesthetic debate of the past decades has concentrated on modernism versus postmodernism. This book refers to this dichotomy throughout. In using these terms, I do not wish to reinforce these binaries but rather acknowledge their continuing cultural force when discussing taste evaluation. The idea of modernism in this study is specific to a particular field of cultural production: narrative film in the United States since 1967. This is the period in which Scorsese becomes a Hollywood director, and this modernist discourse will subsequently shape how his work is received and interpreted. This modernist ideal is heavily involved in the creation of what has been dubbed the New Hollywood cinema, which is usually cited as beginning in 1967 with the films *Bonnie and Clyde* (Arthur Penn, 1967) and *The Graduate* (Mike Nichols, 1967) and continues to be used in connection with the period of the late 1960s and early 1970s, often to define that era as distinctive in quality as compared to the postmodernism of today. However, New Hollywood cinema and the films of Martin Scorsese are not obviously modernist. Compared to previous art practices, such as the novels of James Joyce or the paintings of Jackson Pollock, the Hollywood Renaissance was a very classical movement.[1] There was not a radical consideration of cinema's formal procedures in these films. Stylistic breaks with the past were usually brief and predominantly tied to story. A notable (and often-cited) example is from Scorsese's *Taxi Driver* and its allusion to a sequence from the more clearly modernist *Two or Three Things I Know about Her* (Jean-Luc Godard, 1967). Nevertheless, there emerged at this time a discourse that defined New Hollywood as modernist. And while some academic critics were interested in the avant-garde (such as academic filmmakers like Laura Mulvey and Peter Wollen), there remained a desire to extend ideas of high modernist practice to more mainstream cinema.

Robert Kolker's *A Cinema of Loneliness* is the most explicit example of a critical study of New Hollywood directors explicitly defining
this period as modernist.[2] Kolker's book has undergone three editions,
first in 1980, then in 1988, and most recently in 2000, and it remains
the most important book on the era because it so strongly defines the
dominant approach to this cinema. The validity of his argument is less
important than its effect and influence. Kolker argues that the New
Hollywood was the first extended period of American cinema in which a
modernist sensibility can be located. But this modernism is the creation
of critical method more than the artistic practice itself. This can be
seen from Kolker's own explanation of his approach: "I want to return
cinematic fiction to its proper place as artifice, as something made, and
to reduce the emotional aura that most American film narratives create
in the viewer."[3] The emphasis on formal elements and the downplaying of emotion are indeed modernist, but it is a modernist approach to
interpretation rather than a modernist artistic practice. This is not to
argue that New Hollywood cinema completely lacked these elements.
But the creation of American modernist film required both critics and
filmmakers, which Kolker himself acknowledges: "There has been no
direct joining of forces of critic and filmmaker, but there has been an
occasional paralleling of inquiry and an acknowledgment on both sides
that film is a serious business."[4] The joining of forces between critic
and filmmaker are more important than Kolker realizes. In fact, they
were crucial in the forming of American modernist film. To use Pierre
Bourdieu's terminology, modernist discourse has become the "habitus"
of film academics and reviewers alike.[5] This modernist discourse led to
New Hollywood directors rarely being approached in any other way.

In order to move away from the discourse of modernism in aesthetic debates, a sociological theory of art and artistic production is
needed. The key figure in this field is clearly Bourdieu, partially because
he lies outside these modernist/postmodernist discussions altogether. As
opposed to poststructuralists and postmodernists, Bourdieu launches his
critique of modernism at the whole of the artistic institution itself. As
an alternative, Bourdieu calls for a sociology of the aesthetic and its
institutions, arguing that in order to effectively critique this category,
the critic must break with the field of the aesthetic altogether. Otherwise, the traditional categories continue to dominate the discussion. As
Bourdieu writes in the Postscript to his seminal work *Distinction*, "The
reader may have wondered why, in a text devoted to taste and art, no
appeal is made to the tradition of philosophical and literary aesthetics;
and he or she will no doubt have realized that this is a deliberate refusal."[6]
Bourdieu instead concentrates his attention on "the indivisibility of taste,

the unity of the most 'pure' and most purified, the most sublime and the most sublimated tastes, and the most 'impure' and 'coarse,' ordinary and primitive taste."[7] To look at culture in any other way is to argue in favor of some ideal, pure, and mythical form that ignores the importance of the social altogether.

He thus offers an alternative of "radical contextualizing" that moves beyond these aesthetic categories. I take this term from Randal Johnson's description of Bourdieu's practice in his introduction to *The Field of Cultural Production*:

> Bourdieu's theory of the cultural field might be characterized as a radical contextualization. It takes into consideration not only works themselves, seen relationally within the space of available possibilities and within the historical development of such possibilities, but also producers of works in terms of their strategies and trajectories, based on their individual and class habitus, as well as their objective position within the field. It also entails an analysis of the structure of the field itself, which includes the positions occupied by producers (e.g., writers, artists) as well as those occupied by all the instances of consecration and legitimation which make cultural products what they are (the public, publishers, critics, galleries, academics and so forth). Finally, it involves an analysis of the position of the field within the broader field of power.[8]

Bourdieu's work allows Scorsese to be theorized beyond aesthetic categories and even beyond his own place in the Hollywood industry. Radically contextualizing Scorsese requires a thorough study of how the many aspects of film culture interact with each other in the production of any individual figure in the cultural field. Bourdieu's approach has become more influential in recent years within the film studies discipline, as can be seen in the work of such scholars as Barbara Klinger, Karen Frances Gracy, and Michael Z. Newman.[9] But Bourdieu's influence remains minor and is especially absent from studies of individual authors. This is due to the seeming paradox of using a broad theory of culture that de-emphasizes the artistic field while dealing with a discourse such as auteurism, which concerns itself primarily with the text. Scholars favoring Bourdieu tend to see work on individual directors as unnecessary and even old-fashioned, while scholars attracted to the work of a single filmmaker choose to ignore the more sociological approach of Bourdieu in order to concentrate on individual filmic examples of their chosen director. This has been especially true of work on Scorsese. My objective is to use historical and sociological approaches to offer a corrective to the prevailing scholarship, not so much in terms of what has been written, but rather what has not been written.

While Bourdieu is the key theorist to this work, we can draw on other sociological models, most notably Howard Becker and Herbert Gans.[10] More important, Michel Foucault's writings provide a historical model for the whole notion of authorship. In chapter 4, Foucault's essay on genealogy is used specifically in relation to Scorsese's historical efforts. But the whole book is indebted to Foucault's poststructuralist approach, particularly the removing of subjectivity from its central position and the need to subordinate it to structural systems and discourses. More specifically, Foucault's influential essay "What Is an Author?" provides a questioning and skeptical analysis of the whole notion of the author and what this commonsense term ultimately signifies. Foucault's concept of the "author function" is not concerned with the author's factual relationship to a text (did he or she write this work or not), but rather what social and cultural roles the authored work fulfills. It stresses the social construction of authorship. My analysis of Scorsese's texts aims to demonstrate how Scorsese's authorship has structured these various works, and how Scorsese himself has become a text with various connotations and meanings.

Using these methodologies, each chapter focuses on an area of Scorsese's career from a different perspective than has dominated thus far. Chapter 1, "Scorsese and the University," considers the importance of Scorsese's university background to situating Scorsese as a film director. The reception and mediation of Scorsese's cultural work within academic and popular circles can be traced back to this university connection. But the university also offers an opportunity to examine Scorsese within a very different environment than the profit-driven world of Hollywood where he would eventually work for the majority of his career. The chapter analyzes the films of this period within the context of the time, not as merely "early" works in the career of a great director. The result is a vastly different appreciation of these films, along with the first extended scholarly work on the documentary *Street Scenes 1970*, a collective protest film Scorsese organized while teaching at NYU.

Chapter 2, "The Formation of Scorsese's Critical Reputation," examines Scorsese's move from NYU to Hollywood, from student filmmaker to professional director. It considers how and why Scorsese emerged as the canonized director of his generation, drawing on the connections made between the university and the field of film culture discussed in chapter 1. While most studies of Scorsese emphasize the formal qualities of the films as evidence of Scorsese's greatness, particularly his three most lauded (*Mean Streets*, *Taxi Driver*, and *Raging Bull*), focus shifts away from Scorsese as auteur and toward the critical environment of the early 1970s, which allows for a broader understanding of the period and Scorsese's place within that environment, as well as offering a fresh perspective on the films themselves. This chapter concentrates on the period from *Boxcar Bertha*, Scorsese's first professional directing effort in 1972, until *Raging Bull*, the film many consider Scorsese's masterpiece.

Chapter 3, "Scorsese and the Fall of the Hollywood Renaissance," examines Scorsese's career during the decade of the 1980s, beginning with *Raging Bull*, released in 1980, and continuing to *The Last Temptation of Christ* in 1988. The time between these two landmark films has been downplayed in examinations of Scorsese's career, often dismissed as a transition period. This argument is convincing only if one looks at the films and their marginal place within Scorsese's canon: *The King of Comedy* (1983), *After Hours* (1985), and *The Color of Money* (1986) are relatively ignored when compared to Scorsese's other, more acclaimed works. But when analyzed contextually, this period is crucial due to Scorsese's ability to maintain and even strengthen his place as a prestigious auteur, despite numerous career setbacks. Through his involvement in projects such as film preservation, Scorsese survived the decade with his cultural capital intact, a feat that no other filmmakers of the New Hollywood accomplished.

Chapter 4, "Histories of Cinema and Cinematic Histories: Scorsese as Historian," details Scorsese's role as a chronicler of film history through both the majority of his feature films and his archival efforts. Increasingly, Scorsese presents worlds that no longer exist, emphasizing his own role in re-creating these lost worlds. Scorsese also made many documentaries on cinema history; appeared as an authority in numerous documentaries and shorts dedicated to the cinematic past; edited a book series for the Modern Library reprinting four texts of film literature; and produced a seven-part documentary on the blues for PBS. Like his work in preservation, Scorsese's role as historian and educator was rewarded both officially and unofficially. It also neatly coincided with a move within the discipline of film studies toward history and away from theory. This chapter analyzes how and why Scorsese has been presenting history and the evolution of his concern with the past.

The final chapter, "What Is Scorsese? Scorsese's Role in Contemporary Postmodern Culture," considers Scorsese within the contemporary postmodern environment, beginning with an analysis of *The King of Comedy* and the emerging independent cinema sensibility. It continues by looking at Scorsese as both a film critic and a cultural historian, and concludes with an examination of his campaign for an Academy Award and his role in the controversy over Elia Kazan's honorary Oscar in 1999.

The concern is with what projects Scorsese has chosen and how Scorsese has negotiated his cultural and economic capital as he has become an elder statesman of the industry.

Writing about any living figure offers a challenge, especially in terms of ending the analysis when work continues to be added to the filmography. In 2011 Scorsese released another feature film, *Hugo*, as well as the documentary *George Harrison: Living in the Material World*. While this study cannot keep up with Scorsese's continually increasing cultural output, it can provide a perspective on which to view this new material. Thus, while most reviewers view *Hugo* as simply an unapologetic love letter to cinema, it can also be viewed more critically as another text adding to a biographical legend that Scorsese has worked very hard to cultivate. After reading this study, I hope readers will be able to see each new Scorsese work in a different light and as something beyond just another text in the work of a canonical auteur.

Despite the many years and vast number of topics broached, the book remains coherent because of unifying presence of Scorsese himself. Not every or even most filmmakers of the past few decades would require such a broad range of subjects, and being able to filter all of these topics through Scorsese has hopefully led to a multifaceted work that is of historical interest beyond Scorsese as an individual. At the same time, Scorsese did not create this cultural field, and without it "Scorsese" would simply not exist. Many places throughout the book comment on the liminal position of Scorsese and of a certain duality that he has had to reconcile. This duality can be extended to my approach as well. This is both a broad history of American film culture over the past several decades and a study of one particular individual. It is perhaps this contradiction that has kept most of the studies of Scorsese so narrow in scope, limiting context merely to Scorsese's ethnic and religious background and events within the film industry. To continue this mode of analysis would be to ignore or downplay the vast number of cultural activities in which Scorsese has been and continues to be involved. Thus the analysis of the films focuses less on textual details and much more how each film figures in the broader scope of Scorsese's career and in turn how Scorsese's career is shaped by the cultural forces around him. As a result, films often overlooked, such as the student films and the more obviously mainstream productions are given equal attention with the canonical masterpieces. Furthermore, as Scorsese career progresses, his numerous documentaries, most of which are confined to footnotes in other studies, are given more weight. So while not a conventional authorship study, *Hollywood's New Yorker* is more about the very subject of authorship than approaches that focus primarily on textual explication.

There is a need for a work on Scorsese that matches the breadth of Scorsese's own activities and helps explain his position within the culture. After more than three decades of working for the Hollywood studios, Scorsese has managed to maintain his image as an outsider despite being thoroughly absorbed into the industry structure. How this situation came to be is the subject of this book.

1

Scorsese and the University

[The first film class] was a three-hour course, once a week, called "The History of Motion Pictures, Television and Radio." Most of the kids took the class because they thought they wouldn't have to do anything much except watch films and get two credits for it. But Haig was brutal! He would talk so fast—even faster than me—and he described everything in great detail from the very beginning. . . . Haig would come on stage, hit you with a lecture for one-and-a-half hours, then show a film. Once he showed Stroheim's *Greed* and a student asked why there was no music. Back came the answer, "Do you think this is a show? Get the hell out!" He would weed people out, semester after semester. The idea was to be as serious about it as possible—serious in the sense that you could argue, laugh and joke about the films, but you really had to be there for the love of cinema.

—Martin Scorsese[1]

ONE OF THE GOALS OF THIS BOOK is to analyze Scorsese's films and his career beyond the formal features of his work, and an examination of his relation to academic institutions is a fruitful place to begin. The reception and mediation of Scorsese's cultural work within academic and popular circles can be traced back to this university connection. But the university also offers an opportunity to examine Scorsese within a very different environment than the profit-driven world of Hollywood where he would eventually work for the majority of his career. Pierre Bourdieu has analyzed the field of cultural production as comprising two subfields: "restricted production, in which

11

the producers produce for other producers, and the field of large-scale production, which is *symbolically* excluded and discredited."[2] In Scorsese's case, this division among the two subfields is represented geographically: he attended New York University from 1960 to 1965 and worked part-time as an instructor until 1970, when he moved to Los Angeles to pursue a career in Hollywood. This part of Scorsese's biography is emphasized within the literature, especially NYU's role as an intellectual breeding ground. James Cole Potter acknowledges NYU as a prestige institution and reiterates this romantic, auteurist discourse, describing how at NYU Scorsese developed "an artistic sensibility from which he has not wavered."[3] Ultimately, Potter's lack of detail and examination in the comment reflects his broader aims of textual analysis over context, a recurring trend in Scorsese literature. This chapter illuminates the complex relationship between Scorsese and the university, as well as between the university and Hollywood. With this goal in mind, different questions need to be addressed. What was the reputation of NYU at the time? Did this help establish Scorsese's reputation in a way that would not have been possible if Scorsese had been a graduate of a West Coast institution such as Francis Ford Coppola or George Lucas? Potter's statement about NYU's prestige certainly makes sense retrospectively, and Scorsese's "New York-ness" has been important in the making of his critical reputation, but was this the case at the time? Can Bourdieu's concepts of restricted and large-scale production be mapped onto NYU and Hollywood in the unproblematic way that has been so often implied within the literature? And finally, how do these questions impact on the way Scorsese's filmmaking activities at NYU are understood?

Scorsese entered NYU in 1960, eventually becoming a film major and continuing on to complete a master's degree. Scorsese's filmmaking career began with his work at this institution: the short films *What's a Nice Girl Like You Doing in a Place Like This?* (1963) and *It's Not Just You, Murray!* (1964), the feature *Who's That Knocking at My Door* (a.k.a. *J. R.* and *I Call First*) (1966–1969), and the collective student documentary *Street Scenes 1970* (1970). The current availability of these titles differs significantly, and these differences are telling. *Who's That Knocking at My Door* is the only one of the titles with a wide release on DVD. The short films have had limited home video runs and are available for rental on 16mm through Kino International (an art cinema distributor) and for screening at such institutions as the George Eastman House in Rochester. They have also become available in pirated form on such Internet venues as YouTube. *Street Scenes 1970*, however, is a very difficult film to see. There is no video rental distribution at all. The accessibility of the film through the Museum of Modern Art (MoMA) is restricted by Scorsese himself because it is part of his own personal collection. Because of this limited access and associations with art cinema distribution, many are tempted to consider Scorsese's university career as operating within the subfield of restricted production in which symbolic power takes precedence over economics. And this has certainly been how NYU has been positioned within the cultural field, an association from which Scorsese has also benefited. However, this assumption needs to be examined more closely. How was this rhetoric around NYU established, and how accurate is this portrait of NYU as distinct from the more industry-oriented programs of the West Coast?

New York University in the 1960s

Part of this image of NYU rests on its geographical location away from Hollywood. Its association with the East Coast and especially New York City has been perceived as more authentic culturally than the artificiality of Los Angeles as represented by Hollywood, the place where, to quote Alvy Singer from the quintessential New Yorker Woody Allen's *Annie Hall* (1977), "the only cultural advantage is being able to make a right turn on a red light." The economic power of Hollywood as a field of large-scale production serves to reduce its cultural and symbolic capital while increasing the prestige of those institutions and individuals most distanced from it. Here, the economic hierarchy is reversed. In an article on Scorsese at NYU, Allan Arkush, who was one of Scorsese's students in 1969–1970, at first confirms Potter's assessment of NYU as an artistic rather than industry training ground, stating, "I was a very, very serious film student. The cinema was not fun, it was art. If it was entertaining, it was frivolous and my days of frivolous movie-going were behind me."[4] Scorsese's own recollections quoted at the start of the chapter regarding the head of the school, Haig Manoogian, support Arkush's comments on the "seriousness" of NYU at the time. Anecdotes involving the poverty of the school's equipment further enhanced this reputation of NYU as an institution of art over industry.[5] This coexistence of serious intent and mechanical impoverishment positioned NYU as closer to anticommercial filmmaking (documentary, experimental) than the Hollywood industry.

But Arkush's article then makes the point that Scorsese as an instructor helped to change the situation at NYU, both in terms of the school's equipment and in terms of what was regarded as worthy of study.[6] Arkush recalls Scorsese helping to lead a student protest for better equipment and "better" courses, one of which was "American Movies," taught by Scorsese himself. Arkush describes this course with Scorsese in very loving terms, stating that "those Tuesday afternoon classes changed my view of movies forever. I went to work for Roger Corman, because the films screened in Marty's class helped me see the kind of movies I wanted to make."[7] Arkush has more than forty director credits to his name over the past thirty plus years, the large majority of them for network television series. Another student of Scorsese's, Ezra Sacks, spent years in Hollywood working as a screenwriter. Three of these screenplays were produced: the Universal film *FM* (John A. Alonzo, 1978); the United Artists feature *A Small Circle of Friends* (Rob Cohen, 1980); and the Goldie Hawn comedy *Wildcats* (Michael Ritchie, 1986). Thus, in addition to "auteurs" such as Scorsese, Oliver Stone, Spike Lee, and Jim Jarmusch, NYU has also produced individuals who have felt comfortable working anonymously within the industry. Furthermore, both Arkush and Sacks have cited Scorsese as a primary inspiration for them and their filmmaking careers. NYU's actual legacy, like that of most film schools, is more mixed in its focus on artistic and industrial issues than its reputation would suggest.[8]

The actual course catalogue NYU offered, circa 1970, shows a mixture of art and industry, as well as a mix of filmmaking practice and theory. NYU featured an undergraduate program as well as two separate programs at the graduate level: a production-centered program administered through the Institute of Film and Television, and a scholarly and critical program administered through the Graduate School of the Arts and Sciences. The graduate program in production listed five objectives, two of which are fairly compatible with the image of the school as one focused on aesthetics: "To provide students the opportunity to develop their creative talent through intensive class experiences and actual production experience" and "to provide lectures and seminars in aesthetic, historical and critical studies so that students may be aware of the best of the past and present as it may be applicable to the future." But the objectives also include other factors besides artistic expression. The program guide states that "entrepreneurial competence" is needed, which is why the studies "will provide students with the basic knowledge to deal creatively with professional structures and procedures."[9] This explicitly stated emphasis on the pragmatic details of working in the industry places NYU, despite perceptions, as a rather typical film school: emphasizing artistic expression, but stressing that this can be achieved within the industry. This is exactly the path that Scorsese himself has followed and all of this is not merely coincidental. As Arkush states, Scorsese as an instructor at NYU went a long way toward integrating the study and appreciation of popular cinema into the curriculum. It is important, of course, not to fall into the trap of seeing this strictly in terms of Scorsese's individual influence. By the late 1960s, the auteur theory had begun to influence critical taste within the United States, primarily through the work of Andrew Sarris, who wrote weekly articles in the *Village Voice*, published his book *The American Cinema: Directors and Directions* (1968), and taught courses at New York universities (mostly at Columbia University but briefly at NYU as well). But Scorsese was part of this legitimizing function, representing a certain generational shift within the NYU community.

Arkush's article makes it clear that when he began as a film student, the great divide between high art and mass culture was firmly in place. Scorsese's comments confirm that this was the attitude many of the senior instructors in the faculty, including his mentor, Manoogian, adopted, who dismissed an early Scorsese essay on *The Third Man* as being "just a thriller."[10] Scorsese also acknowledges the influence of the cultural scene happening around him and the adversarial relationship between this new taste formation and the critical stance of the NYU faculty:

> At this time the new American Underground was emerging, and since our campus was in Greenwich Village we had access to all of these films. Jonas Mekas was writing his *Village Voice* column every week, while Andrew Sarris was deploying the *politique des auteurs*, imported from the French *Cahiers du cinema*, in *Film Culture* magazine. Then *Movie* magazine appeared from Britain with its list of great directors, and there were Hawks and Hitchcock at the top. The professors were totally against these critical views, but what we learned was that the new critics liked John Wayne movies, but they weren't just John Wayne movies, but John Ford and Howard Hawks working through him. What had impressed us as good when we were young had impressed other people too.[11]

The question one may ask, then, is how did Scorsese function within this environment whose tastes are seemingly at odds with his own? Manoogian actually produced his first feature film, and he was even brought in as an instructor in 1969, a position he held until he left for Hollywood in the fall of 1970. In Bourdieu's terms, how did Scorsese accumulate this level of symbolic power within this institution, especially given these differences in cultural taste?

Student Filmmaking and the New York Underground

Here a third critical grouping needs to be introduced: the New American underground cinema, which operates much closer to Bourdieu's idea of a restricted field of cultural production than the university. As Bourdieu explains, academic institutions, while certainly operating outside of the field of large-scale production in artistic endeavors, can also be seen as a hindrance to a field defining itself as truly autonomous or disinterested. In fact, "the absence of any academic training or consecration may be considered a virtue."[12] Training in filmmaking at the university level implies a certain "apprenticeship" for the mainstream industry rather than a concern with film as an aesthetic experience. Student films are not aimed at the public at large, but yet they appear to lack the autonomy of an avant-garde practice such as the New American Cinema led by Jonas Mekas, in which opposition to the values of the mainstream cinema is explicit. Like student filmmaking, there is an emphasis on the personal, but the personal filmmaking of the underground defines itself negatively, as being anything but Hollywood: "Our movies come from our hearts—our little movies, not the Hollywood movies."[13] No such explicit rejection is seen at NYU, especially after the influence of Scorsese himself as instructor.

Furthermore, the place of the avant-garde within American film culture and its various institutions during the 1960s is unique. Experimental art frequently relies on cultural institutions as well as government funding to sustain itself in the case of film as well as other cultural forms. However, beginning in the post–World War II period and continuing into the 1970s, MoMA denied support to avant-garde film in New York. Additionally, after its formation in 1965, the National Endowment for the Arts (NEA) similarly rejected experimental cinema. This is despite the fact that these institutions were in general funding abstract, noncommercial artistic expression. As Peter Decherney argues, although the NEA, MoMA, the Rockefeller Foundation, and other institutions devoted themselves to funding avant-garde art in every other medium, with the cinematic medium they supported Hollywood film.[14] Through this exclusion, the restricted field of cultural production represented by avant-garde film was formed, however "accidentally." Because the New American Cinema group and other avant-garde collectives and individuals could not rely on institutional funding, they had to define themselves as anti-institutional. Because of the logic of restricted fields of production, the unintended result was an increase in this avant-garde's cultural capital. This is because the avant-garde has always had a highly problematic relationship with cultural institutions as Decherney points out: "Can the avant-garde have a museum at all? Or do museums necessarily rob art of its avant-garde status?"[15] Indeed, once an archive for experimental cinema was founded at Anthology Film Archives in 1970, the prestige of the avant-garde as anti-institutional was lowered, and through the changing structure of the New Hollywood the avant-garde found a home in the more traditional institutions that it was previously denied. The fact that this anti-institutional stance of the filmic avant-garde in the 1960s was always a fiction, that Mekas and company constantly sought institutional support and created an institutional structure through patronage, is ultimately not the issue. What is important is to understand the multiple fields of film production at this time, how they operated, and how Scorsese is situated within this culture.

Scorsese mentions this New American Cinema group in the context of the new film culture of the 1960s. It is a curiosity of this time and place that Sarris and Mekas were writing for the same weekly paper, the *Village Voice*, often side by side. Sarris and Mekas, in opposing ways, stressed film as a serious art form rather than simply as mass culture. Mekas did this in fairly traditional ways, emphasizing the high modernist values of the experimental movement over the mass culture of Hollywood. Sarris, however, called on the avant-garde's own relationship to film as an anti-institutional art that could yield genuine artistic experiences due to its very lack of pretensions. The key critic in this regard, and Sarris's chief influence, was Manny Farber, the modernist painter/film critic who participated in the development of the New York school of painters only to quickly turn on that school when it began courting the favor of cultural institutions. As Greg Taylor argues, "Farber's cult sensibilities simply prevented him from supporting artists who seemed to be proudly courting fame and acceptance at the expense of artistic integrity."[16] As a film critic, Farber championed what he called "underground films" and "termite art" over what he described as "white elephant art." Farber's idea of "underground" was much different than Mekas's. Farber wanted films that lacked artistic ambition, especially if that artistic ambition was aimed at the mass audience. For Farber, low-budget Hollywood action movies represented a freedom from the bondages of official art.

Andrew Sarris drew on Farber's cultism and the *Cahiers du Cinéma*'s auteurism and established a new film aesthetic and canon in which Hollywood cinema was appreciated as high art. Only within film culture, and only at a time in which postmodern movements such as Pop Art challenged the notion of what art meant, could such a theory actually take hold. Despite championing the most mainstream of films, Sarris could position himself as having vanguard tastes and accuse the avant-garde as being outdated and "boring."[17] But within American cultural institutions, Sarris's approach was not really original. MoMA had a tradition going back to World War II of supporting Hollywood, as had the university system and early programs at Ivy League schools such as Columbia and Harvard. By championing movies, figures like Iris Barry at MoMA had already "altered an idea central to the modernist definition of art: that art shared nothing in common with mass culture."[18] The important point here, however, is to emphasize that the relationship between modernism and mass culture "altered" but hardly disappeared. The avant-garde could still rely on antimass culture rhetoric to advance its claims. In his 1986 study *After the Great Divide: Modernism, Mass Culture, Postmodernism*, Andreas Huyssen discusses how the rise of postmodernism in the 1970s not only challenged the modernist idea that high art had to be separated from the contamination of mass culture, but also notes that this attempt did not have any lasting effect, that "the opposition between modernism and mass culture has remained amazingly resilient over the decades."[19] Indeed, because of (not despite) the rise of auteurism, art cinema and the legitimizing function of cultural institutions such as MoMA and the Film Society of Lincoln Center, the avant-garde strengthened its hold during this period as the truly vanguard movement. Only in the early 1970s, the time in which Scorsese moved into Hollywood filmmaking, does this situation shift once again.

Scorsese's NYU Short Films

The relationship between the avant-garde and student filmmaking at this time was quite close, despite the philosophical differences regarding the industry, not unlike the relationship between Scorsese and senior faculty like Manoogian at NYU. Often, student films and the avant-garde would be conflated. David Thompson and Ian Christie note that this was the case with Scorsese's early short films, which Sarris considered as part of the New American Cinema underground movement.[20] While being condescending to the movement as a whole, Sarris acknowledged a certain potential in Scorsese for "talking features," which for Sarris meant work aimed at a wider audience, preferably Hollywood. The notion of Scorsese placing himself as a filmmaker between two worlds, being inside Hollywood making films while also seeing himself as an outsider to the industry, had its roots in his early formation at the university, which itself shares these same traits. NYU as a student filmmaking center encouraged "personal" filmmaking while also preparing students for a potential career in the industry. The university system thrived on having its students win awards for their films in order to increase their level of prestige and symbolic power, as is often the case within restricted fields, but these awards also served as a way into the Hollywood system for the individual participants. Scorsese's eventual status as a critically acclaimed yet famous and well-known Hollywood director provided an ideal example for NYU to promote. It followed a long history, out of which Scorsese emerged, in which cultural institutions, not only MoMA and the NEA but the university as well, supported Hollywood film and social realist documentary over formal experimentation.

Both of Scorsese's early short films, *What's a Nice Girl Like You Doing in a Place Like This?* and *It's Not Just You, Murray!*, were honored at the 1965 National Student Film Festival, giving Scorsese the prestige he needed to have his film project for his master's degree turned into a feature film and to be able to teach at the institution himself. The National Student Film Festival itself shows the place of student filmmaking within the cultural field. The event was cosponsored by the National Student Association, the Motion Picture Association of America (MPAA), and, by 1964, Lincoln Center, which also began the New York Film Festival in 1963. Along with other cultural institutions like MoMA and the NEA, the New York Film Festival snubbed the avant-garde from 1963 to 1965. Although they reached out in 1966 with a special programming of "independent" filmmakers, the festival as a whole came to represent the type of bourgeois, middle-brow culture the avant-garde opposed. Its exclusion from the New York Film Festival only confirmed the avant-garde's position "as anti-institutional art." It is from within the field of large-scale cultural production such as Hollywood that student films, despite their low budgets and artistic aspirations, ultimately operated. Much like the New York and other film festivals around the world, the National Student Film Festival was a place to earn cultural capital that could be used for career advancement within the Hollywood industry.

Besides Sarris's brief mention of Scorsese's early shorts, little critical attention was paid to these works, and subsequent accounts (which are few, given the limited availability of the prints) discuss the films as apprenticeship work for Hollywood and as miniature examples of Scorsese's later films. A strong autobiographical reading given to each calls on future knowledge of Scorsese as a filmmaker and a personality. But what these short films also reveal is a connection to the classical cinema of Hollywood that is much closer to the art cinema of Europe, particularly the French New Wave and its genre revisions, than to the avant-garde of New York.

What's a Nice Girl Like You Doing in a Place Like This? shows the twin influences of the French New Wave and popular television comedy such as "Sid Caesar's Your Show of Shows." It is a comedic take on the story of the obsessive artist, in this case a writer named Algernon (but called Harry by friends). It consists almost exclusively of voiceover narration by the protagonist, who addresses the audience with a first-person account of his psychological obsession with a picture in his apartment. The style is playful, incorporating stop-motion photography and many cuts in order to make visual jokes to match the voiceover. The most repeated gag is Harry making a comment ("I have a vivid imagination, all my friends say it") and then Scorsese cutting to a man in a dark room repeating the comment ("you know, Harry, you have a vivid imagination"). Thus the rhythm of the 9-minute short is very fast and meant to amuse the viewer. It does, however, conclude rather darkly with Harry finally entering the painting of the ocean and seeming to drown as he is swept out to sea. His final words, "life is fraught with peril," seem to foretell his own future characters and stories, a point Lesley Stern makes in her great, allusive take on Scorsese's work, *The Scorsese Connection*.

It's Not Just You, Murray! combines elements of Classical Hollywood gangster films with a New Wave–style deconstruction of this very genre, with an ending borrowed from Federico Fellini, particularly *8½*. Like *What's a Nice Girl Like You*, it uses voiceover narration (a signal of its low-budget, student film status), but incorporates direct address as well, most notably in the great opening, with Murray showing off his clothes and possessions and telling how much each luxury item costs ("see this tie, twenty dollars"). Murray narrates his story, which begins as a braggart's tale but quickly becomes a deification of his friend Joe, to whom Murray claims he owes all his success. The viewer quickly sees that Murray is a small-time gangster and Joe, far from being Murray's friend,

Figure 1.1. *What's a Nice Girl Like You Doing in a Place Like This?* (Martin Scorsese, 1965).

Figure 1.2. *It's Not Just You, Murray!* (Martin Scorsese, 1965).

is simply using him. Scorsese again uses a running gag throughout, this time involving Murray's mother (played by Scorsese's mother Catherine, her first of many roles in his movies) constantly feeding him spaghetti. Although played as a comedy, it is closer to a satire of gangsters, and Murray is so pathetic and delusional that the tone is rather bleak until the Fellini-inspired finale in which all the characters come together in celebration.

As the June 1992 *Sight and Sound* review states, *"It's Not Just You, Murray!* is not an experimental film, but it is vigorous and refreshing."[21] In other words, the film is a youthful reinterpretation and reexamination of popular cinema (à la the New Wave) rather than a rejection of it. A similar note is sounded in Jonathan Romney's take on *What's a Nice Girl Like You Doing in a Place Like This?* for the same *Sight and Sound* issue.[22] With this review, Romney situates the film within Scorsese's personal history as an obsessive cinephile, as well as within the trajectory of Scorsese's career and its ambiguous relationship with mainstream entertainment. Leighton Grist's reading of the two films takes this argument further: "While the films display a delight in cinema, they also suggest a suspicion of its possibly amoral, possibly

deracinating, possibly dehumanizing seductiveness."[23] While these readings of the films are perceptive and convincing, a question arises: What
"cinema" is being referred to here? Should we collapse all cinemas into
one singular notion, or is one specific type of cinema to be regarded
with suspicion due to its seductiveness? To address these questions, we
need the context of NYU.

As mentioned earlier, according to Scorsese, the aesthetic position
of Haig Manoogian and other senior faculty at NYU was highly critical
of Hollywood mass entertainment and disagreed strongly with the view
that the personal expression they so valued could exist within such a
system. This was part of a cultural perspective known as the mass culture critique of which Hollywood was a particularly common example.
Sociologist Herbert Gans has summarized the "mass culture critique" as
having three major themes, all of which apply to Hollywood cinema: (1)
mass culture is produced solely for profit and thus is completely beholden
to the audience rather than personal expression; (2) mass culture borrows
from and thus debases high culture, both the product and its individual
(for example, Hollywood's luring of the great novelists William Faulkner
and F. Scott Fitzgerald); and (3) mass culture has negative effects on
both the audience as individuals (producing mindless automatons) and
on society as a whole (can lead to totalitarianism).[24] While Scorsese has
stated that he disagreed with this sentiment and instead aligned himself
with the cultural movement in which Hollywood would be taken seriously, an element of this critique appears in his early films. The use of
the Warner Bros. gangster genre in *It's Not Just You, Murray!* recalls the
early work of Jean-Luc Godard in both celebrating and critiquing this
style of filmmaking. Scorsese may have intended the critique to be more
general and include all types of filmmaking, but the standard type of
cinema felt to be detrimental at this time was Hollywood. This critique
would be especially pronounced with his first feature film.

Who's That Knocking at My Door

Who's That Knocking at My Door tells the story of J. R. (Harvey Keitel), a
young man living in New York's Little Italy. He is lower-class, had little
education, and hangs around with small-time hoods from his neighborhood. On his way to run errands on Staten Island, he meets a woman
(Zina Bethune) reading a magazine with a picture of John Wayne. J. R.
strikes up a conversation because of his cinematic knowledge, and the
two start dating. The film cuts between scenes with J. R. and his friends
and scenes between J. R. and "the Girl" (as she is identified in the credits). Eventually the vast differences in background between the couple

(she is higher class, better educated, non–Italian Catholic) lead to their breakup. She tells J. R. she was raped, which he responds to negatively. When he later tries to forgive her and "marry her anyway," she rejects him. He ends up in his old neighborhood, and a high angle overhead shot of J. R. parting with a friend and going home concludes the film.

Who's That Knocking at My Door began as a graduate project at NYU. It also marked Scorsese's first attempt at, as Leighton Grist puts it, "entering the marketplace, [and] developing a style."[25] Or, to phrase it differently, Scorsese was developing a style in order to enter the marketplace. Subsequent writing on the film, which is rather substantial compared to the writing on the short films, emphasizes the work as an apprenticeship for the masterpiece to come, Mean Streets (1973), and hence judges the film in relation to this more professional standard: "Who's That Knocking at My Door presents a patchwork of jerky transitions, unintegrated stylistic contrasts and varying standards of cinematography and picture quality."[26] Leighton Grist's comments represent a wide consensus on the film as technically crude because Scorsese still had not learned to "properly" channel his talent. This view contrasts drastically with one prominent early account of the film by Roger Ebert, who viewed an early version (titled I Call First) at the Chicago Film Festival in 1967. Ebert's review is worth quoting at length:

> As a technical achievement, it brings together two opposing worlds of American cinema. On the one hand, there have been traditional films like Marty, View from the Bridge, On the Waterfront and David and Lisa—all sincere attempts to function at the level where real lives are led and all suffering to some degree from their makers' romantic and idealistic ideas about such lives. On the other hand there have been experimental films from Jonas Mekas, Shirley Clarke and other pioneers of the New York underground. In The Connection, Shadows and Guns of the Trees, they used improvised dialogue and scenes and hidden and handheld cameras in an attempt to capture the freshness of a spontaneous experience. Both groups have lacked the other's strong point. The films like Marty are technically well done and emotionally satisfying, but they lack the flavor of actual experience. Films like Shadows are authentic enough, but often poor in technical quality and lacking the control necessary to develop character and tell a story. I Call First brings these two kinds of films together into a work that is absolutely genuine, artistically satisfying and technically comparable to the best films being made anywhere. I have no reservations in describing it as a great moment in American movies.[27]

To unpack Ebert's remarks here, the film has to be looked at relationally, not only with regard to the different styles of filmmaking but in terms of the different and rapidly changing conceptions of art.

Ebert is positioning Scorsese as Scorsese himself will situate his career: as in-between the world of Hollywood and independent film-making. For Ebert, *I Call First* represents the best of both worlds. It is an aesthetically rich film that has a coherent story and a controlled use of technique. This is in marked contrast to the view of the film as an amateurish and self-indulgent debut feature—a viewpoint that has come to dominate discussions. Instead, Ebert admires the film's ability to be technically competent and authentic without sacrificing storytelling. Ebert's review provides the standard description of the film's plot and thematics, but additionally makes special note of two relatively nonnarra-tive sequences: "Two scenes—one in a bar, another at a party—are among the most evocative descriptions of American life I have ever seen."[28] Compare this with Grist's comments on the same material: "Centred on a long, static front-on take, the characters' inebriated antics, as they laugh inanely, throw napkins and annoy each other, are allowed to drift until the scene teeters on the brink of actualizing rather than represent-ing irritating behaviour."[29] The presence of such scenes, whether viewed positively or negatively, shows the film's debt to independent filmmak-ing and the aesthetic of personal expression. Ebert is able to relate this personal expression to a broader conception of "American life" whereas Grist sees an irritating self-indulgence, but both share the conviction that great filmmaking negotiates between the two extremes of Hollywood and the avant-garde. It is in this aesthetic that will become increasingly popular throughout the years, that Scorsese's reputation will be built.

Like *What's a Nice Girl Like You Doing in a Place Like This?* and *It's Not Just You, Murray!*, *Who's That Knocking at My Door* negotiates between a fascination with Hollywood and a critique of that very cin-ema, as evidenced by the two direct references to Hollywood Westerns: *The Searchers* and *Rio Bravo* (Howard Hawks, 1959). In particular, the film shows how J. R.'s central psychological problem, the inability to see women as anything other than "virgins" or "whores," is not only part of his Italian-Catholic background but is present in the Hollywood cinema that he loves. Ironically, this very cinephilia allows J. R. to have a conversation with his eventual girlfriend in the first place, an indica-tion of how cinema was gaining in cultural prestige during the 1960s. J. R. recognizes a still of *The Searchers* in the Girl's French magazine (a clear reference to auteurism's origins) and is able to use this cultural link as a way to bridge the obvious class differences between them—if only temporarily. During the final confrontation at her apartment, their cultural backgrounds are made very apparent through her high culture music and literary choices (jazz records, F. Scott Fitzgerald's *Tender Is the Night*). And as the sequence concludes, the Girl tells J. R. to "go home," echoing their first meeting when they discuss a scene from *The Searchers*. As Grist argues, J. R.'s investment in the star image of Wayne implies another factor in his determination.[30] J. R. discusses *The Searchers* and *Rio Bravo* without ever recognizing the racism and sexism of Wayne's lead characters. Given the contempt for Hollywood the senior faculty at NYU felt at the time, as well as the general liberal disdain felt toward a figure like John Wayne, Scorsese's film can be easily read as a critique of the dangers of this mass culture and the harm it can inflict on individuals who consume it. But at the same time, one can argue that Scorsese is not so much criticizing Hollywood films as much as those who take an uncritical view of this cinema. Thus J. R. does not see *The Searchers* as problematizing the lead character's racism or *Rio Bravo* as undermining the initial sexism toward the female lead (J. R. can only see her as a "broad"). The problem lies not with Hollywood, but with an uncritical audience that is unable to appreciate the complexity of the films. Or, to phrase it differently, with a view of Hollywood as mass culture rather than art, a perspective that Scorsese, as a future maker of Hollywood films, had a vested interest in changing. Read retrospectively, the film is much more interesting as an example of the kind of high art/low culture negotiation of the period than as a simple fledgling tale in the saga of an auteur.

Also worth noting is the film's relation to the distribution system with this being Scorsese's first commercially released project. After failing to find distribution for the film following its showing at the 1967 Chicago Film Festival, Scorsese received an offer from Joseph Brenner Associates, which agreed to release the film if Scorsese added a nude sequence. Grist argues that this compromised the film's integrity: "The need to include a nude scene plainly highlights the constraints that impinged on the film's production, and Scorsese cut the scene almost contemptuously into the middle of a conversation between J. R. and the [G]irl."[31] While clearly the vagaries of distribution altered the film, Grist is focusing only on the types of obvious influences (such as a direct demand from the distributor) rather than the more implicit type of restraint always found in the distribution of art works. From one perspective *Mean Streets* can be seen in auteurist terms as representing a maturation of the young Scorsese, which is how Grist and almost all book-length studies of Scorsese frame the film: "As an example of film authorship, it bodies forth the maturation of Scorsese's authorial discourse."[32] Grist's chapter serves as an endorsement of Hollywood, whose constraints allowed Scorsese to mature. This is unlike the economic forces that compromised *Who's That Knocking at My Door*, in large part because the constraints of *Mean Streets* promote a certain aesthetic that Grist and most critics often uncritically accept.

For a different perspective, consider former NYU and Scorsese student Peter Rea's illuminating comments on both films:

> I think *Who's That Knocking* has some of the most creative things he's ever done. I think it blows away *Mean Streets*. The use of slow motion when it is going across the people laughing, and, I just think there are things in that movie that are so powerful. I mean he's jump-cutting, he's playing with the medium and having fun with it. Of course I think *Mean Streets* is great as well. I went to L.A. after NYU, I was there for a brief period of time, and he [Scorsese] was cutting *Mean Streets*. And one of his other students was there working on it as well. So I saw an early cut of it. I saw a lot of stuff that I thought was amazing but they cut out of the movie. Kind of outrageous stuff, dream sequences.[33]

Rea, primarily as a filmmaker and a production teacher, appreciates very different aspects of Scorsese's work than those within the academic interpretative community because he belongs to this field of cultural production himself. The changes in style from *Who's That Knocking at My Door* to *Mean Streets* are best considered not as a maturation (which implies

Figure 1.3. *Who's That Knocking at My Door* (Martin Scorsese, 1969), stylistic expression or authorial immaturity?

a clear hierarchy), but as a shift in the type of audience that appreciates each respective work. The vagaries of distribution that Grist uses to denigrate *Who's That Knocking at My Door* apply equally to *Mean Streets* or any other work of art. As Howard Becker argues, "Since most artists want the advantages of distribution, they work with an eye to what the system characteristic of their world can handle. What kinds of work will it distribute? What will it ignore? What return will it give for what kind of work?"[34] With this in mind, comparing the two films with the reception of John Cassavetes' *Shadows*, a film that went through two versions and thus can be considered as two separate texts, may be useful. Jonas Mekas praised the first cut of the film, which unfortunately is no longer available for screening, as a great example of underground cinema, and Mekas used it to promote the idea of a New American Cinema. However, when Cassavetes reedited the film in order to de-emphasize formal experimentation and focus more on characterization, Mekas rejected the film as overly conventional.[35] For Cassavetes, the second version represented a maturation of his filmmaking, rejecting the overindulgence in cinematic style of the first version. A similar split in critical perspective is possible with *Who's That Knocking at My Door* and *Mean Streets*. The later film may be more mature, but it is also more widely acceptable and intelligible in terms of style. To place this opposition within a hierarchy, as most critics of the two films have, not only works well as an auteurist narrative of growth, but also justifies and defends a certain approach to cinema (namely Hollywood, however "New") while rejecting another (experimental). Throughout his career, Scorsese's work will be repeatedly used to mediate different ideas and notions of what cinema should be. And although Scorsese is often seen as an outsider to Hollywood, this mediation usually takes the form of an implicit justification of its approach to cinema.

The Big Shave

After making *Who's That Knocking at My Door*, but before finding distribution for the film, Scorsese received financial support from Jacques Ledoux, curator of the Cinémathèque Royale de Belgique in Brussels, to make a 6-minute short. The result was Scorsese's most experimental and most overtly political work to that point, *The Big Shave* (1967). The differences between this film and Scorsese's earlier shorts can be related to their differing institutional contexts. The fact that Scorsese's only completely experimental work of this period is financed from Europe rather than any American institution is a reflection of the lack of institutional funding available in the United States at this time. Similarly, Scorsese did not produce *The Big Shave* within the academic institution, and the film differs dramatically from those earlier shorts. Rather than being a New Wave exercise in Hollywood revision, *The Big Shave* exists as a narrative in only the barest sense: an unknown man shaves in front of a mirror in an all-white room until he cuts himself and is covered in blood, all to the tune of Bunny Berigan's version of "I Can't Get Started." The film then ends with two title cards: "Whiteness by Herman Melville" and "Viet '67." The film won the Prix L'Age d'Or at the Festival of Experimental Cinema in Belgium and clearly belongs to that particular field of restricted production.

Not surprisingly, the film has been depoliticized by many Scorsese scholars (and Scorsese himself) and brought into line with the auteurist orthodoxy: "Consciously it was an angry outcry against the war. But something else was going on inside me. It was a very bad period."[36] The fact that Scorsese's comments depoliticizing *The Big Shave* are repeatedly used in criticism around the film not only points to a general tendency toward the intentional fallacy still present in even academic writing, but it also reflects a more specific trend in Scorsese scholarship to write a coherent narrative about Scorsese as both a filmmaker and a subject. In all of these examples, the various authors begin by mentioning the

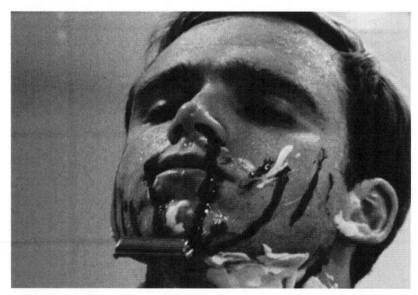

Figure 1.4. *The Big Shave* (Martin Scorsese, 1967), experimental (and political) avant-garde.

Vietnam context, and then finish by quoting Scorsese's remarks about the film's personal rather than political nature, thus rhetorically privileging the latter. One need not deny the veracity of Scorsese's comments to question their particular relevance to a consideration of the film. The hermeneutic maneuver of Scorsese and these auteur critics removes the social context, which allows the film to be seen as a timeless expression of a (male) artist's angst. This positioning allows this formally experimental work to be placed within the tradition of the avant-garde that emphasizes art as personal expression and that can easily and safely be placed within an institutional context. However, as Peter Wollen has argued, historically there are "two avant-gardes." One emphasizes personal expression, usually derived from other art forms (particularly painting), and the other focuses on political expression (often with ties to the theater and literature but with a greater emphasis on cinematic specificity).[37] *The Big Shave* is best approached from the latter of these traditions. The film is made by a filmmaker born in the United States where an explicitly political avant-garde did not really exist, but within a European context with a long and continuing tradition of combining artistic experimentation with political activism.

Furthermore, as an outsider to this context, the European avant-garde Scorsese would have been most familiar with would be precisely this political avant-garde of Sergei Eisenstein and Dziga Vertov on through to contemporaries such as Jean-Marie Straub and Danièle Huillet. And, fittingly, the film won the Prix L'Age d'Or, named after Luis Buñuel and Salvador Dali's 1930 example of political avant-garde provocation. And while the film shows the tendency toward abstraction especially prevalent in American avant-garde painting since World War II, best exemplified in the institutionally celebrated work of Jackson Pollock, the two title cards, "Whiteness by Herman Melville" and "Viet '67," also clearly cue the contemporary viewer (in lieu of any direct access to Scorsese's personal mental state) to the film's political relevance. Lawrence S. Freidman's analysis of the film is rare in making this political aspect (rather than Scorsese's personal crisis) the focus of his comments: "An obscure object of desire, the white whale ultimately resists definition, sharing its inscrutability with that of America's [then-]longest war whose aims grew cloudier rather than clearer with time."[38] The very abstractness of the film thus provides an apt political metaphor for the vagueness of the war itself, and thus works in the best tradition of an avant-garde that works, to quote Godard, "to make films politically" rather than just make political films. If Scorsese had submitted the film for a weeklong antiwar rally with stock footage of the war included, as he once imagined, the film would have had a much more explicit but also less evocative message, as well as owing more to the social realist documentary tradition rather than the avant-garde. The fact that the film has the form it does owes not so much to Scorsese himself as to the very field of cultural production in which he made the work. The film's "Americanness" (rather than its "Scorseseness") makes it a rather unusual specimen within this experimental field. Made by an American about an American political controversy with a literary allusion to a great American novelist, the film is nevertheless unthinkable outside of its European context. The reference to Melville is thus particularly appropriate. Melville is an American author who is known less for his storytelling ability and more for his philosophical investigations, which have put him more in the category of a European sensibility, often as a precursor to the rise of French existentialism (see especially Melville's short story "Bartleby the Scrivener," a staple of literature and existentialism courses). And as most cinephiles like Scorsese know, the director Jean-Pierre Grumbach would take on Melville as his pseudonym, an identification that actually begins before his directorial career. It was his alias during his involvement in the World War II French Resistance.

Woodstock

In 1969, while Scorsese was still teaching at NYU, he joined with a group of NYU alumni and students led by director Michael Wadleigh (who worked as a cinematographer on *Who's That Knocking at My Door*), to film the Woodstock music festival. Scorsese acted as assistant director on the shoot and over the next several months worked with Wadleigh, Thelma Schoonmaker, and others in editing the film, often staying up all night and teaching morning classes the next day at the university. Although the resulting film is one of the major countercultural events of the 1960s, anecdotes around Scorsese's involvement in the film stress his outsider status. Schoonmaker comments, "Marty, of course, was very amusing talking about it. He said he brought his cufflinks. He brought his cufflinks to Woodstock because he thought it was maybe going to be that kind of thing!"[39] Similar comments have been made about *Who's That Knocking at My Door*, stressing how odd a film about sexual repression seemed in the middle of the sexual revolution. These examples de-emphasize any social environment that may be said to have influenced Scorsese during this period. Because Scorsese was outside of this context, his work can be constructed as timeless and universal. And because Scorsese's subsequent work in Hollywood did not relate to this counterculture in any direct manner, it becomes tempting to read this as personal indifference and to view *Woodstock* as simply a job.

A notable exception in this regard is again Friedman, who sees *Woodstock* as part of a politically committed period in Scorsese's career that would undergo a transformation when he moved to Hollywood: "Changing times, shifting priorities, economic imperatives—or 'utter hopelessness': whatever the cause(s), the ensuing cinema of Martin Scorsese lacks the political urgency of *The Big Shave*, *Woodstock*, and *Street Scenes*."[40] Friedman's work is important in recognizing the politics of this period, but he still insists on framing these films within "the cinema of Martin Scorsese." Thus the collective nature of the *Woodstock* project is downplayed and, following from James Monaco's early book on the New Hollywood,[41] the success of *Woodstock* is attributed to Scorsese. A flawed and yet unfortunately common auteurist logic is at work here. Because Scorsese went on to have a more successful career in Hollywood after the film, some argue that he must have been the main creative force behind the project. In order for *Woodstock* as a film to be labeled as an "authentic" piece of art, its maker must be deemed worthy. A masterpiece needs a master: "If we judge the artist on the basis of the work, we must know who really did the work, and therefore [who] deserves the judgment we make of its worth and the worth of its makers."[42] Within the art world of film that now exists, the question of who the authentic artist actually is assumes greater importance, even within obviously collective activity. For if one is not an artist, one is simply personnel, as Howard Becker aptly describes, "It is unfeeling to speak of the people who cooperate in the production of art works as 'personnel' or, worse yet, 'support personnel,' but that accurately reflects their importance in the conventional art world view."[43] This issue of artistic authenticity within the collective nature of filmmaking is most evident in the last project Scorsese embarks on at NYU before departing for Hollywood: *Street Scenes 1970*. Indeed, the issue of collectivity above all else explains the film's controversial status within Scorsese's oeuvre.

Street Scenes 1970

In May 1970, while an instructor at NYU, Martin Scorsese helped to organize a series of short films about the war protests that had erupted following the invasion of Cambodia and the student shootings at Kent State. The New York Cinetracts Collective was formed to produce newsreel shorts documenting the political struggle, including an eventual trip to document a march on Washington the following weekend. The collective consisted mostly of students but also volunteer professional filmmakers and others sympathetic to the enterprise. Over the course of that summer, Scorsese supervised the editing of the footage into a 75-minute feature-length film that premiered at the 1970 New York Film Festival in September. Following this screening, the film traveled to various festivals and was in circulation throughout the 1970s, but it never received a commercial release and eventually fell into obscurity, despite the involvement of such a high-profile figure as Scorsese. A reconsideration of this film, including both its production and reception, is needed, as well as an examination of the reasons for its marginalization.

The film premiered at the New York Film Festival in September 1970. As a result it received a review in the *New York Times*, which praised the film for its "frightening vitality of actuality as recorded on raw film" and its "balanced, accumulative tone of utterances, from all sides."[44] But because the film failed to receive a commercial release, no other reviews or comments were made on the film outside of festival settings. No full-length articles remain on the film—only the occasional brief discussion in books on Scorsese's work. In many cases, the film is only described in passing or as part of a filmography. The two exceptions are Lawrence S. Friedman and Les Keyser, both of whom discuss the film in slight detail and in relation to the context of the time. Friedman, for example, sees the film as part of a brief period of "political urgency" in Scorsese's work that his subsequent films would lack and sees the project as perhaps instigating this move away from the overtly political.[45] Similarly, Keyser describes the extremely political environment of the period that Scorsese himself had helped create: "Instructor Scorsese had so embroiled himself in diverse political film projects that his house had become an impromptu commune for the dissidents and radicals."[46] Keyser states that the film's conclusion represented an endpoint for Scorsese politically as well: "Scorsese's editing in this last sequence, the only part of the film he shot himself, suggests an end to any age of reason."[47] The fact that Scorsese left NYU for Hollywood shortly after the film's premiere only enhances this linear chronology of *Street Scenes 1970* marking a break within Scorsese's career, and symbolizing his move away from the political.

What is most noticeable is the film's absence from texts emphasizing interview material with Scorsese himself. The interview collection *Scorsese on Scorsese* includes a brief description of the film by the book's editors, but no direct comments by Scorsese. The edited collection *Martin Scorsese: Interviews* contains no references to the film, and former Scorsese assistant Mary Pat Kelly's two collections of interviews with Scorsese and his various collaborators, *Martin Scorsese: The First Decade* and *Martin Scorsese: A Journey*, contain only a brief description by Kelly and a few comments by actor/participant Harvey Keitel, as well as a reprint of the original *New York Times* review. Again, no direct quotations from Scorsese are included. In a recent interview published in *Film History*, Scorsese was asked if he was ever interested in collective documentary filmmaking. He answered negatively, thus denying his own history with *Street Scenes 1970*.[48]

The only interview collection to contain Scorsese's actual comments on the film is *Martin Scorsese: Entretiens avec Michael Henry Wilson*, a series of interviews conducted with Wilson, longtime critic for the journal *Positif* (where most of the interviews were first printed) and eventual Scorsese collaborator on the documentary *A Personal Journey with Martin Scorsese through American Movies*. The first of these interviews is from May 1975, held at Paris and Cannes at which time Scorsese was promoting *Alice Doesn't Live Here Anymore* (1974). In this interview, Scorsese makes the following statement about his experiences with the film:

> I edited throughout the night over a period of ten days, trying to give a formal structure to the ensemble, swearing that I would not let myself embark into a political film if I could not direct it from one end to the other. When I showed the film to the participants, they hated it: they didn't find that it was contestable enough. They felt betrayed, they didn't recognize what they had lived through. However, I believe that the film was honest: I showed the sad reality, the anger, the frustration, the irresponsibility, the general sentiment of powerlessness. It didn't concern the Weathermen, the real radicals, but the average student, the sons of families, the weekend leftists. And that was something that they did not want to admit. I was extremely bitter, and the film ended on a very pessimistic note, in the middle of a sentence, by a brutal fade-out. Each time that we projected the film, the spectators, even the non-engaged students, spontaneously pursued the debate in the room, the arguments of the discussion in Washington. That was the only merit of *Street Scenes*.[49]

This bitterness on Scorsese's part thus becomes an obvious explanation as to why he dissociated himself from the film over the years. These comments indicate that Scorsese sees the film as having merit only as a tool to provoke political discussion, strongly implying that the film lacked aesthetic distinction and providing one explanation for his distancing of himself from the project.

The only other comments Scorsese made on the film are included in a long essay profile by Bella Taylor.[50] In this piece, Taylor includes several quotations from Scorsese on *Street Scenes 1970* taken from her own interview:

I always make it very clear that while the film was my idea, I didn't shoot most of it. I only filmed one small segment of it, but, of course, edited it along the lines of what I wanted it to say. I used footage that showed nobody knew what to do, neither radicals or [*sic*] conservatives. Everybody was yelling at everybody, and the picture ends in the middle of an argument because that was when the film literally ran out! I just left it that way. I thought, 'Perfect,' it was God-sent. I wanted to show the humanistic, rather than the political, nature of the issue. All I wanted to show was that no side had the answer. At the end, all we saw was utter hopelessness . . . not futility, but the impotence of the people. They were just sitting around and just arguing and arguing.[51]

Taylor selected all of these comments to validate a fairly standard auteurist discourse. Crucial to this is the separation of true "artists" from the world of politics: "Like many artists, Scorsese deplores the brittle, humorless provincialism of the politically-minded. He detests the dogmatic thinking of those who can only see the 'rightness' of their cause." The major problem with Taylor's piece, however, is that it does not contain or include proper citations. There are vague statements of the film being "condemned by left and right alike, as well as some of the students who shot footage for the film,"[52] but no actual names are used. Taylor seems to be simply paraphrasing comments on the film, perhaps from Scorsese himself. No actual research appears to have been done in the film or conducted with its various participants. Furthermore, the film is being downplayed within Scorsese's overall oeuvre whereas Taylor attributes what praise is given to the film to Scorsese himself. For Taylor, *Street Scenes 1970* stands as the final film of Scorsese's university career before he removed himself from politics and entered into truly "artistic" filmmaking. Given the few comments that Scorsese has made on the film, Taylor's piece influenced future writers, who frequently cite these quotes from Scorsese.

Instead of relying solely on Scorsese's own comments and on an auteurist/teleological argument that sees Scorsese's distancing of the film purely in terms of his eventual political disengagement, I reexamine the film's production and reception through interviews with other participants: NYU students Harry Bolles, John Butman, Peter Rea, Ed Summer, and Nick Tanis, as well as professional filmmaker Don Lenzer. While interviews with participants who are recalling events from more than thirty years ago are obviously not going to reveal any absolute truth (as if it exists in any case), collectively they give a much more detailed and nuanced account of the production as well as suggest another interpretation for why Scorsese dissociated himself from the film.

To begin, the extremely politicized time of the late 1960s and early 1970s is important because it had a direct impact on the environment at NYU and even within the film production classes at the time. When I asked John Butman if the reception of *Street Scenes* was as heated and debated as Taylor describes in her article, he answered, "Everything was contentious at that time, to the point where political debates kept taking over classes, which annoyed me because I was rather apolitical and simply interested in learning about film technique."[53] Furthermore, Scorsese was regarded as the instructor most sympathetic to those on the political left.[54] Far from being the apolitical artist Taylor described, Scorsese was at the vanguard of the NYU faculty, both aesthetically, in his championing of commercial cinema over the objections of senior faculty such as Manoogian, and politically, in his tolerance of political debate within a film production context.

This environment that led to the production of *Street Scenes 1970*, which began with the idea of producing a series of short films on the political situation following the U.S. invasion of Cambodia (with the subsequent shootings at Kent State eventually contributing to this unrest as well as distracting from the original outrages). Scorsese, as a faculty member, was crucial in giving students access to the equipment as well as protecting them from institutional interference. As Harry Bolles recalled, "the administration of NYU was not immediately supportive of any of this activity, which disrupted classes and put equipment at risk, and Scorsese was the one who really worked to stand in between the students and the administration." The situation on the NYU campus following the invasion of Cambodia and the Kent State shootings was extremely tense and bordering on widespread police intervention. On May 5, 1970, a day after the shootings, a group of more than 150 radicals led by a nontenured professor, Dr. Robert Wolfe, and a graduate teaching assistant in physics, Nicolas Unger, had taken over the university's main frame computer in the basement of the Courant Institute of Mathematical Sciences.[55] According to Nick Tanis, because the computer was owned by the U.S. Department of Defense and leased to the university, it was an obvious target. While this was only one of many incidents across the country, it had a more direct connection to the NYU film school given the involvement of Haig Manoogian in the negotiations. The involvement of Scorsese's mentor Manoogian is appropriately symbolic: Manoogian as representative of the establishment, to the point where Bolles remembers him finding the bomb. Manoogian may have been functioning as a symbolic establishment/father figure to some students, even though he had little actual administrative power. Nick Tanis recalls Manoogian acting much more as a mediating figure trying to bring the two sides together. Scorsese finally left NYU to accept an editing job on *Medicine Ball Caravan* (Francois Reichenbach, 1971), but he has also claimed that NYU fired him: "I was offered a job teaching film in NYU; I got very involved in political films and the students were practically living in my house. Also I was away a lot of the time trying to set up projects on the outside. So I ended up getting fired from that as well."[56] We should note, however, that whatever problems Scorsese had with NYU administration, he and Manoogian apparently remained close (and it was not Manoogian who was responsible for Scorsese's firing). Manoogian participated in a panel discussion held during the first Scorsese retrospective in 1977 and was interviewed by Scorsese's assistant Mary Pat Kelly for her two books on Scorsese's career. And, of course, *Raging Bull* is dedicated to Manoogian's memory.

With regard to the actual shooting taking place at this time, Nick Tanis recalls that while several student and professional crews were filming, only some planned on producing actual cinetracts: "While crews were scouring the city, covering every major event we learned about, some of us, inspired by the cinetracts in Paris, began making short films. Our intention was to emulate the French and project these films on the walls and in storefronts." As early as May 21, 1970, a notice appeared in the *Village Voice* on the cinetracts initiative.[57] However, this initial goal of the project was never realized: "none of these short films were ever screened because none were ever finished." Instead, Scorsese and others began to assemble the vast amount of footage into a feature length documentary. This began less than a month after the footage was originally shot, as a press release dated June 2, 1970, makes clear. Eventually, the idea for several shorts was abandoned and only the feature film remained. This shift from several short films projected in public spaces toward a feature-length film that would be shown at festivals was a move away from its original political purpose. Indeed, the film seemed to be heading in the opposite direction from the key French figure of May 1968, Jean-Luc Godard, who abandoned festivals and his own authorship to make political films within the Dziga Vertov Group. But even Godard could not erase his authorship that easily. The same year *Street Scenes* played the New York Film Festival, a screening of *Wind from the East* (Dziga Vertov Collective, 1970) was held. Not surprisingly, the film was hailed as a "Godard" film; in other words, political films could circulate within the festival only if attached to a name director. More telling is the film that played opening night, François Truffaut's *The Wild Child* (1970), a humanist drama by the now thoroughly integrated Truffaut. The "tradition of quality" had come full circle. Once *Street Scenes 1970* enters into this arena, the original intention of the filmmakers to be "the information arm of the revolution" became dramatically altered.

Ed Summer recalls that he probably shot more of the scenes included in the final cut than anyone else, often working in a three-man team with camera assistant Dick Catron and soundman Ian Gale.[58] He was also involved in the editing of the film, which was a difficult task because of the nature of the on-the-fly shooting. Summer describes the finished film as having a clear narrative arc. It begins in New York with many small scenes of people talking about the Vietnam War and the current situation. It then moves to Wall Street with more dramatic footage of larger scale protests and confrontations, and finally to Washington to film the planned protests. As Summer remembers, they were able, purely by chance, to capture a key establishing scene shortly after arriving. It was early in the morning, and Summer was shooting as all the buses started to arrive. The buses were empty and were simply being used to block the streets to control the expected crowds. Most of the scenes in Washington showed the protesters blocked into a controlled area, guarded by the army and police. There was also footage of tear gas being used to further subdue the crowd. The last scene of *Street Scenes 1970*, which Summer shot, takes place in a Washington hotel room after a day of filming. As he recalls, it is a roughly 10-minute sequence shot, filmed quite simply and capturing the rather unfocused mood of the situation. Thus the documentary took shape as a clear narrative with a beginning, middle, and end. However, this account of the events, particularly of the final scene, would be interpreted quite differently by the various participants.

Most of the footage edited into this feature came from the street demonstrations, captured cinéma verité style by the various filmmakers. Clearly staged scenes, most notably the film's conclusion, are also included, as well as at least one or two other sequences. Both Nick Tanis and Harry Bolles describe these scenes, and their details are so close that one wonders if they are discussing the same scene but remembering it differently. As Tanis recalls, "The camera was set up in the control booth of one of our small recording studios, Studio C. A student acting as a newscaster was reading a story when he was mobbed by a group of students acting, as I remember the story, as police shutting down the news." Bolles's version differs quite dramatically: "One of the students, Harry Narunsky, was in a sound booth reading [President] Nixon's speech about Cambodia, while behind his words there is a big pounding on the door, and eventually a group of students burst into the booth and overwhelm him." These sequences imply very different politics: one suggests a fight against government repression of free speech and the other a more radical overthrow of those in power. Given that it is a firsthand recollection, Bolles's account is more likely to be accurate, although whether this sequence is in the final film is questionable. Such scenes indicate that the film is more than a direct cinema observation of the events. It suggests the style of what Bill Nichols refers to as an interactive mode of documentary practice.[59] The filmmakers of *Street Scenes* situate themselves within the action, interacting with the local context of the street as well as reflecting on their own experiences.

This notion of interactivity is especially applicable in the experiences of one of the small student crews consisting of Harry Bolles (camera) and Josh Stein (sound). Bolles recalls his experience filming in the Wall Street area in the middle of a mostly pro-war, pro-military crowd and a particularly dramatic encounter that took place. A man climbed on the George Washington statue and ripped up an American flag, throwing the pieces into the frenzied crowd. Bolles is filming this event when the same man is attacked by one of the pro-military demonstrators: "I'm yelling to him to watch out, which is futile of course from where I'm filming, there's no way he could hear me. And this other guy comes around and punches the man in the head, causing him to fall into the crowd, and I remember screaming at this, even as filming." Bolles filmed this scene as an observer, unable to influence or directly interact with the events. Yet he spontaneously responded with a scream to the man being attacked. In doing so, he situated himself as a local participant, revealing his own sympathies and transforming his observational direct cinema shooting. Unfortunately, this scene is not in the finished film because of another event occurring shortly afterward. Bolles and Stein film a parade of war supporters, thinking it would make great footage but forgetting about the dangers involved:

> As I'm shooting this approaching parade, I see these people break off from the main section and come right over to us. I'm watching this through my viewfinder, which gives it a distanced feel so I don't do the right thing which would have to been to get the heck out of there. Several guys come over and want our footage, which maybe they thought was incriminating. They rough us up a little, kicking us, and take the footage, breaking the camera as they twisted off the film magazine. We still had the sound recording, but the footage was gone.

Here, the distance of the observational filmmaker was broken down in the most violent of ways—a metaphor for the very real conflict and division within the country as a whole. But Bolles's comments also reveal how the camera distanced even the filmmakers from the very danger they entered, ignoring the very social interaction in which they were obviously participating.

Although the visuals Bolles captured were lost in the interaction, the incidents remain in the finished film, providing key drama to the conclusion of *Street Scenes*. This sequence takes place in a Washington hotel room and is the scene Scorsese claims to have "directed," although he was not the cameraman. By "directed," we can assume that Scorsese was the one responsible for planning the scene and choosing the participants involved: Scorsese, Jay Cocks (Scorsese's friend and then-critic at *Time*), actress Verna Bloom (Cocks's partner and one of the stars of Haskell Wexler's protest semidocumentary *Medium Cool*), actor Harvey Keitel (who had already starred in Scorsese's debut feature, *Who's That Knocking at My Door*), and students Harry Bolles, Josh Stein, Bruce Tabor, Dan Schneider, and Deborah Litmar. Because Bolles and his crew partner Josh Stein were involved in this violent and dramatic incident, they were asked to talk about this experience: "The telling of that story is backed up very vividly with screams and shouts——mine!—but it really is something of a cheat, because those are the sounds we recorded as the fellow at Washington's statue was being attacked. I think I was much quieter when those fellows were beating me up." Thus the double absence of visual material recorded and then lost is reconstructed aurally through both the recollections of Bolles and Stein as well as Bolles's now-recontextualized scream. The originally recorded observational scenes have now been thoroughly constructed as fiction and even as metaphor for the failed Washington trip. The notion of failure is here doubled: the inability to retain the original footage because of direct violence by the pro-war protestors and the inability to attain footage because of the indifference of a pro-war government. Thus Scorsese reorganized of Bolles and Stein's experiences to express the futility felt at the time.

The hotel room sequence concludes with a discussion of the current situation that reflected the discouragement of the failed revolution but also the continued devotion of the participants. Most accounts of this scene stress the depressed mood and the lack of consensus, particularly because this is what Scorsese himself emphasizes in his few interviews on the film. The reading Scorsese offered and critics following his lead is only partial and very much informed by Scorsese as auteur: the abrupt ending in which the camera runs out of film reflecting Scorsese's retrospectively defined feelings of the futility of the political situation (and thus of political filmmaking). Bolles argues that those involved were still committed. He reads the conclusion not in terms of the form of the film (the abrupt ending) but in terms of its content, stressing the final line, "Watch the skies!" spoken by student Bruce Tabor. Fellow participant Nick Tanis recalls the scene in a similar fashion: "The concluding line of the film, as I remember it, came from a student who has since passed away, Bruce Tabor, 'Watch the skies! Watch the skies!' This is a quote from a 1950s science fiction film about invaders from outer space. The implication was that we were being threatened by unseen forces." In fact, the line is not only a reference to *The Thing from Another World* (Christian Nyby, 1951), but also became an infamous anticommunist watchword during the 1950s, warning of possible enemies within. The use of the line in this film is an ironic commentary on the student rebellion sharing the legacy of earlier critics of U.S. foreign policy and the need for a revival of a forceful opposition that had earlier been silenced in the cold war witch hunts. The advantage of this reading of the film as remaining politically engaged is that it emphasizes the collective and political nature of the enterprise rather than a decontextualized reading that sees the ending only in terms of Scorsese's later work. As Nick Tanis argues, the objective of the film was to record the demonstrations, which it succeeded in achieving, and it was the only film made about the events of 1970 on the streets of the East Coast. To call this a failure is a distortion only possible if read through Scorsese's authorship.

Of all the footage in the final film, there is unanimous consensus that professional cameraman Don Lenzer captured the most striking material. In addition to Scorsese, both Nick Tanis and Peter Rea recall, after more than thirty years, the quality of Lenzer's work on the film. We should not be surprised that Lenzer, an experienced cameraman, would capture the most compelling footage, but this cannot be attributed solely to technical skill. It also needs to be explained in terms of Lenzer's approach to filming the demonstrations. In the following comments, Lenzer explains both how and why he got involved in the project as well as his cinematic inspiration for what he filmed:

> We concentrated on interviews with pro-war demonstrators— among them were a lot of "hard hats," who were working on the construction of the World Trade Towers. We felt that was much more interesting than simply shooting footage of the protestors or interviewing the anti-war people. At the time, I was very much influenced by the work of Chris Marker. In particular, his film *Le Joli Mai* (1963) and its use of experiential encounters very much influenced what I shot, and I was somewhat pleased when Richard Roud, director of the Festival, noted the connection. After we shot, we simply handed the footage over to the people responsible for putting the film together. I had no hand in the editing of it at all. At the time I was very much in favor of the idea of a collective film, of the documentary as a collaborative work.[60]

Lenzer's comments reveal both his main influence in how and what he filmed, as well as why he was interested in participating in the film: to engage in a collective political project. But when this collection of footage was turned into a feature length film and then entered into the New York Film Festival, the collective dimension was downplayed.

In the original festival program sent out to members of the Film Society of Lincoln Center, the program notes for *Street Scenes 1970* read as follows:

> Cinéma Verité is not dead yet. This is a film about the demonstrations on Wall Street and in Washington this spring. But its virtue is not just that it shows us what the media didn't. Like Chris Marker, director Martin Scorsese [*sic*] is committed without being blinkered. He does not pretend to know what truth is. His truth, yes; but truth, no. Even the interviewees whose opinions are least sympathetic to him come out as recognizable human beings. Doubtless, this is because Scorcese [*sic*] is an artist.[61]

The emphasis here is very much on Scorsese as the author of the film with no mention of the collective nature of the project. Even the influence of Marker is attributed, rather erroneously, to Scorsese. Understandably, Lenzer was upset at this distortion of the film and its collective nature, despite his pleasure in seeing the film receive a public screening:

> I had mixed feelings. Of course I was happy the film was shown at the festival. But at the same time I was angry—I felt that Richard Roud, in his program notes, gave most of the credit for the project to Scorsese. And I felt that the nature of the project was fundamentally a collaborative one—that was so much a part of the times—and that this aspect of it wasn't emphasized. Now, I don't believe that Scorsese himself promoted this idea or tried to take credit for the film. In fact, he wrote me a long letter apologizing after he found out I was upset. I never responded at the time, which I regret now. But I think Marty was sincere, and in any case I don't think it represented anything intentional on Marty's part.

Lenzer's opinion that Scorsese did not intentionally try to take credit for the film seems accurate according to most of the evidence. Nick Tanis stressed that Scorsese was very supportive throughout the making of the film: "He urged people to make short films and trusted very inexperienced students to go out and make this film. At every stage along the way, he included as many people as he could in planning and executing the film." In addition to writing Lenzer a letter apologizing for the program notes, Scorsese appears to have corrected the organizers of the festival. When the advertisement appeared in both the *New York Times* and the *Village Voice* the week before the festival, the program note had been rewritten:

> Cinéma Verité is not dead yet. This film about the demonstrations on Wall Street and in Washington this spring tells you what the media forgot to. It was made by a group of concerned students and professional filmmakers called the New York Cinetracts Collective; they are committed without being blinkered. Even the interviewees whose opinions are least sympathetic to the Collective's political position come out as recognizable human beings. Doubtless this is because postproduction director Martin Scorcese [*sic*] and the other filmmakers are artists.[62]

This rewritten program note stresses the collectivity of the project instead of Scorsese as author and removes the previous reference to Chris Marker, although that Scorsese's name is the still the only one given is telling. What this controversy demonstrates is the incompatibility of the original nature of the project with the demands of a feature-length film. The festival organizers clearly felt the need to fit this collective film into an auteurist box. The rest of the collective needed to be reduced to the status of "personnel" in order for an artist to be celebrated and the film to fit into the art world of the festival circuit.

This authorship controversy around *Street Scenes* is arguably the major factor in both Scorsese's reluctance to discuss the film and his desire to distance himself from the film as much as possible. It is a much more convincing explanation than the one usually given that stresses that the main controversy over the film was of a political nature. While none of the interviewees mentioned anything about the political debate around the film, both Harry Bolles and Peter Rea recall the authorship controversy:

> Bolles: There did end up being a debate around the authorship of the film, not necessarily in the auteurist sense, but literally in terms of ownership. I remember Don Lenzer in particular was upset that Scorsese had turned this student footage into a feature film with Scorsese as the editor/producer. His attitude was that it wasn't Scorsese's film.

Rea: People were saying that he was taking credit for this thing, well, they really weren't, but he felt it that way. So he felt awkward positioning himself as the filmmaker. It wasn't the politics of the film, if anything it was too mild as far as he was concerned.

Furthermore, given the counter culture of the time period, to have been involved in a political protest documentary, even one in which all of the participants were not satisfied with the end result, would hardly be damaging. While there is no direct evidence that there was political debate around the film besides Scorsese's own account, I do not question the truthfulness of this claim but rather its significance. Clearly at the time political discussion was taking place about everything, and the film, no matter what its form, would not be able to avoid this. But a controversy over the authorship of the film and over taking credit for the work of others would be far more damaging to Scorsese's image as prestigious auteur.

Two incidents occurring years after the film's initial screening provide additional evidence that Scorsese remained sensitive over the authorship of the film and any suggestion that he was selfishly profiting from it. Nick Tanis recalls the final meeting he had with Scorsese over the film:

> The last conversation we had about *Street Scenes 1970* took place just after the release of *Mean Streets* [fall of 1973]. Again if my memory is correct, I saw Marty at an early screening of his film. He asked me to join him at his hotel room to tell me that *Street Scenes 1970* had made a small profit. He wanted someone connected to the project to discuss his plan for the money and to give him approval on what to do with the money. I believe he donated the money to the NYU Department of Film and Television.

Scorsese's gesture here is a noble one and is true to the initial collective impulse behind the project, but it also speaks to his anxiety about profiting from the film, either culturally or, in this case, economically. Decades later, this same anxiety was still present. Peter Rea recalls meeting Scorsese at a retrospective of his work at the Walter Reade Theater at Lincoln Center in 1996 and mentioning that he wanted to see the film again:

> I said that I'd love to see *Street Scenes*, I hadn't seen it in so many years. He said he had a copy, but that I'd need to rent it, he wasn't going to rent it to screen it himself. Now here's a man who in

that period of time has directed a body of work that is considered to be one of the premiere in all of American film. And he's still uncomfortable about a student film that someone said he may have taken credit for!

Scorsese's unease toward *Street Scenes* continues today, as can be seen in his infrequent comments on the film (none since the 1981 interview with Bella Taylor) and his tight control over his own print.[63]

The film today functions very much like a "lost" film, a work that failed to be preserved and exists only through contemporaneous reviews or later recollections. Ironically, Scorsese is known today for his commitment to film history and to preserving the cinematic past even as he plays a role in repressing a part of his own history. Of course, we can find other examples of directors denying access to their own work in the interests of preserving a certain image. One example is the aforementioned Cassavetes, who refused to allow his original cut of *Shadows* (1959) to be seen, despite its historical importance in the creation of the New American Cinema. For years this first version of *Shadows* was thought to be lost, but recently Cassavetes's scholar Ray Carney discovered a print and even screened it at the Rotterdam Film Festival without receiving permission from Cassavetes's estate. Cassavetes's wife Gena Rowlands has filed suit to keep the film from being screened, insisting that the film is the intellectual property of Cassavetes and that he did not wish that early version (which she considers a work print) to be shown publicly.[64] While the ethics of this can be debated, the situation of *Street Scenes 1970* is somewhat different and perhaps even unique so far in film history. Scorsese's ownership of the film as the textual "author" is not being used to keep the film from being seen. On the contrary, Scorsese has actually tried to disavow his connections to the project and the film's authorship controversy is the main impediment to greater access to the print. Because of his role as an archivist, Scorsese is able to control access to his print of the film, and with a film with so few known prints and no commercial distribution, this has significantly reduced the already limited access to a film that was made, as a collective, to contribute to the public discourse and debate around the United States and its role in foreign countries.

One cannot help but note an obvious contradiction regarding Scorsese and *Street Scenes 1970*. Scorsese's involvement in the film has probably saved it from the dustbin of history, linking it to the work of an "important" filmmaker in the "Great Man" tradition that is still very much with us. At the same time, the fact that Scorsese now owns and controls a print of the film as an archivist has limited the film's distribution and access. As we move forward in film history and the preservation of this past, the issues arising from artists in the archive will be of greater and greater importance. While Scorsese is one of the most prominent of these artists/archivists, he is no means unique and will most likely become less of an exception. Scorsese may be nobly preserving the world's film heritage, but he is also carefully shaping and constructing his image. As Scorsese knows very well, this image relies on telling his history in a very particular way, one in which issues of authorship and politics are downplayed as much as possible. This idea of a singular auteurist authority needs to be challenged and works of history, especially works of relatively recent history, are always in constant need of other voices that revise and question the dominant accounts. Given the huge amount of capital involved in film preservation, a situation that threatens its cultural autonomy in the services of those with economic power, the necessity of multiplying the voices heard within the cultural discourse is all the more urgent.[65]

Street Scenes 1970 marks a break in Scorsese's career, being the last project he was involved with before moving to Hollywood. Unfortunately, this divide has caused the production and reception of *Street Scenes* to be distorted. A similar teleology would continue to influence the reading of individual Scorsese projects. Additionally, the divide between New York and Hollywood would reoccur throughout Scorsese criticism. In leaving behind the New York film and university community, Scorsese was certainly risking the small reputation he had built as a talented young director. For the first time, Scorsese had literally "gone Hollywood." Figuratively, this question of going Hollywood would continue to structure the remainder of his career.

2

The Formation of Scorsese's Critical Reputation

More than ever before, the movie studios are terrified to try anything new. They want to repeat past successes, and they have found a new generation of filmmakers willing to oblige them. During the sixties young directors dreamed of becoming the American Bergman or Fellini. Today's young filmmakers are more likely to emulate Peter Bogdanovich, the film-buff-turned-director who has built his career on clever reproductions of the genre movies of the thirties and forties.[1]

❧

THIS CAUTIONARY *NEW YORK TIMES* article by Stephen Farber concerning the fate of the talented young filmmakers of the Hollywood Renaissance is intriguing from several perspectives. First, this is written in 1975, in the middle of the so-called last Golden Age of Hollywood before the releases of *Jaws* (Steven Spielberg, 1975) and *Star Wars* (George Lucas, 1977) would move Hollywood into the blockbuster era. Farber's comments show how contemporary discussions of Hollywood at this time often paint a very different picture of the period than later, more nostalgic recollections. Second, the opposition Farber establishes here between the genuine, pure artistry of a Bergman or Fellini and a genre filmmaker like Bogdanovich is mapped onto Scorsese's first two Hollywood films, with *Mean Streets* representing the work of "an unconventional artist" and *Alice Doesn't Live Here Anymore* showing Scorsese having "capitulated to Hollywood." Farber strongly upholds the dichotomy between authentic art and commercialism, ignoring the challenges made over the preceding decade to overturn this notion of aesthetic purity. Farber sees in Scorsese both the qualities of a genuine artist as well as those of a commercial craftsman: "At his best he is an intransigent artist committed to unvarnished truth on the screen; but, like Peter Bogdanovich, he is also a film buff with a taste for Hollywood showmanship."[2] Looking back on this article, Farber both realized the dangers inherent in Scorsese's commercialism while misrecognizing the cultural field as it had developed. The very qualities Farber admires in *Mean Streets*, such as cultural authenticity, were seen as being overly sociological in nature and possibly detrimental to notions of universality so key to canonization. Moving into Hollywood genre filmmaking was an attempt to further reduce (although not eliminate entirely) Scorsese's ethnic specificity as well as appeal to a critical community invested in the notion that a true auteur can work within Hollywood's genre system.

Scorsese's move from NYU to Hollywood signaled his move from student filmmaker to professional director. While most studies of Scorsese emphasize the formal qualities of the films as evidence of Scorsese's greatness, particularly his three most lauded films (*Mean Streets, Taxi Driver*, and *Raging Bull*), I shift focus away from Scorsese as auteur and toward the critical environment of the period. This will allow for a broader understanding and Scorsese's place within that environment, as well as offer a fresh perspective on the films themselves. Although a consideration of Scorsese's critical reputation and his more recent films will continue throughout the rest of the study, this chapter concentrates on the period from *Boxcar Bertha*, Scorsese's first professional directing effort in 1972, until *Raging Bull*, the film many consider Scorsese's masterpiece. The field in which Scorsese's reputation emerges can only be understood by tracing the history back to the immediate post–World War II years in both the United States and Europe. From this point, we can begin to contextualize Scorsese's emergence as the most critically acclaimed director of his generation. Several critics have noted the mixture of American and European influences on Scorsese and his cinematic style, but have not examined these connections beyond the texts themselves. Many have tended to see these influences as dialectical rather than dialogical. Examining the commonalities rather than the divisions between classical and modernist styles and approaches is much more fruitful instead of insisting on the division between Hollywood and Europe.

Cahiers du Cinéma and Its Influence

A good place to start is with the auteur theory as espoused by the critics at the *Cahiers du Cinéma*. Since many *Cahiers* critics would become filmmakers themselves, this journal is often associated with a European, modernist sensibility (New Wave innovation as opposed to Hollywood convention). This argument can only be made at the level of the text itself: *Les Quatre Cents Coups* (François Truffaut, 1959) and *À Bout de Souffle* (Jean-Luc Godard, 1959) both break with the classical style of Hollywood. When looking beyond the film texts and at the level of the broader culture in which works are discussed and consumed, these distinctions begin to immediately break down. These French critics were the most influential of all in removing Hollywood from the realm of "mass culture" and having these films taken seriously as art. Part of this was recognizing a certain modernist complexity in Hollywood directors, but also of critical importance was how these films were discussed. As Greg Taylor argues, the notion of the critic who served as an aesthetic and moral guide to great art was challenged within American film criticism as early as the 1940s with writers such as Manny Farber and Parker Tyler, who worked very much as artists/critics. This same approach can be seen in the criticism of Godard, a good example being his review of Douglas Sirk's *A Time to Love and a Time to Die* (1957).[3] Taking this approach to film aesthetics is not surprising given that Godard and many other writers for *Cahiers* were interested in moving beyond being critics and toward being filmmakers, eliminating the boundaries separating the two. As Godard stated in an interview shortly after completing his first feature film: "Today I still think of myself as a critic, and in a sense I am, more than ever before. Instead of writing criticism, I make a film, but the critical dimension is subsumed."[4]

With the *Cahiers* group, an interpretive community is already rejecting the notion of Hollywood mass art versus high European modernism. But what is often forgotten about this group (probably due to Godard's later politicization) is the degree to which they depoliticized and desocialized French cinema, calling for a certain brand of modernist criticism that argued form over content. Thus the main aesthetic criticism labeled against the "tradition of quality" Truffaut so despised was that it was a cinema of writers, not directors. It lacked the concern with the formal specificity of the medium that was a prerequisite of modernist high art. But at the same time, Truffaut angrily denounced the screenwriters Jean Aurenche and Pierre Bost for having an attitude of high art elitism toward the cinema as a mass medium. The filmmakers of the "tradition of quality" were thus both elitist snobs who valued literature over film, and philistines when it came to the notion of cinematic form. Any conclusion that characterized the *Cahiers* group as early cinematic postmodernists who wanted to demolish the notion of high modernist art would be inaccurate. Rather, the argument centered on whether literary high art produced cinematic high art, or whether cinema had to develop its own aesthetic specificity, a very modernist notion that was only radical in its application to a culturally negated art form like film, not in the application itself.

This relates directly to Scorsese and his historical position. If the French influenced how Americans viewed their own cinema, European cinema then had a profound influence on the postwar American film culture, particularly in major cities like New York in which Scorsese was raised. Consider the brief DVD introduction Scorsese gave viewers to *The Golden Coach* (Jean Renoir, 1953), a film Scorsese helped to restore (and the film after which Truffaut names his production company). In this short clip, Scorsese stated that he is neither a Hollywood director nor a European director, but rather somewhere between. The same lack of clear distinctions along these binaries can be seen in Scorsese's description of the film. He focuses on the emotional effect the film has, thus emphasizing its popular dimension rather than its intellectual (read political and social) sophistication. At the same time, the medium specificity is stressed through the admiration of the film's use of Technicolor. Simply stating that Scorsese was influenced by the European cinema is insufficient. What specifically within European cinema influenced him? What was the ultimate effect of this influence not only on Scorsese but also on American culture as a whole?

John Hess, in his two-part critique of "La politique des auteurs" that appears in *Jump Cut* in 1974, argues that despite the aesthetic innovation and sense of youthful rebellion associated with the movement, the French New Wave itself, especially the *Cahiers* group, was "a culturally conservative, politically reactionary attempt to remove film from the realm of social and political concern."[5] Part of this process was praising of Hollywood directors, and the success of the French New Wave brought an imprimatur to these views when applied in the United States by Andrew Sarris. Similar to the process of depoliticizing the French cinema, Sarris sought to change the focus in U.S. film criticism from the sociological approach of critics such as James Agee. This had already been started in the United States through the blacklist years of the 1950s and was supported by cold war apologists such as Robert Warshow. Sarris used this cultural environment to shift the American film canon, as Peter Biskind argues:

By the time Sarris began to write, the pages of American newspa-
pers and magazines had been made safe for democracy. The lefties,
radicals, fellow travellers, independents, anarchists, pacifists, and
general riffraff who had infected the press with their pink prose in
the thirties and forties had been flushed out by almost a decade of
witch hunting. . . . All Sarris had to do was to conduct a mopping-up
operation, and he saw to it that auteurism would play the same role
in America that it had played in France; the American "tradition
of quality" that it was used to demolish was precisely the Jacobs,
Rotha, Griffith, Macdonald, Agee group that Warshow had already
softened up. More so than Warshow, Sarris saw them as a "tradition," and attacked them directly. His strategy, borrowed from the
French, was to dump the silents, whether Russian or American, the
"art films" so dear to the old guard, and privilege "movies" instead,
claiming they were true "art."[6]

The field of American cinema popular criticism thus became seemingly
free of sociological concerns while making possible cultural legitimacy
through popular forms.

Of course, this criticism was still ideological and even sociological,
as it had been in France. Hess asked the question of what an auteur was
according to the *Cahiers* critics and found that it had very little to do
with film technique. The *Cahiers* group was attracted to a single tale: an
isolated character placed within an extreme circumstance eventually finding acceptance, understanding, and redemption. Whenever the auteur
critics saw this tale on the screen, they called its creator an auteur.[7]
The aesthetic concerns (realism, mise-en-scène, and acting) had to do
with how a director presented this interior life of isolation and eventual
transcendence: "The most important determinant of an auteur was not
so much the director's ability to express his personality, as usually has
been claimed, but rather his desire and ability to express a certain world
view."[8] This worldview needed to be able to express art's autonomy and
be divorced from the social and political world. Thus the criticism of
the "tradition of quality," although argued on aesthetic grounds, had a
great deal to do with objectionable content, such as Truffaut's criticism
of blasphemy and homosexuality in these films. As a result, the revolution
of the New Wave and the auteur theory was easily assimilated because
it was essentially about art rather than politics.

Likewise, Sarris was superficially concerned with aesthetics and
argued explicitly for its separation from social and political concerns:
"I still find it impossible to attribute films and directors to any particular system or culture. If directors and other artists cannot be wrenched

from their historical environments, aesthetics is reduced to a subordinate branch of ethnography."[9] On closer inspection, Sarris, like the New Wave critics, was not only or even primarily interested in aesthetics. His own writing was just as ideologically charged as the sociological criticism, only it was beneath an aesthetic argument: "The adoration of American film meant the adoration of American ideology. The action films auteurists liked were clean, mean, tough, and generally right wing. The films they didn't like were [Sarris's] 'liberal' "[10] reviews, such as his harsh critique of *Dog Day Afternoon* (Sidney Lumet, 1975), were often purely sociological, just from a different political perspective: "It suddenly became clear that there was good sociological criticism and bad sociological criticism. Good sociological criticism wasn't sociological at all; it was redefined as 'aesthetic,' and it was practiced by 'us'; bad sociological criticism was practiced by 'them.' 'Us' in this case meant centrists like Sarris."[11] This is important to keep in mind because Sarris's influence, like that of the New Wave critics, was enormous, both in the field of film criticism and among filmmakers themselves.

In the case of Scorsese, who was both a filmmaker and a film teacher during this early period, the influence is doubled. Scorsese, as an instructor, followed Sarris's lead in both content and style, initiating an early course on "American Movies" at NYU. Former student Harry Bolles recalls Scorsese approaching the material in a manner reminiscent of Sarris: "His method was very similar to that of Andrew Sarris, whose book *The American Cinema* had just been published and which was a very popular text amongst film students. I was personally very excited by the book; I read and re-read it over and over at that time. It was very fun and accessible and made you interested in the subject. I had a similar response to Marty's class and his style as a teacher." Even at this early phase, Scorsese responded to Sarris's views on American cinema while popularizing them with a new generation of film students. Although he cannot be said to have the same influence as the critic turned directors of the French New Wave, the purpose was comparable: to open a space within the culture for his filmmaking within a Hollywood context. Sarris's position was challenged almost immediately, but from the similarly apolitical position of Pauline Kael. The resulting war between Sarris and Kael and their respective supporters concealed the fact that both had worked toward a similar goal: to remove politics, sociology, and "ideology" (which were all equated) from the realm of artistic discussion. Kael's main objection to Sarris was in terms of taste. She accused him and his followers of being elitist, of wanting to transform popular film into high art. For this same reason, Kael opposed the academic study of film. But Kael also critiqued the emerging postmodern sensibility of a Sontag or a Warhol, which seemed to want to eliminate the high/low culture distinction. Within the circle of film criticism, the idea of high art may have been transforming, but it was hardly eliminated.

Contingencies of Value and the Politics of Film Canons

Whatever value as art one may want to assign to Scorsese's films, that value is highly contingent. This is not to say that the aesthetic worth of Scorsese's films is purely relative or that all other films could be praised with the same validity, but rather that there are no pure or absolute evaluations. As Barbara Herrnstein-Smith argues, "the value—the 'goodness' or 'badness'—of an evaluation, like that of anything else (including any other type of utterance), is *itself* contingent, and thus a matter not of its abstract 'truth-value' but of how well it performs various desired/able functions."[12] The evaluation of any work cannot be separated and divorced from its social value and social function. This is not to claim that evaluation simply reflects the political values of the time in any straightforward fashion, but rather that art has a use-value within society and is praised for the functions it performs for certain groups (either dominant or marginal) within that society. These contingencies or conditions are usually unspoken or sometimes even denied; for example, there are the continued claims for the "universality" of certain artists. These arguments of universality are connected to another common concept within evaluation: the notion of timelessness. As the argument is conventionally told, art that survives must have lasted because it says something "essential" about the "human condition." But as Herrnstein-Smith argues, this idea, so central to canon formation, is fundamentally flawed:

> What is commonly referred to as the "test of time" is not, as the figure implies, an impersonal and impartial mechanism: for the cultural institutions through which it operates (schools, libraries, theatres, museums, publishing and printing houses, editorial boards, prize-awarding commissions, state censors, etc.) are, of course, all managed by persons (who, by definition, are those with cultural power and commonly other forms of power as well), and, since the texts that are selected and preserved by "time" will always tend to be those which "fit" (and, indeed, have often been *designed* to fit) their characteristic needs, interests, resources, and purposes, that testing mechanism has its own built-in partialities accumulated in and thus *intensified by* time.[13]

For these reasons, canons have a strong tendency to be self-perpetuating. Once an artwork achieves classical status, it is much less prone to the risk of nonsurvival than other works. This is the case even when features of the canonized work tend to conflict with the political and social values of a particular society. Once canonized, an older text that is out of fashion with current values will be rationalized or its offensive material repressed. And while Herrnstein-Smith is primarily referring here to literature, within the area of film this timelessness is even more problematic. Because of the fragile nature of the medium, a great deal of film history, barely a century old, has been lost. The movies that do survive tend to be works that have had a degree of critical acclaim. For this reason, film canons are thus even more self-perpetuating than those in most other cultural fields.

There is not a huge body of literature around the subject of film canons and axiology, and Janet Staiger's 1985 essay, "The Politics of Film Canons," remains the most thorough discussion of the topic. Staiger argues that film studies as a discipline needs to address questions around its own evaluative activity: "By what standards do we make value judgments? What are the political implications of various standards? What ends do these standards promote? How do we, if we are to make selections based on value, choose among the standards? If evaluative standards are for the social good, who determines the social good? Are standards for the society at large, for segments of the society, for individuals? What about those outside a particular hegemonic culture?"[14] To answer these questions, Staiger considers the two groups of critics that helped shape the formation of the film canon as it stood at the time: the auteur critics and the ideological critics. Auteurism was the methodology that helped secure film as a legitimate art form worthy of academic study, which helped establish film studies as an academic discipline. The auteur critics were concerned with three main criteria of value: (1) universality and endurance; (2) personal vision; and (3) consistency of statement. The Romantic auteur critics were concerned with the elevation of their chosen group into an elite category (the "Pantheon") that often took on spiritual overtones, "as if they were members of a spiritual priesthood."[15]

The problem, however, was that the content was of much less importance (at least overtly) than the criteria of universality, endurance, personal vision, and consistency across a group of films. The reconsideration of the criteria used for evaluation and the process of evaluation itself were precisely the questions that the ideological critics who overtook the discipline in the 1970s asked. After the political upheaval of May 1968, the editorial stance of the *Cahiers du Cinéma* shifted from its former auteurism to an avowedly Marxist stance. The new group of critics, led by Jean-Luc Comolli and Jean Narboni, critiqued dominant filmmaking practices for supporting and reinforcing bourgeois ideology and explicitly called for a new agenda for the magazine. The editorial piece,

"Cinema/Ideology/Criticism," was published in the October 1969 issue of *Cahiers*, and it outlined the new purpose of ideological film criticism: "The question we have to ask is: which films, books and magazines allow the ideology a free, unhampered passage, transmit it with crystal clarity, serve as its chosen language? And which attempt to make it turn back and reflect itself, intercept it, make it visible by revealing its mechanisms, by blocking them?"[16] This editorial signaled the turn in film criticism toward issues of ideology that would dominate film studies as a discipline throughout the 1970s.

But, as Staiger argues, despite this seemingly dramatic shift in emphasis, the auteur critics and the ideological critics often discussed the same films and filmmakers. Although the ideological critics did champion previously marginalized work, they concentrated on rescuing films and filmmakers who were previously discovered by the auteur critics. Although Comolli and Narboni outlined seven categories of films for film critics to analyze, by far the most influential of these has been the now infamous "category e": "Films which seem at first sight to belong firmly within the ideology and to be completely under its sway, but which turn out to be so only in an ambiguous manner."[17] Comolli and Narboni argue that through film style, certain directors can transform content that seems very conservative into a critique of itself. In the case of films in "category e," the critic's task becomes to point out how certain formal aspects of film style can call into question the apparent ideology on the surface. The reason "category e" becomes so influential is because it allowed auteurism, which was previously at the forefront of film criticism, to continue despite the change within the politics of the time. Many film critics, who tended to be left-leaning, needed a way to justify their aesthetic tastes, and "category e" allowed these critics to salvage their favorite films of the past by claiming them as "subtly subversive." This is not to claim that this criticism is wrong or incorrect, but merely that this way of reading Hollywood films has a history. Ironically, the method of Comolli and Narboni, two Marxist critics, has rescued the centrist methodological approach. We see the influence of both auteurist and ideological critics in the making of Scorsese's reputation, and as further evidence of self-perpetuation, these two interpretive communities strongly influence Scorsese's own documentaries on film history discussed in chapter 4.

Becoming a Professional: *Boxcar Bertha*

Based on Bertha Thompson's autobiographical novel, *Boxcar Bertha* takes place during the Depression-era 1930s, and much more explicitly than its

forerunner, *Bonnie and Clyde* (Arthur Penn, 1967), it shows the antago-
nism between the rich people in power and the poor that have to resort
to crime to survive. Following the death of her father, a pilot who is killed
in an airplane crash because he is overworked, Bertha (Barbara Hershey)
takes to a transient life on the railway boxcars of the country. She soon
reunites with the union leader Big Bill Shelley (David Carradine) and
the two become lovers, but they are separated because of persecution
by the railway owners. She starts a relationship with the hustler Rake
Brown (Barry Primus) and ends up killing a man to protect him. As the
two flee onto yet another boxcar, she is reunited with Bill, along with his
African-American friend Von Morton (Bernie Casey). The four form a
gang, robbing the railway company and fighting against southern racism
and police brutality. Eventually, Bill is caught and put in jail, Rake is
killed, and Bertha escapes and is forced into prostitution. At the conclusion, she finds an escaped Bill once again, but the reunion is short-lived.
Railway company thugs attacked them, and Bill is crucified against the
boxcar as Bertha watches. Von returns and takes revenge, in a violent
scene shot as an homage to Sam Peckinpah. The final shot shows a crucified Bill being taken away by the train as Bertha chases behind in vain.

From the beginning of Scorsese's career, one can see an example
of the Herrnstein-Smith discussed contingencies. Scorsese's first "professional" directing job actually took place two years before his move
to Hollywood and four years before he worked for Roger Corman on
Boxcar Bertha. In 1968 Scorsese was hired to direct *The Honeymoon Killers*,
scripted by Leonard Castle. But after a week of shooting, Scorsese was
fired from the job and replaced by Castle himself. The film was released
in 1970 and has developed a significant cult following, eventually being
distributed by the prestigious Criterion Collection DVD company. Scorsese's comments on this incident reveal a great deal about the cultural
field of filmmaking:

> I had been fired from *The Honeymoon Killers* in 1968 after one week's
> shooting, and for a pretty good reason too. It was a 200-page script
> and I was shooting everything in master shots with no coverage
> because I was an artist! Since the guys with the money only had
> enough for a $150,000 black and white film, they said we just
> couldn't go on; there would have to be close-ups or something. Of
> course, not every scene was shot from one angle, but too many of
> them were, so that there was no way of avoiding a film four hours
> long. That was a great lesson. From 1968 to 1972 I was very much
> afraid I would get fired again. So when I started on *Boxcar Bertha*
> I drew every scene, about 500 pictures altogether.[18]

Scorsese's comment here that he was an "artist" is clearly meant to be self-mocking, but it is also a conventional parody of the self-important experimental filmmaker who will not submit to the demands of working in the industry. Given that Scorsese was making these comments retrospectively in order to position his own subsequent career, they served as a self-justification as well as self-critique. Because of the auteur theory, the idea of producing art within the system was considered possible. Art was no longer contingent on being separate from commercial concerns. When Scorsese looked back on his younger filmmaking self as pretentious and unreasonable, he implicitly passed judgment on others who insist on this point of view. Moving from New York and independent filmmaking and into the world of Hollywood commercialism can be read as "selling out" to the system. Scorsese's comments argue against this by seeing financial interests as inevitable to the making of film. What was a very clear professional and ideological decision by Scorsese is turned into "common sense."

Boxcar Bertha stands as Scorsese's entrance into Hollywood as a director because of its unambiguously commercial nature, even if it was made on the margins of this industry. It is an example of a Roger Corman–produced "exploitation" film, one of the many in the lovers-on-the-run genre. These same qualities excluded the film from serious consideration as art, as Scorsese's now often-told anecdote about the film shows:

> I showed *Boxcar Bertha* in a rough-cut of about two hours to John Cassavetes. John took me back to his office, looked at me and said, "Marty, you've just spent a whole year of your life making a piece of shit. It's a good picture, but you're better than the people who make this kind of movie. Don't get hooked into the exploitation market, just try and do something different." Jay Cocks, who was then the *Time* film critic, had shown him *Who's That Knocking at My Door* and he had loved it. He said I must go back to making that kind of film and was there anything I had that I was really dying to make. I said, "Yes, although it needs a rewrite." "Well, rewrite it then!"[19]

The frequency with which this story gets told and retold proves its symbolic value to the narrative that is Scorsese's career.[20] The story both praises and critiques Scorsese, stressing his immense talent as an artist as well as the failure of that talent to be properly realized within the exploitation market. It features Cassavetes in the role of supportive yet critical mentor/father, guiding the young disciple to his proper place as an artist, stressing the importance of "personal" work. Although the exploitation market was the contemporary equivalent of the Classical Hollywood B films that Scorsese so admired, it was not the place, according to Cassavetes, in which serious, personal work could be accomplished. "Personal work" for Cassavetes meant stories about people, not about film technique, as in auteurism. As previously mentioned, Cassavetes's first film, *Shadows*, had an early version that was more experimental in technique that he eventually abandoned for a second version that was more focused on the characters and their relationships. He argued, "the first version was an interesting film from a technical point of view, but it had nothing to do with people."[21] Throughout the rest of his career Cassavetes continued to follow this principle, and although he would become an almost mythical figure within the context of "independent" cinema, he would be relatively ignored by film studies as a discipline and marginalized within the canon.[22] Scorsese avoids this marginalization by virtue of his closer ties to Hollywood, a closeness foreshadowed by his involvement with Corman and Corman's own relationship vis-à-vis the major studios.

Although Corman began as a low-budget alternative to Hollywood, he was at the same time fulfilling a role within the system that Hollywood had abandoned: the B film. After the breaking up of vertical integration throughout the 1950s and the loss of guaranteed distribution, major companies no longer produced nor exhibited B pictures. This caused the differences between low-budget B films being made within the confines of the Production Code and the exploitation films made outside of the

Figure 2.1. *Boxcar Bertha* (Martin Scorsese, 1972), low genre, overt politics.

system to disappear.[23] Corman was one of the low-budget producers who emerged from this split, providing cheap, low-budget genre films using exploitation material that appealed to the increasingly youth-oriented market. Gradually, Corman and low-budget exploitation would integrate into Hollywood. The New Hollywood films of the Hollywood Renaissance (what Geoff King has dubbed "New Hollywood Version I"[24]) like *Bonnie and Clyde* and especially *Easy Rider* (Dennis Hopper, 1969) relied on previously taboo (for Hollywood) subjects of sex, violence, and in the case of *Easy Rider*, drugs for their breakout success with the youth audience. The New Hollywood films of the blockbuster cycle (what King refers to as "New Hollywood Version II") relied on the generic elements and exploitation marketing strategies Corman favored, eventually forcing him out of the business. Hollywood, with films such as *A Clockwork Orange* (Stanley Kubrick, 1971) and *The Godfather* (Francis Ford Coppola, 1972), was pushing the boundaries of sex and violence, and later blockbusters such as *Star Wars* and *Raiders on the Lost Ark* (Steven Spielberg, 1981) were using similar advertising strategies, all with the huge budget of a Hollywood studio behind them.

Boxcar Bertha served as an important work for Scorsese (as with similar films by other New Hollywood directors) by displaying his ability to work successfully within a commercial system, delivering a film on time and on budget. More important, it began to establish the niche within which Scorsese could operate within the changing conditions of New Hollywood: as a filmmaker who took violence as a subject matter. The few early reviews of the film that do exist concentrate on the representation of brutality. Roger Ebert comments, "Scorsese has gone for mood and atmosphere more than for action, and his violence is always blunt and unpleasant—never liberating and exhilarating, as the New Violence is supposed to be."[25] Likewise, Jeremy James praises the depth of Scorsese's violence, his ability to fill the picture "with a paranoid and ultimately justified dread, a constant sense of impending atrocity."[26] Even though the criticism was not always positive, it created a debate over representations of violence that has continued throughout Scorsese's career. *Boxcar Bertha* serves as an effective bridge in Scorsese's career, a work with "limits" of "possibilities" in which he nevertheless "succeeds"[27] The film anticipates the debates over violence that would continue within Scorsese's work, debates that would also be central in discussions of the New Hollywood. In the end, Scorsese did and did not take Cassavetes's advice. He moved away from the exploitation ranks of Corman and into more "personal" (that is, more autobiographical) material with his next film, *Mean Streets*. But he never left the more exploitative material of sex and violence behind, which allowed him to work within an industry in which these elements were increasingly felt to be imperative to box-office success.

What was the left behind was the more overtly political material dealing with the oppression of the working class, racial minorities, and women to which Scorsese would never really return. It would take ideological critics to draw out implicitly in Scorsese's Hollywood films what was explicit in *Boxcar Bertha* and some of the earlier student work. With the essential disappearance of *Street Scenes 1970* from Scorsese's oeuvre, the politics of *Boxcar Bertha* can seem very antithetical to his career arc. But read as the first film after *Street Scenes*, the early credit sequence of *Boxcar Bertha*, detailing the clashes between the police and the workers, can be seen as a direct continuation of the police–student battles featured in the earlier documentary. And while it was a commercial picture, its political agenda was to the left of anything coming out of Hollywood. It features a group of heroes that include a communist union leader, an African American justifiably fighting racism with violence, and a woman who lives freely with different lovers and even as a prostitute without being punished for it. Its villains are rich, powerful white men and their underlings. And while the character of Bertha and the actress Barbara Hershey are still treated as sexual objects for the voyeuristic gaze of the camera (after all, this is exploitation filmmaking), an argument can be made that Bertha is a more progressive female character than any of the women in Scorsese's future pictures. Although labeled a "whore" by those in power, Bertha is constantly seen as sympathetic despite her breaking of the social conventions of womanhood. The constantly lauded movement of Scorsese away from this exploitation material and back into more personal work constantly overlooks the fact that a more progressive social vision was abandoned as well.

Scorsese becoming "Scorsese": *Mean Streets*

Mean Streets represented Scorsese's return to the subject matter of his first feature, *Who's That Knocking at My Door*, detailing life in the Little Italy neighborhood where he grew up. The lead character, Charlie (once again played by Harvey Keitel), is a small-time gangster working for his uncle Giovanni. He suffers from a great deal of Catholic guilt and is tormented by the "fires of hell." He sees himself as a modern day Francis of Assisi, wanting to help others and be a saint within his underground world. He is having a secret affair with Theresa, who is also the cousin of his friend Johnny Boy (Robert De Niro). Giovanni disapproves of both Theresa because she is epileptic and Johnny Boy because he is irresponsible and "half-crazy." Johnny Boy falls into debt to Charlie's friend Michael, a small-time hood, and eventually Charlie, Johnny Boy, and Theresa have to flee the city. At the conclusion, Michael and his gunman (played by Scorsese) shoot Johnny Boy and injure Charlie and Theresa in the subsequent car crash.

Who's That Knocking at My Door, despite some early positive notices, has generally been seen as a technically crude and overindulgent apprenticeship work. The film was positioned very much in the tradition of the New York independent film, with a strong New Wave, European influence. Even the references in the film to John Wayne, the most American of all movie icons, begin with a picture of Wayne in a French magazine. Clearly, if Scorsese had remained in New York, attempting to make small, personal independent films in the tradition of Godard or even Cassavetes, he would not have the reputation he has today. Within the world of film, especially American cinema, saying that the cultural field is the economic field reversed is not quite accurate. Surely, cultural capital relies on the symbolic function of prestige that is difficult to achieve with a great deal of box-office success. Steven Spielberg, despite all of his economic success and even his recent Academy Awards, has not achieved the kind of highbrow esteem bestowed on Scorsese. Even Classical Hollywood entertainers such as John Ford and Alfred Hitchcock did not achieve canonical status until their careers were in decline, with their respective masterpieces, *The Searchers* (1956) and *Vertigo* (1958), not entering the *Sight and Sound* polls until 1982, more than twenty years after their initial release. Nevertheless, the films that comprise the canon of American cinema are all very commercial in nature, films that were made as part of the Hollywood system.[28] American silent films, once considered the pinnacle of cinema as a visual art, have fallen off the list with no silent appearing since *The General* placed tenth in 1982, a fate that has not befallen their European counterparts *The Battleship Potemkin* (Sergei Eisenstein, 1925) and *The Passion of Joan of Arc* (Carl Theodor Dreyer, 1928). As silent films have increasingly been seen as esoteric and difficult, the tendency has been for critics and scholars to remove them from the core of the American film canon. The two mangled masterpieces of Hollywood, *Greed* and *The Magnificent Ambersons*, have not appeared since 1982, representing an increasing trend to justify and celebrate the Hollywood studio system as a positive rather than negative influence on film art. This same impulse lies behind the campaign to have *Citizen Kane* situated as a Hollywood rather than an independent film, attempting to explain the film's greatness in terms of its collaborative nature, the "genius of the system."[29] As Jonathan Rosenbaum argues, a lot is at stake in this labeling because once *Citizen Kane* is recognized as a studio film, we arrive at a platonic ideal of Hollywood.[30]

Given this climate, Scorsese's move to making films for Hollywood was a necessary contingency for his eventual canonization. Although *Mean Streets* is produced independently, it was made for studio distribution and has a technical polish and generic grounding that *Who's That Knocking at My Door* lacks. Scorsese rewrote an earlier draft of the script, at that point titled *Season of the Witch*, following Cassavetes's advice in 1972. In the process, Scorsese attempted to remove some of the more explicit cultural signifiers that would confuse a mainstream audience. Following the advice of then-partner Sandy Weintraub, the daughter of studio executive Fred Weintraub who first brought Scorsese to Hollywood to edit *Medicine Ball Caravan*, Scorsese worked to streamline his sensibility to fit the marketplace: "I took out a lot of religious stuff—it was still called *Season of the Witch* at this stage—and put in things like the pool-hall scene."[31] What results is a curious mixture of elements that allows *Mean Streets* to be discussed as an authentic, personal vision of New York's Little Italy as seen through one of its own members while eliminating some of the more obscure religious and ethnic specificity. The two titles of the film, the original *Season of the Witch* and the subsequent *Mean Streets*, encapsulate this duality. Understanding the title *Season of the Witch* requires a deep knowledge of Italian culture, as Robert Casillo argues:

> The title *Season of the Witch* has its merits and is arguably preferable to the present one, being more closely related to the film's themes, narrative and characters. Such an argument, however, depends partly on the likely possibility that Scorsese grasped the significance of witches, witchcraft, and the related belief in the evil eye or *mal occhio* in both southern Italian and Italian American society. . . . Its unsuitability lies in the fact that, while witches have a specific significance in southern Italian society and its earlier Italian American off-shoots, these meanings would have been lost on most American viewers.[32]

However, Casillo ignores the fact that more than just the title of the film had changed. Although the specific references to Italian-Catholic culture are still present in the film, they are no longer of central importance to the film's meaning. The change to the title *Mean Streets* was not isolated; it was part of a larger movement within the script and film as a whole to make the film more socially intelligible to a wider constituency.

The reference to Raymond Chandler in the title is merely one of many allusions the film makes to American popular culture, especially Hollywood cinema, as Scorsese attempts to locate *Mean Streets* within a filmmaking tradition. The characters in the film may be from a culturally specific group, but this culture has now been transformed by its connection with the world of mass entertainment Hollywood cinema represented Scorsese's own comments on the film stress these twin influences: "[A]t the same time as giving this accurate picture of Italian-Americans, I was trying to make a kind of homage to the Warner Brothers [*sic*] gangster films."[33] In fact, the film is full of references to Hollywood that situate *Mean Streets* as the New Hollywood film it was trying to be. Three clips are shown from other films, *The Searchers*, *The Big Heat* (Fritz Lang, 1953), and *The Tomb of Ligeia* (Roger Corman, 1964). Two Hollywood World War II films, *The Pride of the Marines* (Delmer Daves, 1945) and *Back to Bataan* (Edward Dmytryk, 1945), are referenced in the dialogue, and one scene features a poster for *Point Blank* (John Boorman, 1967) and *Husbands* (John Cassavetes, 1970). The variety of films here and how they are deployed speaks to *Mean Streets* as a film consciously trying to position itself within a group of ambitious Hollywood films reworking the conventions of its past.

The attitude is certainly not purely celebratory; the references to World War II films show a clear disconnect between that war and the one currently raging in Vietnam. This point is made explicit by the presence of the Vietnam veteran who is presented with an American flag and an allusion to John Garfield's line in *The Pride of the Marines*: "Get 'em in the eyes, get 'em right in the eyes." Charlie makes this reference to a

Figure 2.2. *Mean Streets* (Martin Scorsese, 1973), allusion to New Hollywood film *Point Blank* and, below it, less prominently, the independent *Husbands*.

physically disabled veteran of World War II, but is completely oblivious to the actual man he is addressing, a psychologically damaged veteran of the Vietnam War. This damage is revealed when the man turns violent and attacks a woman at the party, having to be physically restrained and calmed down by the words, "You're in America, Jerry." The mythology of Hollywood and its war propaganda is revealed as inadequate for people to comprehend their current social and political reality. But at the same time, the references are used to suggest continuity with the past, made especially apparent by the more recent films alluded to, *The Tomb of Ligeia*, *Point Blank*, and *Husbands*. The Corman film was, according to Scorsese, included as a thank you for getting Scorsese's professional career started.[34] But more than this, it presents the film as part of an American commercial tradition, even as it is working to reimagine that legacy. *Point Blank* cements this idea because it is a film that already uses an experimental formal approach to traditional genre material, suggesting an artistic direction that had been opened up and which *Mean Streets* was following.

But ultimately, *Mean Streets* would not move into the heavily formalized, nonlinear editing style of *Point Blank*, a film with clear echoes of Alain Resnais's experiments with narrative, *Hiroshima Mon Amour* (1959) and *Last Year at Marienbad* (1961). Despite its stylistic flourishes, *Mean Streets* is concerned with assimilating into classical filmmaking to a much greater extent than the earlier *Who's That Knocking at My Door*. Part of this is its larger budget. Despite being made independently and in less than a month, *Mean Streets* nevertheless was made according to professional standards, not as a student film put together over several years. With the larger budget and commercial interests came a film style that removed many of the nonclassical elements, especially the New Wave inspired jump cuts and flash forwards. Despite Roger Ebert's claim that *Who's That Knocking at My Door* managed to combine the Cassavetes-style independent film with a mainstream sensibility, it would really take *Mean Streets* to effectively make this transition. One of the biggest supporters of the film was Ebert's mentor Pauline Kael, who admired the film for both its personal nature and for its lack of formalism. The film was a "triumph of personal filmmaking"[35] in which Scorsese showed the audience what he knew. According to Kael, Scorsese was able to combine this with a cinematic style that was at once expressive and naturalistic: "The picture is stylized without seeming in any way artificial; it is the only movie I've ever seen that achieves the effects of Expressionism without the use of distortion. 'Mean Streets' never loses touch with the ordinary look of things or with common experience; rather, it puts us in closer touch with the ordinary, the common, by turning a different light on them."[36] Crucial for Kael is the idea that truly great films must be immediately accessible and not lose touch with the "common" or the "ordinary."

Kael combines this populism with a taste for modernist art as she was harshly critical of auteur critics and their attempts to make high art out of genre films. Hence the comparison of *Mean Streets* with a modernist movement such as expressionism within a review that stresses the film's everyday naturalism. She concludes her review by claiming that *Mean Streets* is "a blood thriller in the truest sense."[37] James Naremore, in his book *More than Night: Film Noir and Its Contexts*, draws out the connection between modernism and melodrama in the noir genre, dubbing many of these thrillers "blood melodramas."[38] Not coincidentally, noir discourse was starting to form at the particular historical moment. In 1972 future Scorsese collaborator Paul Schrader (himself heavily influenced by Kael as a critic) published his influential "Notes on Film Noir" in *Film Comment*.[39] In this piece, Schrader argues for the aesthetic greatness of the noir films but in rather nonauteurist terms similar to Kael. For Schrader, dark modernist impulses combined with American pop culture to produce a high point of Hollywood cinema. This noir discourse would extend beyond critical writing and into the films of the New Hollywood: *The Long Goodbye* (Robert Altman, 1973), *Thieves Like Us* (Robert Altman, 1974), *Chinatown* (Roman Polanski, 1974), and *Night Moves* (Arthur Penn, 1975), along with Scorsese's *Mean Streets* and *Taxi Driver*, began a noir revival during this period. But crucially all but Scorsese's films are revisionist genre films. Only Scorsese aims to keep this tension between realism and expressionism that defined noir as an aesthetic movement. In other words, this noir revival cycle was all modernism and very little melodrama, a modernism without the vernacular quality. Scorsese had the ability to locate his modernist aesthetic vision within a naturalist, everyday setting that was at once ethnically specific without being obscure.

Beyond Kael's glowing review, *Mean Streets* received almost unanimous support from the mainstream press and it was the first Scorsese film to receive widespread critical attention. But the few negative notices of the film strongly convey the critical environment and how *Mean Streets* was positioned within it. These reviews also indicate the direction Scorsese would turn in his subsequent work. Richard Schickel's review for *Time* is ambivalent, noting both admiration for the film's realism and dissatisfaction with the lack of connection to the characters: "It is impossible to care as deeply as he does about people whose minds and spirits are stunted."[40] Because of this inability to relate to the characters, Schickel concludes, "one leaves the film with the sense of having endured a class in social anthropology rather than an aesthetic experience." One recalls here Andrew Sarris's argument that truly great cinema needed to be decontextualized from its social and historical milieu. The connection is not accidental. In 1973 Schickel produced the television series *The Men Who Made the Movies*, featuring seven Classical Hollywood filmmakers: Alfred Hitchcock, George Cukor, Howard Hawks, Vincente Minnelli, King Vidor, Raoul Walsh, and William Wellman. This series would have been inconceivable without the influence of auteurists such as Sarris, and the selections greatly reflected the overturn in critical taste Sarris promoted (all but Wellman were highly regarded by Sarris in his rankings). For Schickel, these classical filmmakers offered aesthetic experiences not on display in *Mean Streets*, and they grounded their personality in their formal style rather than their social milieu. Despite the mainstreaming of the text, *Mean Streets* remained too grounded in sociology for many auteurists.

From the opposite perspective, John Simon's negative review of both the film and its supporters sees a crass and adolescent spirit keeping the film from reaching a high aesthetic quality:

> The enthusiastic reception of *Mean Streets* may be due in part to its being largely child's play, and rather sloppily written, improvised, acted, photographed and edited child's play, at that. But in a period when movie-making has reached a high plateau of soulless slickness and glitter, when any number of directors can put together neat little scenes into a triumph of the art of assemblage—the only trouble being that the entire thing is hollow and pointless—a movie oozing amateurishness from every hole in the plot and every crevice in the continuity may come across as endearingly genuine, unassuming, and direct.[41]

The high modernist Simon, who looks down on the medium of film in general as lacking the aesthetic quality of other arts, sees an inferior mass culture product that passes itself off as folk art relative to its debased competitors. Simon points out the film's inferiority to Federico Fellini's "masterpiece" *I Vitelloni*, stating that Scorsese lacks Fellini's humanity and structure. For Simon, the few examples of film art that do exist come not from Hollywood but from the European cinema, not from mass culture but from high modernism with the great divide continuing to separate them. But even as Simon maintained his place as a prominent critic throughout the 1970s, his aesthetic position was becoming increasingly outdated. Similar to Scorsese and his students at NYU overtaking the previous aesthetic positions held by senior faculty like Haig Manoogian,

Simon's idea of great cinema needing to possess a modernist purity was being replaced by critics as seemingly opposed as Kael and Sarris. The main danger facing Scorsese's reputation at this point was the possibility of being seen as an ethnic filmmaker of sociological films. He thus needed to appeal not only to Kael and her critical followers (for example, Roger Ebert), but also to auteur critics who took Hollywood genre cinema seriously. His next films would move increasingly in this direction.

"Has Martin Scorsese Gone Hollywood?" (Part One): *Alice Doesn't Live Here Anymore*

Alice Doesn't Live Here Anymore opens with a flashback to both the lead character's childhood and to the style of film popular in her youth. It shows Alice singing on an old movie set reminiscent of *The Wizard of Oz* as her mother yells for her to come home. After this dreamlike beginning, the film leaps forward to the present, where Alice (Ellen Burstyn) is an unhappily married woman with an eleven-year-old son. Soon after, her husband is killed in a car accident, and Alice decides to travel to Monterey, California (her childhood home), to pursue her dream of becoming a singer. Along the way, she goes through a disturbing relationship with the abusive Ben (Harvey Keitel) before getting a job as a waitress and forming a friendship with her coworker Flo (Diane Ladd). She begins dating David (Kris Kristofferson), a farmer, but breaks it off after he disciplines her son too harshly. The two reunite at the restaurant with David saying he will take Alice to Monterey and the two embracing before a cheering crowd of customers. The last images show Alice and her son walking down a road to an uncertain future.

In 1974, following the critical success of *Mean Streets*, Scorsese would make his first film financed by a Hollywood studio. As Mary Pat Kelly puts it, *Alice Doesn't Live Here Anymore* would be "his first real Hollywood movie."[42] This was very much a film of the period. How the personnel were assembled, how the film was shot, and how the genre of the woman's melodrama was dealt with were indicative of how New Hollywood worked.[43] The driving force behind the film was Burstyn, who was coming off a major hit, *The Exorcist* (William Friedkin, 1973). Burstyn had a script written by Robert Getchell, and she and Warner Bros. were looking for a director. As Scorsese describes the situation, "because I was receiving a lot of scripts now, Sandy Weintraub read it first and said it was really interesting. I thought it was a good idea too, dealing with women for a change."[44] At one level, the film was a calculated move on Scorsese's part, as he has admitted in certain interviews: "I needed to do something that was a major studio film for a certain amount of money and to prove that I can direct women. It was as simple as that."[45] However, it was not quite that simple. *Alice Doesn't Live Here Anymore* cannot be explained as a Hollywood mass cultural product to be defined in opposition to the modernist rigor of Scorsese's "masterpieces." Rather, it needs to be seen, as do all Scorsese's films, as playing an important role in establishing Scorsese's reputation, and its mass culture status was paradoxically both a detriment to its critical reputation while playing an important role in establishing Scorsese's eventual high art status.

Discussions of the film's style show a split between critics seeing Scorsese's use of technique as a concession to the classical style of Hollywood and others maintaining that the film's style provides a self-reflexive commentary in the best tradition of a Hollywood auteur. The radical journal *Jump Cut* featured a series of articles on the film critiquing the lack of directorial control Scorsese exhibited working within a genre context with one article comparing the film unfavorably to newly discovered auteur favorite Douglas Sirk, whose "controlled poetic visual style [black-and-white Cinemascope] seem striking contrasts to Scorsese's intuitive cinematic ramblings. . . . [I]t is Douglas Sirk who should be honored as a truly worthy women's director."[46] The comparison here to Sirk is no doubt negative, but it nevertheless shows how, within academic film journals, Hollywood was no longer seen as beneath serious consideration. If Sirk can be taken seriously, then theoretically at least, so could a film such as *Alice Doesn't Live Here Anymore*. The problem the film has from this perspective is not its Hollywood conventions; rather it is the lack of deliberate artifice to render those conventions critically. The film is at once too Hollywood and too realistic. It is tied to genre conventions while stylistically following the new codes of realism, especially with regard to mise-en-scène and performance. We should not be surprised therefore that the sequence most commented on and most admired is the opening with its deliberately artificial Classical Hollywood studio look. In addition, Christine Geraghty, writing in *Movie*, makes an argument for the use of style in the film as expressing the tensions inherent in the social situation, not unlike the use of style in classical melodrama: "There is, I think, a tension in the film between the emphasis on choice and freedom which is used to create Alice as a character and the control which the men represent. This tension is expressed in the mixing of styles in the film, the effect of which is to underplay the resolution of the narrative."[47] Within this review, one can see the seeds of Scorsese's eventual canonization, combining the traditional auteurist argument with ideological criticism. Scorsese's subsequent films would all build on this foundation, offering up ever more convincing examples of Scorsese's uniqueness both as an artist and as a critic of American culture with the two often intimately linked.

But ultimately with *Alice Doesn't Live Here Anymore*, this interpretive approach remains marginal due to the film's strong association with the social movement of feminism, which grounds the film in a specific time and place. It does not transcend its time, partly because the film itself is difficult to place within Scorsese's subsequent work and partly because the way in which feminism is dealt with is overdetermined by the economic structure of Hollywood itself. Much of the film's critical attention at the time debated its status as the first Hollywood picture that explicitly confronted the feminist movement. In addition to the reviews of the film, most of which mention the film's relation to the women's movement, the feminist scholar Marjorie Rosen interviewed Scorsese for *Film Comment*[48] and discussed the film along these lines. There were promotional pieces arranged by the studio in *Ms. Magazine*, which Warner Communications had just purchased.[49] All of this served an important purpose for Scorsese. It established his name within the mainstream press beyond the niche market *Mean Streets* provided. Scorsese had now become a player within the industry, and he had shown he was capable of working within a genre system. But the film's sociological interest as a film of the moment, promoted by the studio and the

Figure 2.3. *Alice Doesn't Live Here Anymore* (Martin Scorsese, 1974), two endings: ironic romance . . .

Figure 2.4. *Alice Doesn't Live Here Anymore* (Martin Scorsese, 1974), . . . and mother-son sincerity.

popular press, denied the film its personality as a "Scorsese" picture, despite Scorsese's best efforts to discuss formal elements in interviews. In the 2004 documentary *Scorsese on Scorsese*, Scorsese would try once again to remove the feminist elements of the film and focus on its personal connections. He compared the relationship of Alice and her son with that of himself and his mother. Responding to the feminist criticisms of the film, Scorsese simply shrugged his shoulders and stated, "That's me." Richard Schickel directed the documentary, and like his film series *The Men Who Made the Movies*, its purpose is to emphasize Scorsese as auteur. In this documentary, Scorsese films that do not do this well, such as his studio project *The Color of Money* (1986), are dropped altogether. Films such as *Alice Doesn't Live Here Anymore* are discussed from a very particular personal point of view, very unlike how they were originally conceived and mediated within the culture. As much as possible, context is stripped away.

Transcendence, Redemption, Irony (Take One): *Taxi Driver*, Scorsese's First Masterpiece

Taxi Driver opens ominously with Bernard Herrmann's score playing over an image of a yellow cab emerging from the steam and smoke of the city. The atmosphere of dread is established and never relents, despite the fact that the story does not contain much action until well into the narrative. We follow Vietnam veteran Travis Bickle (Robert De Niro) as he drives a cab through some of New York's worst areas. His voiceover tells his disturbed thoughts and feelings, as does the expressive camerawork and editing, much of which breaks with classical convention. Not until a failed relationship with Betsy (Cybill Shepherd), however, does Travis begin to seriously unravel and become a threat. He hatches a plan to assassinate presidential candidate Charles Palantine for whom Betsy works. He also begins a tentative friendship with Iris (Jodie Foster), a twelve-year-old prostitute. When his plan to kill Palantine is foiled, he turns his violence toward Iris's pimp Sport (Harvey Keitel) and massacres three people in a bloody shootout. Because he murders social outcasts and returns Iris to her family, the press praises him as a hero. The film concludes with Travis back in his cab, drifting through the city.

Following the financial and industry success of *Alice Doesn't Live Here Anymore* (the film won an Academy Award for Ellen Burstyn, which Scorsese himself accepted in her absence), Scorsese returned to New York City to film *Taxi Driver*. Produced by Hollywood independents Michael and Julia Phillips, Scorsese was packaged along with screenwriter Paul Schrader, who had just sold his script for *The Yakuza* (Sydney Pollack, 1974), and lead actor Robert De Niro, who had just won an Academy Award for *The Godfather: Part II* (Francis Ford Coppola, 1974). *Taxi Driver* would make Scorsese's reputation both critically and financially, combining the cultural prestige of *Mean Streets* with the box-office success of *Alice Doesn't Live Here Anymore*.[50] This can be attributed to its combining of previously successful elements. The film's mixture of expressionism and realism along with its New York City location recalled *Mean Streets*, but it further assimilates these elements with a lead character foreign to this environment. A strong contemporary strain echoes through the references in Schrader's script to would-be political assassin Arthur Bremer[51] along with the film's implicit use of the social movements of the 1960s: feminism, the sexual revolution, civil rights, and the counterculture. References are made to New Wave favorites such as *Diary of a Country Priest* (Robert Bresson, 1950) and *The Searchers* (previously referenced by Scorsese in earlier films), with a score conducted by Bernard Herrmann, famous for his work with Welles and Hitchcock. Finally, the sensational elements of violence and sex connect the film to the exploitation movie with the film's look even recalling many of the earlier films of 1970s blaxploitation.[52] As much as the quality of the filmmaking itself, these factors contributed to *Taxi Driver* becoming Scorsese's first acknowledged masterpiece.

An examination of the contemporary writing on the film is revealing in two ways. Compared with *Mean Streets* the film received little
critical praise from the mainstream press, and the film received an enormous amount of attention from cinema-specific publications. Numerous
rather negative or at best mixed reviews were written, which extends to
the reception at the Cannes Film Festival, where it was awarded the top
prize of the Palme d'Or amidst booing at the press conference announce-
ment.[53] The mixed or negative reviews included prominent names such
as Andrew Sarris, Manny Farber, Stanley Kauffmann, Richard Schickel,
David Sterritt, and Jonathan Rosenbaum; only Pauline Kael and Roger Ebert were among prominent critics giving the film an enthusiastic
reception.[54] One could conclude that the film's subsequent reputation is
an example of Kael's enormous power as a critic at that time, but that
would be simplifying matters. Kael exalted many films and filmmakers
who no longer held a great deal of critical prestige (for Exhibit A, see
"De Palma, Brian"). Instead, the film's transcendent thematic combined
with an incoherence toward this theme accounts for the film's ability to
maintain its popularity with audiences and critics alike. In fact, even those
reviewers who dislike the film, especially those in the cinema-specific
journals, contribute to the film's reputation by debating its artistic and,
more crucially, its ideological merit. Of all Scorsese films, *Taxi Driver*
splits critics interested in aesthetic merit and those concerned with issues
of ideology, not unlike the classical film on which it is loosely based,
The Searchers. Thus the film's "incoherence" led both to its mixed critical
reception and its eventual canonization.

Screenwriter Paul Schrader's interview in *Film Comment* initially
established the theme of transcendence as he discusses Bresson's influence on the structure of the screenplay.[55] Schrader had already written
Transcendental Style in Film: Ozu, Bresson, Dreyer (1972) in which he had
outlined his ideas about transcendence and film form. What Schrader's
book emphasized were the spiritual qualities of the three directors while
removing each of them from their social and historical specificity. While
Schrader claims this style in relation to the spiritual, clear associations
exist with the canon formation of both the *Cahiers* critics and Sarris, both
of whom link aesthetics with spiritual experience beyond historical, political, or cultural context. Schrader does make cultural distinctions, however
broad and highly contentious they may be, such as his claim that transcendental style could only be commercially successful within a Japanese
(and Asian) culture.[56] But this transcendental core remains imbedded into
Taxi Driver and has allowed this particular reading of the film to survive
despite the obvious social context that even Schrader himself analyzes:

I saw the script as an attempt to take the European existential hero, that is, the man from *The Stranger, Notes from the Underground, Nausea, Pickpocket, Le Feu Follet,* and *A Man Escaped,* and put him in an American context. In doing so, you find that he becomes more ignorant, ignorant of the nature of his problem. . . . We don't properly understand the nature of the problem, so the self-destructive impulse, instead of being inner-directed, as it is in Japan, Europe, any of the older cultures, becomes outer-directed. The man who feels the time has come to die will go out and kill other people rather than kill himself.[57]

Schrader here is being culturally specific while criticizing this tendency for obscuring the true nature of the problem, which is existential (which, for Schrader, is linked with the transcendental). Schrader is thus critical of Bickle's violence toward others, but not in the context of that violence because for Schrader the problem is ultimately metaphysical rather than social.

What Schrader was able to contribute to the story was the single tale that the *Cahiers* critics consistently celebrated: the central hero experiences isolation, which is then followed by an extreme circumstance ending with acceptance, understanding, and redemption. As John Hess describes it, "the individual is trapped in solitude morale and can escape it—transcend—if he or she comes to see their [*sic*] condition and then extend themselves [*sic*] to others and God."[58] The films that are cited as directly influencing *Taxi Driver* the most, *Diary of a Country Priest* and *The Searchers,* share this plot formation and can likewise be read as films about the central hero's redemption and transcendence. *Taxi Driver* is certainly a more difficult film to read in this manner because its central character is so obviously unstable, but nevertheless the anecdotes of cheering audiences reveal a continuing identification with Travis Bickle. Scorsese recalls:

[I] was shocked by the way audiences took the violence. . . . I saw *Taxi Driver* once in the theatre, on the opening night, I think, and everyone was yelling and screaming at the shoot-out. When I made it, I didn't intend to have the audience react with that feeling, "Yes, do it! Let's go out and kill." The idea was to create a violent catharsis, so that they'd find themselves saying, "Yes, kill"; and then afterwards realize, "My God, no"—like some strange Californian therapy session. That was the instinct I went with, but it's scary to hear what happens with the audience.[59]

These comments were made many years after the film and differ strikingly from Scorsese's discussion of the film at the time, especially with regard to the ending. In an interview published in the *Village Voice* at the time of the film's release, Scorsese commented, "I like the idea of spurting blood, it reminds . . . it's like a . . . God, it's . . . it's really like a purification, you know, the fountains of blood."[60] Clearly, from both these comments and the title of the article itself ("Martin Scorsese Tells All: Blood and Guts Turn Me On!"), *Taxi Driver* traded very much on the audience's desire for violent spectacle. Originally, Scorsese related this violence to the idea of religious purification and transcendence. His comments on the film years later reveal how the film's reception within academic circles shaped Scorsese's more cautionary explanation of the film's conclusion.

Although Pauline Kael celebrated *Taxi Driver* for its refusal to make a "moral statement" about its lead character, many others saw problems with the film's ideological underpinnings. This is especially the case within the cinema-specific journals, beginning with Patricia Patterson and Manny Farber's essay in *Film Comment*. Patterson and Farber begin the essay by praising the film's aesthetic quality, not unlike Kael's appreciation of the film's acting and expressionism, although with considerably more impressionistic flourish.[61] This review recalls the earlier film criticism of Farber in which his own skills as a critic describing a film mean more than the evaluation of the film itself. But the essay mixes this approach with a strong critique of the film's fetishization of gun violence and attitudes toward women and racial minorities: "its immoral posture on blacks, male supremacy, guns, women, subverts believability at every moment."[62] Jonathan Rosenbaum similarly expressed reservations about the ideology of the film while admiring its ravishing form.[63] Thus, despite the film's aesthetic quality and appeal to the apolitical transcendental theme, *Taxi Driver* was in danger of being seen as an ideologically reactionary piece.

Slowly and due to the context of later films the blame for the film's reactionary elements was shifted almost exclusively to Schrader. Scorsese began to be seen as the classical "category e" filmmaker, subverting the originally conservative material through his own auteurist style. The beginnings of this argument can be seen in early reviews of the film. Michael Dempsey, writing in *Film Quarterly*, noted a contradiction between Schrader's Calvinist concern with Bresson and the transcendental as opposed to Scorsese's Catholic expressionism.[64] Robin Wood sees this contrast between Schrader and Scorsese as leading to the film's status as an "incoherent text,"[65] arguing that this contrast was not so much religious as ideological, placing the blame for the film's reactionary elements on Schrader alone. This is done by reference to their other films with Wood referring to Schrader's overall oeuvre as being "quasi-fascist" while Scorsese is seen as "relatively open to social issues."[66] This ideological reading of the film in reference to its two auteurs is echoed in Leighton Grist's more recent account. Grist sees Scorsese as offering "a discursive appropriation through which the text not only inscribes Scorsese's stylistic and thematic emphases, but would appear seriously to compromise the script's implicit spiritual and redemptive trajectory."[67] In particular, Grist points out that the final massacre "salutarily 'corrects' our identification with Travis." The credit for this correction is given completely to Scorsese.

Grist's reading of the film relies heavily on Robert Ray's interpretation of *Taxi Driver* in his influential text *A Certain Tendency of the Hollywood Cinema, 1930–1980* (published in 1985). This ideological overview of American cinema concludes with a chapter discussing *Taxi Driver* and Francis Ford Coppola's *The Godfather*, and it is important to stress this connection. If another filmmaker from this era can be said to challenge Scorsese's place as the key artistic figure, it is Coppola. With films like *The Godfather*, *The Conversation* (1974), and *The Godfather: Part II* (1974), Coppola emerged both as a commercially and critically acclaimed filmmaker as well as a director making subversive films within the Hollywood system.[68] Ray's analysis of the two films challenges this assumption about Coppola's ideological progressiveness in relation to Scorsese and would be one of the first of many arguments about Scorsese as a radical

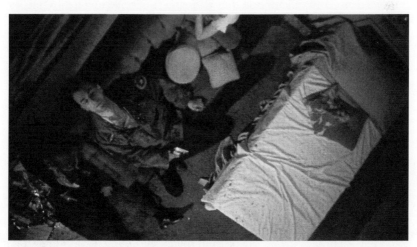

Figure 2.5. *Taxi Driver* (Martin Scorsese, 1976), transcendence or irony?

auteur working within the Hollywood system. For Ray, *Taxi Driver* was an important artistic achievement because of its ideological intervention. It was a film that followed the conventional plot of the "Right" cycle of vigilante films only to "correct" that audience's assumptions. It thus lured the popular, "naïve" audience and achieved popular success (crucial to being politically consequential) while "attack(ing) that audience's sustaining myth, the belief in the continued application of Western-style, individual solutions to contemporary complex problems."[69] *The Godfather*, however, was more compromised. It may have "corrected" the "Left" cycle of films by showing its outlaw hero gangsters as being part of the corrupt capitalist system, but it ultimately failed to be truly progressive in its politics. Ray acknowledges that the sequel made Coppola's original anticapitalist message more explicit, but nevertheless claims that the critiques "operated squarely within the traditional American mythology, working variants on frontier imagery and the ideologically determined platitude, 'It's lonely at the top.'"[70]

The validity of Ray's argument concerning the two films and their ideological relationship to the American cinema does not concern me here. Rather, what is of interest is how this argument encapsulates an overall movement that would see Scorsese recognized and discussed as a great artist not only for the artistic quality of his films, but for his ideological progressiveness as well. If, as Ray claims, both a naïve and an ironic audience within the United States at the time, it can also be said that there were naïve and ironic film critics. *Taxi Driver* succeeded not only with the naïve auteur critics who were interested in themes of transcendence and redemption, but also with the ironic ideological critics as well. Scorsese's next films would continue this trajectory.

Scorsese's First "Failure": *New York, New York*

New York, New York opens on V-J Day, as saxophonist Jimmy Doyle (Robert De Niro) meets singer Francine Evans (Liza Minnelli) during the celebrations. Although she is initially annoyed by his abrasive manner, Francine and Jimmy start a romantic and professional relationship, going on the road with the Frankie Harte Band. They get married and Jimmy eventually takes over as the band leader. However, Francine gets pregnant and has to return to New York. Without her, the band fails and a resentful Jimmy returns home. Their relationship becomes more antagonistic as Francine succeeds and Jimmy flounders. This reaches a climax with an ugly verbal and eventually physical confrontation that prompts Francine to go into labor. Following the birth of their son, Jimmy leaves. The story concludes years later when both have achieved professional success. They see each other following Francine's show and agree to meet afterward. In a last departure from the conventional musical, neither shows up because both are convinced they cannot be happy as a couple.

Following the box-office popularity of *Taxi Driver*, Scorsese was given the freedom to undertake his first big budget picture, *New York, New York*. The film represented the first clear disappointment of Scorsese's professional career, unpopular both at the box office and with critics. With very few exceptions, at the time of release the popular press received the film negatively, including publications such as the *New York Times* and the *New Yorker*, which had previously received Scorsese's work favorably.[71] Vincent Canby's review was particularly telling, suggesting that the failure of the film was intimately linked with Scorsese being given too much directorial freedom.[72] Many subsequent career studies of Scorsese or overviews of New Hollywood would echo these comments. Les Keyser's discussion of Scorsese's career saw *New York, New York* as the beginning of "the most frenzied and self-destructive period of his life."[73] Peter Biskind's book *Easy Riders, Raging Bulls* would add to this argument: "Fuelled by an I-am-a-genius ego and surrounded now by an adoring circle of friends, with *New York, New York* shaping up as an unprecedented triumph, Scorsese had begun to change."[74] The director-as-celebrity model that had brought such power to the directors of the New Hollywood had as its dark mirror a resentment of this idea of the rebel auteur. Following the failure of the film, critics compared Scorsese to Peter Bogdanovich, both for their failures with big budget musicals (in Bogdanovich's case, *At Long Last Love*) and for their marital infidelities and scandals. Just as Bogdanovich had been criticized for his extramarital affair and subsequent working relationship with actress Cybill Shepherd, Scorsese and actress Liza Minnelli were attracting gossip columnists with their romance.[75] This only increased when Scorsese agreed to direct Minnelli in the theatrical production *The Act*. Scorsese wisely backed out of this production at the last minute, breaking off his association with Minnelli and avoiding the tarnished reputation of Bogdanovich. Nevertheless, *New York, New York* is included in a group of films that represent the excesses of the auteur generation and its eventual fall, an early forewarning of the eventual disaster of *Heaven's Gate* (Michael Cimino, 1981) and, to a lesser extent, *One from the Heart* (Francis Ford Coppola, 1982).

But at the same time, the very "failure" of *New York, New York* on initial release has been used to justify its success on an artistic level. This begins with the film's reissue in 1981, in which the "Happy Endings" musical number is restored. This reissue is received much more favorably, which Scorsese himself explains as follows: "I think the reviews were better (in 1981) because by that time the industry had changed. In 1977, a week or so after we first opened, *Star Wars* opened. The whole industry went another way. It became megabucks. I'm not condemning it, and I'm not criticizing it either. *Star Wars* was a wonderful film. It started a whole new way of thinking, and of looking at films. It's just that people became interested in something else entirely, and *New York, New York* looked hopelessly old-fashioned."[76] This comparison with *Star Wars*, which initially worked to the film's disadvantage, has become a sign of *New York, New York* and Scorsese's authenticity. As Leighton Grist argues, it is "precisely the film's artistic success that helps explain its commercial failure."[77] Despite Scorsese's claims to the contrary, this has come at the expense of blockbuster films. It is not simply that *Star Wars* made more money than *New York, New York* and thus must not be aesthetically interesting (although this mass culture critique still has some influence, as Grist's statement shows). *Star Wars* was also seen as ideologically reactionary, and this factor as much as its popular appeal has led to its lack of cultural prestige. Conversely, *New York, New York*'s lack of commercial success was increasingly linked to its ideological critique of both the Hollywood musical and the romantic myth of the heterosexual couple it embodies.

The best example of this can be seen in the winter 1986 *Movie* special issue on "Reaganite Entertainment," which contains Andrew Britton's lengthy piece on the poor state of the American film industry, a critique that links the lack of aesthetic quality with a lack of ideological critique.[78] Following this lead piece several articles are devoted to Scorsese, most of which focus on Scorsese's ideological challenge to this very "Reaganite Entertainment" that the issue as a whole works to critique. *New York, New York* is regarded as a key text in this regard, partly because of its firm generic basis. Bryan Bruce's argument here vividly shows the combination of auteurist and ideological readings that form the basis of *Movie* criticism at this time. It is telling that the use of genre enhances Scorsese's own authorial obsessions. This is not unlike the older Hollywood auteurs, many of who were increasingly being reclaimed as radical by auteurist/ideological critics. This strategy of associating Scorsese with the previous Hollywood auteurs who are privileged as subversive can be seen most clearly in two articles, one by Richard Lippe in *Movie* and another by Susan Morrison in a special issue on Scorsese in *CineAction!*, a journal initiated by a collective consisting of former *Movie* critics. Lippe made explicit the connections between Scorsese's film and Vincente Minnelli's work, arguing, "Minnelli doesn't need to parody the musical tradition because he believes in its potential to communicate the complex issue of the individual's attempts to confront and expose restrictive societal positions. It is this kind of belief in the tradition and a desire to extend it rather than an interest in nostalgia (*That's Entertainment*) or parody (*All That Jazz*) that is the basis for Scorsese's *New York, New York*."[79] Scorsese is being compared favorably here to another generic deconstruction, *All That Jazz* (Bob Fosse, 1979), and Lippe positively notes the modernist continuity with tradition in Scorsese's film versus the postmodern parody of Fosse. This is echoed in Morrison's comparison of *New York, New York* with *Written on the Wind* (Douglas Sirk, 1956): "Unlike *Written on the Wind*, *New York, New York* does not have a conventional melodramatic content. What sets this film firmly within its time period, the mid-'70s, is the freedom that its director had in regards to flaunting the conventions of Classical Hollywood film. Untied to a studio system, imposed script, or even need to please/appease the public, Scorsese put together a film whose narrative strips away ideological pretense to function as an obvious critique of society's values."[80] These readings by Lippe and Morrison both link Scorsese with the classical era, differentiating him from his contemporaries, while emphasizing Scorsese's ability to go further in his ideological critique than previous filmmakers. Despite its initial box-office and critical disappointment, *New York, New York* ultimately proved to be anything but a failure to Scorsese's critical reputation.

Authenticating the Fiction: Scorsese's 1970s Documentaries

While working in Hollywood during the 1970s, Scorsese still managed to direct three documentaries: *Italianamerican* (1974), *American Boy: A Profile of Steven Prince* (1978), and *The Last Waltz* (1978). The first two were roughly hour-long films of a highly personal, noncommercial nature. *Italianamerican* shows Scorsese interviewing his parents Catherine and Charles in their New York apartment. It details their individual family history (especially how they immigrated to America) as well as their history with each other. It begins with Catherine describing the history of her spaghetti sauce and veers into a discussion of the history of the Little Italy neighborhood itself, particularly the history of the various ethnic groups. Scorsese cuts in documentary footage of Little Italy, both past and present. The end credits famously finish with the recipe for the sauce.[81] *American Boy* is a profile of Scorsese's friend, Steven Prince. It takes place at the house of actor George Memoli (who had a role in *Mean Streets*) on January 13, 1977. It opens with home movies of Prince as a baby over the opening credits as Neil Young's "Time Fades Away" plays on the soundtrack. It tells of Prince's family history, but mainly consists of stories told by Prince himself, usually of a fantastical nature and many involving drug use. The most famous of these tales involves Prince reviving a woman having a drug overdose by stabbing her in the heart with a shot of adrenalin, which Quentin Tarantino uses in *Pulp Fiction* (1994), and of Prince shooting a knife-wielding, drug-crazed man with his .44 magnum pistol, which Prince himself would later retell in Richard Linklater's *Waking Life* (2001).

The two films are fascinating to compare and contrast. They obviously have wildly different subject matter and show a marked difference in Scorsese himself, from his New York family home to the decadence of the drug world of Los Angeles. But the style is quite similar. Both begin with the very amateur, student-film style titles: "Film Is about to Start" (*Italianamerican*) and "Film Starts Here" (*American Boy*). Most of all they are extremely self-reflexive, especially in their opening and closing segments. Scorsese is always present and is directly addressed in both. In *Italianamerican*, his mother Catherine asks him questions about how to begin, and at the conclusion she complains about the camera crew's presence in her house without knowing that the camera is continuing to film. Likewise, *American Boy* starts with Scorsese and Prince in a hot tub and proceeds to film an extended playful wrestling match between Prince and Memoli. The conclusion is particularly intriguing, with Prince telling an emotional story about his last words with his father, which is undercut by Scorsese asking him to tell the story again, both of which are shown. Thus, although both works have direct cinema elements,

Figure 2.6. *Taxi Driver* (Martin Scorsese, 1976), mirror images: Travis Bickle . . .

Figure 2.7. *American Boy: A Profile of Steven Prince* (Martin Scorsese, 1978), . . . and Steven Prince.

Scorsese uses these distancing techniques to remind the viewers that they are watching constructed objects.

The Last Waltz was a very different type of film, a large concert documentary of The Band's farewell performance, accompanied by a large number of famous rock star guests, which has become famous as one of the finest in the "rockumentary" genre as well as being the subject of parody in *This Is Spinal Tap* (Rob Reiner, 1984) and *The Last Polka* (John Blanchard, 1985). Scorsese was able to plan the shooting of the concert itself and enlisted Boris Leven as production designer and Michael Chapman as cinematographer with additional photographing by well-known cameramen Laszlo Kovacs, Vilmos Zsigmond, and others. The result is some of the most beautiful concert footage ever shot, a look very different than previous rock films, most notably *Woodstock*, which is much more about the event itself than about the performers on stage. In *The Last Waltz*, the crowd is much less important. There are even two performances shot on a sound stage. The narrative moves back and forth between musical numbers and Scorsese's interviews with various members of the group who describe the history of the band, the end of the rock era, and the plans they have moving forward.

What all three documentaries have in common is their status as complementary texts to Scorsese's fiction films of the period.[82] *Italiana-merican* is often discussed in relation to *Mean Streets*, reinforcing both the autobiographical and anthropological nature of Scorsese's first Hollywood film. *American Boy* has a direct relation to *Taxi Driver* in that Prince plays the character of the gun dealer in that film. Furthermore, both films can be linked thematically in exploring marginal, disturbed figures. Finally, *The Last Waltz* is, like *New York, New York*, an elegy for a lost musical era. In all of these cases, the documentaries work to authenticate Scorsese's feature films, which are already immersed in a discourse around their "realism" and "truthfulness," despite their status as Hollywood texts. The place of the nonfiction film within the canon is pertinent to the discussion here. Rarely are documentaries considered as "art" in the same way as fiction films. As a result, they are often excluded from the canon of "greatest films." For example, the *Sight and Sound* poll has never included a documentary film in its Top Ten. The few documentaries that are taken seriously as art are highly aesthetic in their construction: *Berlin, Symphony of a City* (Walter Ruttman, 1927), *The Man with a Movie Camera* (Dziga Vertov, 1928), and, most infamously, *Triumph of the Will* (Leni Riefenstahl, 1934) and *Olympia* (Leni Riefenstahl, 1938). At the same time, some feel that documentaries are the peak of cinematic achievement, completely rejecting the inauthentic nature of most fiction films. Realist critics like André Bazin praise documentary filmmakers such as Robert Flaherty, especially his *Nanook of the North* (1922), along with fiction filmmakers such as Jean Renoir and the Italian neorealists for their faithfulness to cinema's true nature as a photographic device capturing reality. Within this transvaluation of cinematic aesthetics, documentary filmmakers like Riefenstahl would be critiqued along with other cinematic movements such as Soviet Montage and German expressionism that likewise manipulated reality.

The generally noncommercial nature of documentary films also conferred on them a cultural status distinct from that of the fiction film, particularly Hollywood films. There have been exceptions to this, from travelogues such as *This Is Cinerama* (1952) to the *March of Time* newsreels, but these have usually been seen as distinct from the classical definitions of documentary.[83] This situation changed slightly in the 1970s when some documentaries received theatrical runs and gained some small measure of commercial success, such as *Hearts and Minds* (Peter Davis, 1974), *Grey Gardens* (Albert and David Maysles, 1976), and *Harlan County*

U.S.A. (Barbara Kopple, 1976). Nevertheless, the concept of a mass audience documentary would not emerge until decades later with Michael Moore. As William Rothman argues, "In the seventies, a handful of documentaries enjoyed relatively significant theatrical runs, and a larger handful reached audiences nationwide through public television. . . . But audiences for documentary films were usually small, and sometimes quite specialized. Except on the occasions in which they were screened at the venues in major cities and college campuses around the country that were open to the work of contemporary independent filmmakers, most documentaries received little or no public notice."[84] If documentaries can be considered to have a similar status as Cassavetes-style independent films, Scorsese's continued commitment to this form in the 1970s can be seen as another mediation on his move away from New York and toward Hollywood.

Thus, Scorsese's documentaries of this period did more than simply complement his fiction films; they acted to distinguish Scorsese as an important filmmaker even among critics who are dismissive of Hollywood films in general. James Monaco's judgment of Scorsese's career was reflective of this view. He begins by crediting Scorsese as editor with the true artistic achievement of *Woodstock* and noted that Scorsese did a similarly fine job editing the massive amounts of footage from *Street Scenes 1970*. Monaco continues, "[d]ocumentary work has provided Scorsese with a second, hidden career ever since. . . . They may be less publicized than his Hollywood features, but they indicate an important second side to his personality as a filmmaker. There's no better example of a contemporary director seriously crippled by trying to accommodate himself to the system of commercial film production than Martin Scorsese. If he'd been left to his own devices, his films, I think, would be a lot more interesting than they are."[85] Monaco continues his section on Scorsese chronicling the various weaknesses he saw in the fiction films, only to return to the documentary form in his conclusion:

> There's no doubt Martin Scorsese is an exceptionally interesting and imaginative director, but for more than ten years now he's been setting self-destructive traps for himself, then stepping smartly right into them. He's capable of a great deal more, one surmises. In 1974 he shot a forty-eight-minute essay (originally meant to be a part of a television series) called *Italianamerican*. Basically a documentary visit with his parents, it had many of the qualities missing from the feature films he has made since *Mean Streets*. The people weren't characters, they were people. The film wasn't a self-conscious parody of movies dead and gone, but honest and straightforward. Scorsese

spoke for himself rather than hiding behind the pretentiously anxious film-noir mask. *Italianamerican* was relaxed, broadly humorous, not excessively ambitious, direct.[86]

Obviously a much different taste culture is represented here than in that of the *Movie* critics. For Monaco, Hollywood was seemingly incapable of allowing for the free expression of an artistic sensibility. But even for a critic as harshly critical of the contemporary mainstream film as Monaco, Scorsese retained a level of authenticity through this work in documentary. More than any other filmmaker of his era, Scorsese has been able to sustain the idea that he was making authentically personal films from his own cultural experiences, even while working from within the Hollywood framework. However admired filmmakers such as Robert Altman and Stanley Kubrick may be for their unique, modernist film styles, critics do not link their filmmaking to their personal roots to the same extent.

The first Scorsese retrospective, held at La Guardia Community College in May 1977, provides a concrete example of how Scorsese's films were established as being authentic even amid Scorsese's move into Hollywood filmmaking. The program, titled *Going to Look for America: The Urban and Ethnic Experience through the Films of Martin Scorsese* and organized by Scorsese's assistant Mary Pat Kelly, included several panels discussing Scorsese's films and included participants such as Scorsese childhood friend Dominic Lo Faro; Scorsese's mentor Haig Manoogian; Professors Allen Mendelbaum and Marco Miele, both specialists in Italian culture; film critic Stanley Kauffmann; actors Peter Boyle, Amy Robinson, and Robert Shields; and Scorsese's parents. Eventually, Kelly would collect this material into the book *Martin Scorsese: The First Decade*, published in 1980, which includes an introduction by filmmaker Michael Powell that serves very much as an imprimatur, conferring on Scorsese the status of an artist, "the Goya of Tenth Street," as Powell states.[87] The rest of Kelly's text similarly works toward consecrating Scorsese's art, reprinting many reviews of the films as well as working documents such as storyboards from *Raging Bull*.

In addition to this discussion of Scorsese as an artist, equal attention was paid to Scorsese's position as an ethnic minority filmmaker in America. This was hardly unique to the time period. One of the major distinguishing features of New Hollywood was the greater presence of ethnic minorities both in front of the camera (Dustin Hoffman, Al Pacino, Robert De Niro, and so forth) and behind it (Scorsese, Francis Ford Coppola, Michael Cimino, Woody Allen, and so on). But Scorsese was able to maintain his connection with the working-class

Little Italy background from which he emerged. The program itself was organized around the idea of Scorsese as an authentic voice emerging from his community. By far the most interesting of the panels in the program deals with Scorsese's "Neighborhood Films," which are debated by Manoogian, Kauffman, and Professors Mandelbaum and Miele. This panel differed from the rest by including much more debate and critique around Scorsese's work, as opposed to the autobiographical and hagiographic descriptions offered in the rest of the book. Kauffmann was especially critical of the idea of Scorsese as a great artist: "I come here tonight to talk about Scorsese after having shown a second film by a twenty-four-year-old man called Bertolucci—*Before the Revolution*. And Scorsese begins to look like warmed over pasta."[88] The discussion then moved onto the topic of Scorsese's early films, particularly *Mean Streets*, as anthropology, with Professor Miele critiquing the film's limited scope: "From the point of view of films of great success which have a universal appeal, I would like to say that films that portray a little corner, a ghetto, as you call it, can't really travel very, very wide in the world."[89] However, at this point in the panel, an audience member interjected and challenged this interpretation. Mario Carcaterra, identified as a fifty-five-year-old butcher, defended the film and its cultural specificity:

> You've got the wrong idea about what the picture . . . actually you know, people live in . . . the Lower East Side. . . . I come from what they call Hell's Kitchen. . . . I lived in Hell's Kitchen. . . . I've also lived downtown where you're talking about now. What I've seen in this picture here is not fake. It's the truth. In them days, I'm talking about, you know, in the twenties, thirties, forties, and fifties, I don't have no education, and I don't understand some of the words you're using . . . but reading stories . . . reading and actually being born in these places here . . . in what we call the slums—you know what I mean?—that's two different things. . . ."[90]

The inclusion of this audience member in Kelly's book functions rhetorically within the chapter as a whole to defend Scorsese's work. Carcaterra's profession and the grammatical errors of speech confer both an authenticity on this man as representative of the working class and, metonymically, on Scorsese's film as a truthful and legitimate expression of New York's Little Italy. It is hardly coincidental that this man appears during the only chapter in this book in which Scorsese's work is intellectually challenged to any degree. The idea of reading about this place, as presumably the professors do, is considered false, as opposed to living in these places, as this man and Scorsese do, which is real. Because of this, Scorsese's work is inoculated against intellectual criticism by virtue of its truth value.

Beginning with films dealing with his own childhood background and then continuing through his documentary work, Scorsese's works were legitimated as truthful and authentic visions even as Scorsese was taken seriously as an artist of great formalist beauty. Within a single text, he was both considered worthy of comparison to a great master painter and praised for the photographic directness of his depictions of his own ethnic milieu. Although Scorsese was not yet firmly established as the outstanding filmmaker of his generation, he already demonstrated his ability to appeal to very different aesthetic traditions and positions. This versatility would prove crucial to the ascendancy of his prestige. But it would also take efforts and events beyond the context of even the films and their aesthetics to eventually solidify Scorsese's artistic reputation. The films up to and including *Raging Bull* continue to be Scorsese's most acclaimed. But without Scorsese's work within the culture in the coming decades, it is unlikely that these films would be received as the greatest American films of this generation.

3

Scorsese and the Fall of the Hollywood Renaissance

IN THE DOCUMENTARY FILM OF Peter Biskind's book on the New Hollywood, *Easy Riders, Raging Bulls*, a clip from *Raging Bull* is used as a conclusion. The scene is the final fight shown in the film. The lead character, boxer Jake La Motta, withstands a violent beating from his rival, Sugar Ray Robinson. The documentary voiceover introduces the clip stating, "Scorsese let out one last howl of defiance." This is followed by La Motta standing up to a series of punches, blood splattering all over the front row of the audience. La Motta triumphantly says to Robinson, "You never got me down, Ray." Within the context of the documentary and its tragic rise-and-fall narrative of the New Hollywood, Scorsese is similarly seen as never giving in to the studio system, continuing with his vision uncompromised. This same scene within the original film can certainly be interpreted very differently, as being critical of La Motta's senseless masculine bravado. But the film's tragic structure and La Motta's tragic nobility also allow for the film to be reappropriated as a fitting conclusion to the Hollywood Renaissance narrative.

This chapter examines Scorsese's career during the 1980s, beginning with *Raging Bull*, released in 1980, and concluding with *The Last Temptation of Christ* in 1988. The time between these two landmark films has been rarely analyzed, often dismissed as a transition period. This argument is convincing if one looks only at the films and their marginal place within Scorsese's canon: *The King of Comedy* (1983), *After Hours* (1985), and *The Color of Money* (1986) are relatively ignored when compared to Scorsese's more acclaimed works. But when analyzed contextually, this period is crucial due to Scorsese's ability to maintain and even strengthen his place as a prestigious auteur, despite numerous career setbacks. Through his involvement in projects such as the film preservation movement, Scorsese survived the decade with his cultural capital intact, a feat few filmmakers of the New Hollywood match.

Transcendence, Redemption, Irony (Take Two): *Raging Bull*

Raging Bull begins with an older, overweight Jake LaMotta (Robert De Niro), a former boxing champion, backstage at a nightclub practicing his routine. A sudden cut shows LaMotta as a young man, fighting in the ring. We follow LaMotta's career and personal life with the fights themselves shot according to his state of mind. He has two main relationships, one with his brother/manager Joey (Joe Pesci), and the other with his second wife Vicky (Cathy Moriarty) of whom he is insanely jealous. After finally making a deal with the local mob to intentionally lose a fight, LaMotta is victorious in his long-awaited title shot. But his jealousy and insecurity overwhelm him, which leads him to accuse his brother of sleeping with his wife, and he then beats both Joey and Vicky in a jealous rage. He loses the title, absorbing a violent beating almost in penance for his sins. He retires, Vicky finally leaves him, and he spends time in prison. He tries unsuccessfully to reunite with Joey. The final scene shows him alone, back at the nightclub, preparing to deliver his act.

Raging Bull both completed the formation of Scorsese's critical reputation and marked his first public campaign for film preservation. The linking of these two events is important. Looked at retrospectively, the fact that *Raging Bull* is now considered Scorsese's masterpiece can seem rather natural, a seemingly organic progression. When viewed in context, a clearer picture of how the film became Scorsese's most acclaimed work can be reached. Initial reaction to *Raging Bull* was, like that to *Taxi Driver*, hardly unqualified enthusiasm, although it differed from the mostly negative reaction to *New York, New York*. While it received many positive reviews, including from the previously antagonistic Stanley Kauffmann, it received mixed notices from such prominent critics as Andrew Sarris and David Denby, as well as a dismissive pan from Pauline Kael.[1] Negative comments on the film tended to center around the portrayal of the lead character who was seen as too alienating and unlikable a protagonist. Much criticism also centered on Scorsese's failings as a storyteller. This actually prompted one of the film's defenders, Janet Maslin, to address the criticisms in an article two months after the initial release, arguing that the puzzling nature of the lead character was actually an aesthetic choice rather than a failure,[2] which is the first of many subsequent pieces within both the academic and popular press to defend the film against its detractors. These pieces generally fall into one of two categories: (1) defenses of the film on grounds of its spiritual dimension or (2) defenses of the film as ideologically progressive. Like Scorsese's previous "masterpiece," *Taxi Driver*, the film was largely seen as either a story of redemption or an ironic critique of violent masculinity. The ascendancy of *Raging Bull* over *Taxi Driver* as Scorsese's greatest film can partly be attributed to its ability to serve both of these narratives more convincingly.

In many interviews Scorsese often emphasized the spiritual dimension of the lead character, Jake LaMotta. Most dramatically, he has stated, "*Raging Bull* is about a man who loses everything and then regains it spiritually."[3] For Scorsese, LaMotta's profession as a boxer allowed him this greater access to the spiritual dimension of life. But precisely because he is on this higher level of spirituality, LaMotta's redemption is left fairly ambiguous at the film's conclusion. The film closes with LaMotta alone in his dressing room, as he was at the film's opening, and we see no traditional character growth as is typical of the Hollywood bio-pic. In fact, we see no indication that LaMotta has learned anything. Without the closing biblical quote, how much of a spiritual dimension would be read into the character is doubtful. The film's final end card reads as follows:

> So, for the second time, (the Pharisees)
> summoned the man who had been blind and said:
> "Speak the truth before God.
> We know this fellow is a sinner."
> "Whether or not he is a sinner, I do not know,"
> the man replied.
> "All I know is this:
> Once I was blind and now I can see."
> John IX, 24–26
> The New English Bible
> Remembering Haig P. Manoogian, teacher;
> May 23, 1916–May 26, 1980
> With Love and resolution, Marty.

This quote gives the film this spiritual element while anchoring it firmly within Scorsese's authorship. Unlike *Taxi Driver*, which is a film discussed as both a Scorsese and a Schrader film, *Raging Bull* is Scorsese's own. The final quote emphasizes this while connecting LaMotta to Scorsese, suggesting that even if LaMotta himself did not necessarily learn anything in the course of the narrative, Scorsese learned to see through his artistic treatment of the character. Hence the bold text signaling out the line, "Once I was blind and now I can see," and connecting it graphically with his own dedication to his film teacher Manoogian.

Scorsese reworks the classic tale of the *Cahiers* critics: a character faces alienation and achieves grace. It is arguable if the character has achieved redemption, but this is ultimately not as important as the fact that Scorsese has redeemed himself. This redemption is transferred from the character and onto the auteur, but nevertheless remains a key thematic. The fact that Scorsese continued exploring this narrative contributed as much as his skill as a filmmaker as to his critical reputation. This is particularly the case with his reception in France, not surprisingly given the origins of this spiritual auteurism in that country. Throughout the 1970s, Michael Henry (later Michael Henry Wilson) published articles on and interviews with Scorsese for *Positif*. In a piece written before the release of *Raging Bull*, Henry argues that Scorsese is the greatest of the American filmmakers of his generation because he deals with larger, spiritual issues in his work.[4] After years of featuring little coverage of Scorsese, *Cahiers du Cinéma* published several pieces on Scorsese around the release of *Raging Bull*, including Pascal Bonitzer's essay that compares Scorsese with Dosto-evsky in his handling of dark, spiritual themes.[5] This was part of a larger movement within *Cahiers* as a whole, in which the "Red Cahiers" period of the 1970s was replaced with the move into the mainstream of the 1980s.[6]

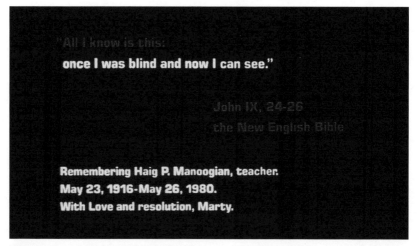

Figure 3.1. *Raging Bull* (Martin Scorsese, 1980), final credits emphasizing Scorsese's redemption.

The solitude of the lone figure striving for spiritual transcendence, the foundational tale of the original auteur critics of the 1950s, was once again taken seriously as the highest expression of cinematic art, and Scorsese was the filmmaker recounting this tale most consistently.

However, this spiritual theme of *Raging Bull* is not the only reading. The ideological critics looked at the film very differently, ignoring the themes of transcendence to focus instead on the issue of masculinity. The key reading in this regard is Robin Wood's piece in *Movie*, which was later reprinted in his study *Hollywood from Vietnam to Reagan* (originally published in 1986, with a revised version in 2003 featuring a still from *Raging Bull* on the cover). Previously Wood considered *Taxi Driver* aesthetically and ideologically unsatisfying because of its close reliance on the transcendence narrative, which he felt derived from the contributions of screenwriter Schrader. With *Raging Bull*, Wood argues that this spiritual dimension was largely downplayed in favor of a psychological portrait of a representative masculine figure.

Wood defends the film aesthetically from critics who argued that the film does not display a coherent narrative by arguing that its structure can only be understood from an ideological perspective. Using psychoanalytic theory, Wood sees the film through its homosexual subtext and argues that La Motta's paranoid violence is a result of this sexual repression. For Wood, the film's greatness lies in its implicit ideological critique of the culture of masculine violence. Although Scorsese does not discuss this reading in interviews to nearly the same extent as he affirms the spiritual reading, he did confirm Wood's reading of the film: "The title of my chapter comes from Martin Scorsese himself: he told me in a conversation that, though he was not aware of it at the time, he now saw that *Raging Bull* has a 'homosexual subtext.' "[7]

Wood's inclusion of this remark is telling. Wood acknowledges in his writing on Scorsese that he is not an explicitly political filmmaker, that instead his greatness as a creative artist leads him to expose the ideological cracks in the system:

> The films express no overt political commitment; one cannot take from them any coherently articulated Marxist critique of capitalism or feminist critique of patriarchy, and they give no reason to suppose that Scorsese would subscribe to either of these ideologies. . . . Yet every subject available must inevitably be structured by the major conflicts within the culture; what distinguishes the major artist is not an explicit ideological stance but his/her ability to pursue the implications of a given subject rigorously, honestly and without compromise, until its basis in those conflicts is revealed.[8]

This interpretative model can be seen in Comolli and Narboni's discussion of "category e" films in their influential "cinema/ideology/criticism." But like Comolli and Narboni, the ideological criticism of Wood does not break with older models of auteurism and thus proves Janet Staiger's point that film canons have a strong tendency to self-perpetuate. Wood continues to insist on the author as the major creative force and even feels the need to validate his own reading through Scorsese's comments. Although Wood rejects the reading of the film that would focus on the spiritual elements typical of traditional auteurism, he nevertheless restricts and limits the meaning of the film through his need to construct Scorsese as a radical filmmaker.

In a perceptive essay written for *Screen* in 1981, Pam Cook challenges the notion that *Raging Bull* is a radical critique of masculinity. Cook's point is that although the film presents the disturbing results of masculine violence, it also views the loss of masculinity through the prism of tragedy.[9] What Cook confronts is the film's ability to appeal to two sets of critics, the auteurist and the ideological, who will each interpret the film according to their own criteria. Cook critiques the ideological critics for failing to account for the film's tragic structure and the way in which masculinity is both criticized and affirmed. Viewed retrospectively, Cook's brief article foretells the reception of *Raging Bull* and the various ways in which it has been used within popular culture. Cook's recognition of the pleasure the film's tragic structure offers and the way

Figure 3.2. *Raging Bull* (Martin Scorsese, 1980), masculinity in crisis or rebellious hero?

in which La Motta can be seen as both a victim and even a hero is borne out by using *Raging Bull* as an icon of the Hollywood Renaissance. Peter Biskind's description of the film combines an admiration of the film with nostalgia for the lost Golden Age of New Hollywood:

> [*Raging Bull*] was very much a movie of the seventies, very much a beached whale on the shores of the new decade. It was an actor's movie, a film that valued character over plot, that indeed contained no one to "root for." With its unromantic, black and white, in-your-face tabloid look, its ferocious violence, and its pond scum characters layered with ghostly images of Italian Renaissance pietas and echoes of *verismo* operas such as *Cavalleria Rusticana* and *Pagliacci*, it was the furthest remove from the smarmy, feel-good pap of the coming cultural counterrevolution. Scorsese had refused to get with the program, had made an anti-*Rocky*, thumbed his nose at *Star Wars*, and he would pay for it.[10]

The film's tragic structure, its elegiac quality that Cook feels heavily qualified the film's critique of masculine violence, serves the film very well in its role as the last great film of the Hollywood Renaissance. Just as Scorsese had served as a surrogate for La Motta over the whole question of spiritual redemption, he also stood in for La Motta's stubborn defiance in the face of defeat.

Cook proved to be just as accurate in her analysis of the role of cinephilia in the film. Although ideological critics often ignore the role of visual pleasure in *Raging Bull*, it is vastly important to its meaning. As Cook argues, "[t]hen there is the film's visual pleasure: the excitement of a mise-en-scène which alternates between long, reflective shots which allow us to contemplate the scene in safety, at a distance, and explosions of rapid montage which assault our eyes and ears, bringing us right into the ring with the fighters."[11] This "assault" on our eyes and ears is suggestive of an aspect of *Raging Bull* that is usually ignored. In giving the audience the spectacle of violence, *Raging Bull* was not as far away from the blockbuster cinema of Spielberg and Lucas as might first appear. In her recent study of cinema in the home, Barbara Klinger argues that there now exists what she labels the "hardware aesthetic" that evaluates films "through the lens of hardware priorities" with special attention to "technological considerations." This involves "a rereading of films through the ideology of the spectacular, and the triumph of a particular notion of form over content."[12] Klinger argues, "in these estimations of films, sound and image may displace other tried-and-true priorities in critical criteria, such as auteurism and existing canons."[13] This would seem to be an overstatement in that the academic canon seems likely to ignore most of the blockbuster films this aesthetic praised. But with a film such as *Raging Bull*, the presence of fight sequences carefully designed to dazzle the senses have definitely contributed to the film's reputation.

A comparison of the DVD releases of both *Raging Bull* and *Taxi Driver* is instructive in this regard. The emphasis in the *Raging Bull* release was clearly on the technical achievement of the film, with four minidocumentaries on the film's various stages of production. One documentary focuses solely on the fight scenes. One of the film's audio commentaries featured Scorsese and editor Thelma Schoonmaker, who similarly devotes much of their discussion to the technical intricacies of the film. The *Taxi Driver* DVD differs significantly, although the disc designs are almost identical (despite being released by different companies). While it includes storyboards of the notorious final massacre and the typical behind-the-scenes features, the *Taxi Driver* DVD focuses much more on intellectual discussions of the film and its meanings. The DVD features audio commentaries by Professor Robert Kolker and screenwriter Paul Schrader, a former film critic and scholar. These contrasting DVD releases are mirrored by the reception of the two films critically. Despite *Raging Bull*'s current recognition as Scorsese's masterpiece, *Taxi Driver* remained the Scorsese film most popular with film critics in the 2002 *Sight and Sound* poll. *Taxi Driver* received six votes from critics, compared to three for *Raging Bull*. It is among the filmmakers polled that *Raging Bull* has earned its reputation, finishing tied for second in the 1992 poll and tied for sixth in the 2002 poll. Among filmmakers, it outnumbered *Taxi Driver* 13–6.[14] Filmmakers as a group are much more likely to share Klinger's hardware aesthetic, admiring the formal achievement of films to a greater extent than critics. But at the same time, they continue to hold to the standards of traditional canons. Films such as *Citizen Kane*, *Vertigo*, and *The Rules of the Game* continue to appear on both lists. Thus the impact of the hardware aesthetic on traditional canons is subtle. Canons are far too self-perpetuating to be subject to radical overhaul by new technology. That said, *Raging Bull* has clearly lent itself to the digital home theater environment and its desire for sound and image spectacle, and these elements have increased its reputation.

Scorsese's First Public Foray into Film Preservation: The Kodak Campaign

Related to this notion of cinephilia is another major factor in *Raging Bull*'s critical reception: Scorsese's involvement in film preservation. Shortly before the film's release in fall 1980, Scorsese launched a campaign against Kodak over the issue of color preservation. His interest in film archiving, although well chronicled, documented, and celebrated, has yet to be the subject of any significant scholarly work.[15] This is a rather large absence given the tremendous amount of cultural prestige these activities have given to Scorsese, not only within the film community but also within the general culture.[16] Scorsese has been rewarded both literally (1991 American Cinematheque Award, 1995 American Society of Cinematographers Board of Governors Award, the International Federation of Film Archives Film Preservation Award) and symbolically because of this his association with film preservation. This lack of analysis and contextualization is characteristic not only of Scorsese scholarship, but also of film preservation discourse. Caroline Frick argues, "[r]ather than actively or critically contextualizing the emergence and growth of the film preservation movement of the last one hundred years, academics and film archivists alike have relied upon key, common sense assumptions about the value of media preservation."[17] Part of this common sense is an uncritical examination of those participating in the preservation process. However noble Scorsese's efforts may be, they have a history. Or, rather, they are a part of at least three distinct histories: (1) the history of Scorsese's role within film preservation; (2) the history of Scorsese's critical reputation; and (3) the history of film preservation itself.

At the 1979 New York Film Festival, Scorsese made public the problem of color fading.[18] The campaign against Kodak began in the summer of 1980 and continued into the fall, using the release of *Raging Bull* as extra publicity for the cause. The U.S. press began to report on the story in trade journals such as *Variety* and *Box Office* and film magazines such as *American Film* and *Film Comment* with the story eventually reaching the mainstream press with pieces in the *Washington Post* and the *New York Times*.[19] Each piece reported on both the problem of color fading and Scorsese's petition sent to Kodak on June 12, 1980, complete with signatures from many in the industry.[20] Scorsese extended this appeal beyond Hollywood with a letter addressed to his European colleagues in *Positif* in the summer of that same year.[21] Follow-up articles appeared later in the year in both *Positif* and *Cahiers du Cinéma*.[22] The campaign proved enormously successful, and Kodak eventually changed to a color stock considerably less vulnerable to fading. The fact that Scorsese embarked on this campaign at this particular point in his career had major consequences for the growth of his critical reputation. This would seem to be coincidental. We find no evidence that Scorsese calculated this move to further his career, and his devotion to film preservation appears to be sincere. Nevertheless, it has become a major factor in how Scorsese is now viewed as a public figure, becoming a key aspect of his persona and influencing how his films would be received in the years to come.

Although the campaign against color fading marks Scorsese's first public foray into film preservation, his career as an archivist can be seen beginning even earlier, back at least to July 1977 when Scorsese presents a special award to director Michael Powell at the Telluride Film Festival.[23] The next year, Scorsese claims that he was asked to help present a new release print of Powell's *Peeping Tom* (1960): "In 1978, I was approached by a New York distributor, Corinth Films, who needed some money to re-release the film (*Peeping Tom*) with a brand-new print. I agreed to put up $5,000 on condition that the poster and print said, 'Martin Scorsese presents . . . ,' because I wanted to have this honor—and get my own 35mm print."[24]

Thus Scorsese's earliest public efforts within preservation are as a "presenter," a role he continues with greater frequency as his career progresses.[25] But, as Scorsese indicates, this interest in preservation is closely linked to another passion: collecting. If Scorsese's collecting can be considered an early version of his work in preservation, Scorsese had been an amateur archivist a long time before he chose to make this a part of his public persona.[26] It was in the interest of preserving his own personal collection that Scorsese first made contact with MoMA, coinciding with the preservation efforts involving color fading.

One of Scorsese's assistants at the time was Mark Del Costello, who was also a MoMA employee. Del Costello believes he was hired in part because of his experience at MoMA, and one of his first jobs for Scorsese involved working on the color preservation campaign and collecting and cataloging on video as many films as possible. He claims that Scorsese's personal collection had grown to such an extent that he was having difficulty paying for the space required to store his assets, resulting in his interest in developing a relationship with MoMA:

> Scorsese's collection was actually quite small—maybe only 30 titles (16mm). His posters collection in the flat file cabinet took up more space then [*sic*] his films did. It was his video collection that was massive (5,000 videos of films recorded from broadcast television and 500 videos made from film to video transfer). He would borrow from various sources prints of films that were not in circulation or distribution on video and have video dubs made. His storage facility was mainly filled with personal "stuff." The stuff that we had hoped MoMA would store included sets, props etc. from his films. Scorsese saw MoMA as a place where he could deposit his films and posters and ephemera and avoid the cost of storage while still maintaining ownership. He also saw that he could possibly gain

access to MoMA's collection of films and its facilities—such as the screening room. I broached the subject of Scorsese "collaborating" with MoMA and MoMA receiving his "collection" on deposit loan with the Film Department administrator Mary Lea Bandy. She was enthusiastic about the opportunity to open a relationship with Scorsese, believing that a working relationship with Scorsese was a coup in getting the "New Hollywood" generation engaged.[27]

For MoMA, Scorsese represented a key figure within the New Hollywood, an individual who would prove valuable if the institution wanted to keep a partnership with the now globalized Hollywood conglomerate.

As Peter Decherney explains, the former collaborations between cultural institutions and Classical Hollywood had now been reduced: "Collaborations between Hollywood and cultural institutions belong to the golden era of the studio system. Like the other constituent elements of the period, such collaborations were transformed during the transition from the studio system to what has been called the New Hollywood, in the 1950s, 1960s, and 1970s."[28] With the focus shifting in Hollywood to a global market, the concern with making movies American by forming relationships with institutions such as MoMA was no longer felt to be a priority. In addition, the introduction of more multimedia opportunities for the corporate conglomerates that now owned the studios meant that "cultural institutions lost their monopoly on the traffic of old films."[29] Because it was now cut off from Hollywood, Decherney argues that MoMA had to turn to the avant-garde director whom they originally rebuffed. Hollywood no longer needed the cultural legitimacy offered by cultural institutions like MoMA to the same extent as in the past: "In the New Hollywood, canon formation and the market for the studios' film libraries is managed by Hollywood with minimal help from museums, universities, or the government."[30] But what Decherney ignores is that while Hollywood studios may no longer focus as much energy on relationships with cultural institutions, individuals from Hollywood, such as Scorsese, were still interested in making these connections. Scorsese's mutually beneficial relationship with MoMA is thus very much contingent on this particular historical moment. Scorsese was the ideal figure to be associated with MoMA for several reasons. He was a native New Yorker. He had a previous association with another New York cultural institution, NYU, which had a long affiliation with MoMA.[31] He was both a Hollywood director and a Hollywood outsider, and he had just begun a campaign against color fading. Decherney overestimates the ability of Hollywood to create its own canon independently. Individuals like Scorsese, through their associations with organizations of cultural legitimacy, can maintain their reputation over contemporary figures more popular with the Hollywood establishment. Scorsese's ability to mark himself as an outsider to Hollywood even while working with the studios is what has allowed his reputation to flourish. His connections with cultural institutions play a key role in making this distinction.

The initial reception of *Raging Bull* provides an early example of how Scorsese's activities outside of filmmaking have had a positive influence on the rise of his critical reputation. Linking the release of the film with the color preservation campaign meant that reviews of *Raging Bull* were appearing simultaneously with articles on Scorsese's color fading petition. The fact that *Raging Bull* was shot in black and white was even seen as a type of protest by Scorsese against the industry: "[At first] we said, no, it's too pretentious to use black and white now. But then it clicked in my mind that color wasn't going to last anyway—the film stock was subject to rapid fading."[32] The problem of color fading gave Scorsese an excuse to use black and white without appearing "pretentious." Scorsese was thus able to give his film the aura of high art without that choice seeming calculated for such an effect. This is in marked contrast to several other films released during this period, such as *Manhattan* (Woody Allen, 1979), *The Elephant Man* (David Lynch, 1980), and *Stardust Memories* (Woody Allen, 1980). In each case, the decision to shoot in black and white cannot help but be seen as one of aesthetic posturing, using the now rare black-and-white images to distinguish the films as art. *Raging Bull* is not immune to these criticisms either, but given that the film was released in conjunction with the color fading campaign, with *Raging Bull* often accompanied by a demonstration at festivals throughout North America and Europe, the use of black and white could be argued to have an importance beyond the formal aesthetics of the film.[33]

In particular, the contrast with Allen is illuminating, with the accusation of artistic pretense always much more present in response to Allen's work. This is despite the fact that in terms of overt use of cinematic technique, Scorsese's work is equally as formalist. The difference lies much more in how each has been able to sell a notion of authenticity. The example of the use of black and white in their respective films of this period is just one instance among many in which Scorsese has been able to position his work as artistically pure in a way in which Allen has not. *Raging Bull* uses black and white for three primary reasons, according to Scorsese's explanations and those of critics given through the years: (1) to protest against color fading; (2) to capture the realism of the period setting of the film in which all of the original fight footage would also be in black and white (similar arguments that were eventually made for Steven Spielberg's *Schindler's List* in 1993); and (3) because

Scorsese, cinematographer Michael Chapman, and Scorsese's friend and fellow director Michael Powell all agreed that color was "distracting" from the images.[34] In all cases, the idea was to offer a justification for the decision that deflected away from any ideas of artistic pretension. This was especially important given that Scorsese's previous film, *New York, New York*, had been received coldly because it was too self-conscious and revisionist. Similarly, Allen had just finished the film *Interiors* (1978), which many regarded as too self-conscious and arty, particularly in its homage to Swedish director Ingmar Bergman.[35] Allen, however, did not feel the need to correct this impression, creating two back-to-back films using high contrast black-and-white images to distinguish the films as aesthetic objects. There was no other explanation, such as with *Raging Bull*, for films such as *Manhattan* and *Stardust Memories* to be shot in black and white other than to consciously create beautiful images. As Allen's career progressed, he felt increasingly comfortable, following his Academy Award in 1977 for *Annie Hall*, to become a cult item, making the films he wanted on limited budgets with a small but loyal following. Scorsese's ambitions were always much higher, and allowed him to be considered as a great artist to an extent that Allen has never achieved.

A class dimension can be added to this, especially as related to Allen's and Scorsese's respective visions of New York City. Scorsese's Italian background has been linked to a broader sense of the city's working class, as can be seen in *Mean Streets*. Scorsese's next New York film, *Taxi Driver*, is even more iconic due in large part to its contradictions as a text, contradictions that extend to its depiction of New York itself. As Amy Taubin writes, "[a]mong the many reasons that *Taxi Driver* has become a classic is that it testifies to both a vanished New York (chequer cabs, rotary phones, typewriters and 3 a.m. coffee at the Belmore Cafeteria) and an absolutely contemporary anomie. The film's love/hate relationship with the city plays into the fantasies of both New Yorkers and those who project from afar their fears, loathings, hopes and desires."[36] The downtown Manhattan on display in Scorsese's work, with its fascination with small-time criminals and the urban poor, became associated with a new realism in American cinema as a whole. Scorsese benefits from this realism while employing a cinematic style in stark contrast to any notion of reality. Scorsese is able to present this stylized version of New York's underclass because he is a native New Yorker as well as a member of the ethnic community of Little Italy. Without this, *Taxi Driver* risks being seen as at best disingenuous and at worst exploitative.

Allen's vision of New York, by contrast, came to be seen as less authentic because of his associations with an idealized conception of the city. As Leonard Quart describes it:

His city is basically limited to a large fragment of one borough, Manhattan—though both *Annie Hall* (1977) and *Radio Days* (1986) reconstruct scenes from his central characters' boyhoods in Brooklyn and Rockaway, the other boroughs are usually treated as if they have been severed from the city—an upscale section that runs from the Upper West Side through Central Park to the Village and Soho and from the east 80s to Gramercy Park. There are scenes set on the Columbia Unviersity [*sic*] campus with its grand McKim, Mead, and White buildings, but Harlem, Washington Heights, and even the Lower East Side barely make an appearance in his films.[37]

If *Taxi Driver*'s Travis Bickle will go "any place" in the city, Allen limits his geographical points of interest and thus can appear myopic and detached from "real world" concerns. This is also true of the more limited racial, ethnic, and class base of his characters. However false one may think this dichotomy between Scorsese and Allen, there nevertheless exists a strong impression that Scorsese remained relevant to "real world" (that is, non–upper-class) concerns and Allen did not. When examining their respective careers film-by-film, especially through the 1980s, a persuasive case can be made that Allen's work was of greater distinction.[38] But the films themselves simply do not account for actual reputations, which are contingent on many other factors.

The contrast between Scorsese and Allen can be extended to their respective relationships to the directors they admire. Allen's homages to European auteurs such as Bergman and Federico Fellini were felt to be too direct, obviously imitations rather than original pieces: *Interiors* as an imitation of Bergman, *Stardust Memories* as an imitation of Fellini. Allen's background in comic parodies such as *Take the Money and Run* (1969), *Bananas* (1971), *Sleeper* (1973), and *Love and Death* (1975) contributed to this reception as well. Scorsese, however, even with such densely intertextual works as *Mean Streets* and *Taxi Driver*, was always received as a more original voice. Scorsese's relationship with previous directors can best be encapsulated by his relationship with Michael Powell, which provides a vivid example of how Scorsese's work in film preservation has worked toward enshrining Scorsese's name in the temple of cinema he wants to protect. Thus Scorsese "presents" Powell's *Peeping Tom*, and in turn Powell wrote an introduction to *Martin Scorsese: The First Decade* in order to provide an imprimatur to the study (as mentioned earlier, Powell actually compares Scorsese to Goya).[39] Subsequently, Scorsese has written forewords to an academic text on Powell as well as Powell's autobiography, not to mention praises within the popular press.[40] While Powell's influence on certain shots in Scorsese's career has been acknowledged (such as in Scorsese's various audio commentaries on the Criterion Collection's DVD releases of Powell/Pressburger films), he has avoided making an entire film as homage to Powell's work. Instead, Scorsese has used his interests in film history and preservation to show his appreciation of past masters, which has in turn led to his cultural prestige being increased.

This claim about Scorsese's artistic ambition being high runs counter to most accounts of Scorsese's career. When compared with many of his New Hollywood compatriots, such as Francis Ford Coppola, Steven Spielberg, George Lucas, or Michael Cimino, all of whom favor dramas more epic in scope, Scorsese seemed much more intent on making smaller, intimate character studies that were more personal. His one attempt at a bigger project, *New York, New York*, was his first commercial and critical failure. This was precisely because there was too much character study in a form (musical epic) in which this was not expected. But when compared to independent, non-Hollywood directors, Scorsese's artistic ambitions are seen more clearly. By coming to Hollywood and opting out of the independent scene, Scorsese was able to make his name and reputation surpass even one of his mentors, John Cassavetes. Like Allen, although on an even smaller scale, Cassavetes has remained a cult taste. Despite his enormous influence and his prestige as an uncompromising artist, Cassavetes has never achieved the level of canonization of a Scorsese. Cassavetes's work is frequently praised for the performances and for the rawness of the emotions presented, but it is also criticized for the crudeness of the technique and for being over-indulgent.[41] There is an ideological dimension to this aesthetic critique, an idea that, at least within the American cinema, technical limitations are sufficient grounds for dismissal from the upper pantheon of great films and filmmakers. An "independent" director in the United States is a figure like Scorsese, someone making Hollywood films that have both aesthetic polish and artistic authenticity. To see how Scorsese has come to be seen as this authentic ideal, we must compare him with his fellow New Hollywood filmmaker.

Scorsese and Coppola

The most obvious figure to compare to Scorsese is Francis Ford Coppola because he is the only filmmaker within the New Hollywood to legitimately challenge Scorsese as the greatest director of his generation.[42] In fact, Coppola's first two *Godfather* films ranked above any Scorsese film in the 2002 *Sight and Sound* poll (although the idea of considering the two films as a single work is highly debatable), and in the poll asking critics to decide the greatest film of the past twenty-five years, Coppola's *Apocalypse Now* (1979) was the top selection. By 1981, the time at which both Scorsese and Coppola had already made their most critically acclaimed films, Coppola was clearly the director with the greater critical reputation. But within the next decade, Scorsese would take Coppola's place as the generation's greatest artist. This is despite the fact that none of the films Scorsese released after *Raging Bull* has been canonized as Scorsese masterpieces. His two most critically acclaimed films continue to be *Taxi Driver* and *Raging Bull*. When one looks at only the films they produced throughout the next decade, Scorsese's and Coppola's careers look strikingly similar. After the respective success of *Raging Bull* and *Apocalypse Now*, each had a major disappointment with *The King of Comedy* and *One from the Heart*. This was followed by both retreating into lower budget projects: Scorsese with *After Hours* (1985), Coppola with a pair of S. E. Hinton adaptations: the rather conventional *The Outsiders* (1983) and the more experimental *Rumble Fish* (1983). Both then made films to move themselves back into the mainstream of Hollywood: Scorsese with *The Color of Money* (1986), Coppola with *The Cotton Club* (1984), *Peggy Sue Got Married* (1986), and *Gardens of Stone* (1987). Both were involved in a project with the most recognized star of the decade, Michael Jackson: Scorsese directing the video *Bad* (1987), Coppola the Walt Disney World theme park short *Captain EO* (1986). Both went on to direct a deeply personal project: Scorsese's *The Last Temptation of Christ* (1988) and Coppola's *Tucker: The Man and His Dream* (1988). These parallels merge when Scorsese and Coppola join Woody Allen to make *New York Stories* (1989), a trio of short films combined into a feature. Both Scorsese and Coppola then return to their roots in the gangster genre, with Scorsese's *GoodFellas* (1990) and Coppola's *The Godfather: Part III* (1990). But despite these parallels, by 1991, Scorsese had managed to increase his prestige greatly, whereas Coppola's reputation fell dramatically. Is this simply because Scorsese's work was of greater quality? Or are there other factors to consider?

When comparing Scorsese and Coppola, one immediate difference is their vision of cinema's history and future. Scorsese, as evidenced by his work in film preservation, looks very much to the past. Scorsese's main concern is preserving America's cinematic heritage. Thus, when faced with the problem of color fading, Scorsese tried both to preserve films that were in danger of being lost and to petition Kodak to make available a film stock less susceptible to deterioration. Unlike many of his colleagues, including Coppola, Lucas, and Spielberg, Scorsese remained committed to film as a medium. At the same time Scorsese was undergoing his preservation efforts, Coppola, on the other hand, was looking forward to the demise of film and the rise of electronic and digital technology. He believed that this would revolutionize the whole process of producing visual narrative by democratizing the process. Because Coppola had always been far more successful at the box office than Scorsese, he was able to do more than simply use his new system of electronic cinema in his own films. Instead, Coppola purchased production facilities and attempted to challenge the reigning Hollywood oligopoly with his own Zoetrope Studios. Believing he could make better films more cheaply and efficiently, Coppola set his ambitions higher than directing. Whereas Scorsese kept to the more modest (and ultimately less threatening) goal of improving film stock, Coppola's vision was to radically transform movies to the point where the medium itself would be forever altered. In 1982 Coppola stated, "I think electronic cinema is going to make art less expensive to make and available to more people. I think in two years there won't be any more film shot."[43]

Two things are striking about Coppola's predictions about the future of cinema: he was in the long run correct, and he was massively misguided in his notions of how quickly change would come about. As Jon Lewis has argued, Coppola failed to correctly read the environment of Hollywood. This led to his failed attempt to run a studio and challenge the Hollywood power structure, which in turn has greatly affected his critical reputation. Lewis's book on Coppola, in fact, was partly inspired by Lewis's conviction that the history of Coppola and Zoetrope Studios was extremely flawed. Lewis's argument is that Coppola's failures as a studio mogul have adversely influenced the reputation of the film texts themselves. Coppola positioned himself as a visionary, aligning himself with the future, and when that vision failed, Coppola and his films, by the logic of auteurism, were seen as failures as well. Many of the reviews of Coppola's films since and including *Apocalypse Now* have focused on issues such as the cost of the production at the expense of the movies themselves.[44]

Even Coppola's one major foray into film preservation reveals the fundamental distinction between Coppola and Scorsese. In 1980 Coppola helped rerelease the restoration of the silent classic *Napoleon* (Abel Gance, 1927). The rather extraordinary box-office success of this release seemed, at the time, even further proof of Coppola's ability to know audiences of the time. The film, reconstructed by Kevin Brownlow and the British Film Institute (BFI), was first shown to Coppola in 1973 in rough-cut form in London. After the film premiered at the London Film Festival in 1980, Coppola purchased the rights to the film from French director Claude Lelouche. As Lewis argues, Coppola's interest in the project was more than simple philanthropy. First, it gave Coppola an opportunity to appear as a patron of the cinematic arts, which would help his own posterity and legacy. Second, it was the type of film that Coppola felt was consistent with his own future work. By 1980 Coppola had already begun developing a multiscreen version of Goethe's *Elective Affinities*, as well as developing *One from the Heart*, which, like *Napoleon*, he hoped would take shape through technological innovation.[45] Coppola, even when dealing with cinematic history and its preservation, still was looking toward the future, not the past.

Coppola's role as a producer in the reissue of *Napoleon* initially appeared to be an unqualified—and unexpected—success. However, even early on, Coppola was criticized for his involvement in the project: "Despite its success at the box office, 'Coppola's' *Napoleon* met with significant criticism from the very community that had once embraced the *auteur* theory, posting for the first time a kind of warning that, in the 1980s, his prestige and success might eventually become something of a liability."[46] The controversy over the film was mainly between Coppola and BFI, which had actually restored the work. As is often the case when film preservation becomes commercial, the debate stemmed from questions of authenticity. For the theatrical release, Coppola replaced Carl Davis's BFI-commissioned score, based on available material dating back to the film's first run with a live orchestra playing a score composed by his father, Carmine Coppola.[47] Because of a court ruling, the BFI version was licensed for exhibition only in the United Kingdom, whereas Coppola's version could be shown anywhere. Coppola attempted to diffuse the situation by making sure all of the profits went to BFI, but this did not quell the dissent. For Coppola as an auteur to be insensitive to the authenticity of Gance's original film seemed paradoxical and even hypocritical, which points to another problem in addition to that of authenticity. Coppola's very success was resented: "Many at the British Film Institute, where the film was restored, bristled that Coppola's success had upstaged their hard work. In the United States, they argued *Napoleon* was just another product bearing the logo 'Francis Ford Coppola Presents.' Coppola, they argued, had somehow become the *auteur* of not Gance's but also *their* film."[48] In attempting to increase his cultural capital, Coppola had failed to negotiate with the cultural institutions crucial to this prestige. His attempt to handle the situation economically by handing over the profits proved how little Coppola understood this field. A decade earlier, in dealing with the authorship controversy over *Street Scenes 1970*, Scorsese had learned the perils of taking credit for the work of others. Since then he has proven much shrewder in handling his cultural prestige.

This incident involving film preservation and *Napoleon* is a microcosm of a larger problem for Coppola. He began to be seen as a studio mogul even as he was an outsider to the people in Hollywood who had the real money and power. His reputation as a great artist was compromised by his desire to be a studio head and producer. Coppola felt he could have the best of both worlds, to be "the studio mogul and resident artist—Zanuck and Welles rolled into one," as *Newsweek* critic Jack Kroll described Coppola in 1981.[49] In reality, both his economic and cultural capital suffered by being combined. Coppola placed too much importance on financial considerations thereby jeopardizing the idea that he was a driven and uncompromising artist. However realistic and practical Coppola's position may have been, it cost him a great deal of his economic and cultural capital. This was only compounded by the actual problems of running a studio. Instead of nurturing an environment of artistic freedom, Coppola proved to be just as interfering as any other studio head. On the Zoetrope production *Hammett* (1983), directed by German art cinema favorite Wim Wenders, Coppola insisted on hiring screenwriters to try to fix the film's problems rather than allowing Wenders the opportunity to solve the problems on set.[50] As a result, and echoing the early criticisms of his handling of *Napoleon*, many saw Coppola as betraying a fellow artist.

By the mid-1980s, both Coppola and Scorsese were reeling from box-office failures and were forced to capitulate to Hollywood and make safe, mainstream commercial fare. But Scorsese had his artistic integrity intact. At the same time Coppola was having problems as a studio head in dealing with *Hammett*, Scorsese was having his first attempt to adapt Nikos Kazantzakis's novel *The Last Temptation of Christ* shut down due to studio reluctance to challenge religious protest groups. Despite the similarities of their actual film outputs, the contextual situations of Coppola and Scorsese were quite different. I have already discussed the work of Robert Ray who, in his study *A Certain Tendency of the Hollywood Cinema, 1930–1980*, compared Scorsese favorably to Coppola in terms of his ability to ideologically challenge Hollywood. Ray's book was released in 1985 during the time when the reputations of both were moving in opposite directions. Another prominent example of the differing critical trajectories of the two filmmakers can be charted in the first two editions of Robert Philip Kolker's *A Cinema of Loneliness*, the first book-length academic analysis of the New Hollywood era. The first edition, released in 1980, includes five representative figures: Arthur Penn, Stanley Kubrick, Scorsese, Coppola, and Robert Altman. Kolker's method is representative of an approach to this period, similar to that of the *Movie* critics, which sees these filmmakers as representing a brief modernist period in Hollywood. Using this modernist discourse helped establish these films as art and their directors as auteurs and went a long way to creating the notion of this era as the last Hollywood Golden Age. The main ideas of the modernist discourse of this interpretive community are clear: reducing the significance of plot, defying traditions, and breaking with convention signal great art. Kolker's approach is thus representative of an entire school of criticism applied to the New Hollywood. Scorsese's and Coppola's presence as the only directors of the film school generation included signaled Kolker's suspicion of this group's modernist credentials, instead favoring older directors such as Penn, Kubrick, and Altman.

When Kolker decided to drop Coppola in favor of Steven Spielberg in the second edition of the text in 1988, it was symbolic of how far Coppola had fallen in critical reputation. Conversely, it left Scorsese alone as the key figure of his generation, the last American modernist. Spielberg's inclusion was simply a commentary on the new direction of digital mise-en-scène and the return of Hollywood to formulaic filmmaking. It can also be read as another critique of Coppola, replacing him with Spielberg to imply that Coppola was always more of a commercial showman (like Spielberg) than an artist (like Scorsese). Kolker's explanation for dropping Coppola from the book's second edition is worth quoting at length:

> Coppola, to whom a chapter was devoted in the first edition, has, it seems to me, proven a much less important filmmaker over the course of time. His cinematic imagination, along with his attempts to remain independent, to operate his own studio, produce or distribute other people's films, has failed. In retrospect, his films seem not to bear the amount of analysis first given them, and certainly the work he has produced since the second has lacked the insight and careful attention to form that marked the earlier material.[51]

As a justification, this seems rather weak, but it is nevertheless extremely telling. Kolker does not simply say that Coppola's "cinematic imagination" has failed. He follows this by saying that Coppola's "attempts to remain independent" and "to operate his own studio" have failed as well, thus clearly linking the two. A strong argument can made that this extratextual failure on Coppola's part led to his being dropped from the second edition of Kolker's study, despite Kolker's close attention to textual analysis. If the work Coppola has produced since 1980 has "lacked the insight and careful attention to form that marked the earlier material," the same can certainly be said of Scorsese. In fact, Kolker even acknowledges this. Discussing *After Hours* and *The Color of Money*, Kolker argues that the films "betray a certain exhaustion of imagination" or "a willing surrender of imagination."[52] Nevertheless, Scorsese was still included in the book because he was able to maintain his reputation as an artist who was having difficulty adjusting to the system. Coppola, however, was seen as attempting to be the system. Curiously, his films made before 1980, which Kolker felt deserved discussion in 1980, now "seem not to bear the amount of analysis first given them."

My own approach is similar to Lewis's in that I want to reexamine the perceived reputation of a noted New Hollywood auteur. However, in the case of Scorsese, the situation is reversed. Rather than reconsidering extratextual factors to explain the downfall of a reputation, what is needed with Scorsese is an explanation for how his reputation continued to flourish during the period of the 1980s. Echoing the massive amount of now-received knowledge about this moment in Hollywood history, Lewis states, "In the aftermath of *Heaven's Gate*, 1970s *auteurs* like Martin Scorsese, Robert Altman, Peter Bogdanovich, and William Friedkin, along with Cimino and Coppola, all proved unable to make a smooth transition into 1980s Hollywood."[53] Examined purely in terms of their film output, Lewis's comments about this group of filmmakers seem accurate. In the case of Scorsese, most critics agree that his films made after *Raging Bull* represent a low period artistically, particularly *The Color of Money*, and overall these films have not become canonized alongside *Taxi Driver* and *Raging Bull*.[54] But when looked at contextually, Scorsese was just as successful during this period in maintaining and even building his cultural capital as directors such as Lucas and Spielberg were in building their economic power. After the commercial failure of *The King of Comedy*, Scorsese was faced with a very different Hollywood environment following big budget failures by such auteurs as Cimino and Coppola. He found this out firsthand when his production of *The Last Temptation of Christ* in 1983 was shut down by Paramount.[55] This disappointment led to Scorsese making two films in the mid-1980s, *After Hours* and *The Color of Money*, and although on the surface these films seem very remote from each other, they are in fact very complementary texts. And despite the general neglect both receive in Scorsese's career overviews, they are key films for understanding the reputation Scorsese has today.

Going "Indie": *After Hours*

After Hours takes place over the course of one night in New York. After a burst of Mozart over the opening credits, the camera moves in dramatically, in mock heroic fashion, toward Paul (Griffin Dunne), a bored office worker. After a banal conversation with a coworker, he leaves work and is next seen in a coffee shop reading Henry Miller's *Tropic of Cancer* (Miller, one of the great American subversive outsiders, would come up again six years later in *Cape Fear*). He meets an attractive young woman named Marcy (Rosanna Arquette) and decides to take a cab to downtown Soho at 11:30 P.M. in order to meet her. His journey becomes a nightmare, not just in its unpleasantness but in its very dreamlike, Buñuelesque structure. Marcy proves to be very unstable, telling extreme stories of sexual abuse in a deadpan manner, and seemingly hiding severe burns and scars. Paul flees only to encounter more bizarre characters. Without any money he is unable to make his way back home and must continue to deal with an increasingly hostile universe. Finally, an angry mob pursues him, convinced he is a serial burglar. His only escape is to be turned into a sculpture. In a final twist, he (it) is stolen by the real thieves, and falls out of back of their truck in the early morning right in front of his office. He returns to his desk where a computer greets him with the message "good morning Paul" as the Mozart and camera movement of the opening return to frame the narrative.

Given the situation as it now existed in Hollywood, Scorsese was faced with one of two options: make a large studio film in which he would have no control, or remove himself from the Hollywood big budgets and make a film cheaply. He was even offered Hollywood projects such as *Beverly Hills Cop* (Martin Brest, 1984).[56] This runs counter to the idea that Scorsese was struggling to "survive" as a filmmaker, as he put it.[57] What was in danger of not surviving this period was his critical reputation, "Scorsese" as the name of the auteur rather than Scorsese the

Figure 3.3. *After Hours* (Martin Scorsese, 1985).

actual director. Instead of staying in Hollywood, Scorsese went back to making a small film in New York City. Working for the first time with cinematographer Michael Ballhaus (best known for working quickly and cheaply with German art cinema director Rainer Werner Fassbinder), Scorsese shot *After Hours* in 40 days for $4 million, similar to the way he put together *Taxi Driver* nearly ten years earlier.[58] *After Hours* was thus seen as an "independent film" and would win Scorsese a prize for Best Director at the first Independent Spirit Awards. It was unquestionably a shrewd move for Scorsese to make. Instead of being seen as a failed Hollywood filmmaker such as Coppola, Scorsese was seen as an outsider to the studio industry. Also, by 1985, as the very existence of an awards presentation suggests, the idea of an American Independent Cinema had begun to take shape. Throughout the early 1980s, numerous younger directors made their films completely outside of the industry: *The Return of the Secaucus Seven* (John Sayles, 1980), *Chan Is Missing* (Wayne Wang, 1982), *Stranger than Paradise* (Jim Jarmusch, 1984), *She's Gotta Have It* (Spike Lee, 1985), and *Blood Simple* (Joel Coen, 1985) to name only the most prominent of these works. But the recognition of these films as part of a larger movement that would eventually be called "American Independent Cinema" depended on other historical factors apart from the films themselves. Most notably, American Independent Cinema rises at the same time as the Hollywood Renaissance is in decline.

There is thus a clear link between the independent cinema and the former Hollywood Renaissance, both artistically and in terms of the industry. Although many independent films are financed, distributed, and even exhibited outside of the industry, a great many are not. By the 1990s, all of the studios had "independent" studios that they financed. Even early on, a film such as *After Hours* is at best codependent. Describing the film, Andy Dougan writes, "*After Hours* was completely independent. [Amy] Robinson and [Griffin] Dunne [the film's producers] had raised the cash through a bank loan secured against a distribution promise from a studio. This meant that Scorsese could do what he wanted with the minimum of interference."[59] The very contradiction of the film's independent status is evident from this short quotation. The film's production cost may not have come from the studios, but the loan required a distribution deal from Hollywood. This highly qualifies Dougan's conclusion that Scorsese therefore had a minimum of interference. This independent cinema movement has two strains of filmmakers: (1) those using independent cinema to produce a "calling card" in order to work for the studios; (2) those wanting to stay on the margins because they are interested in pursuing a style or subject matter that cannot be assimilated into studio filmmaking. Scorsese's goal at the time seems clear: to continue to make Hollywood, not independent, films. He thus was very similar to many other "independent" filmmakers, such as Spike Lee, the Coen Brothers, and countless others who began in independent films in order to move into making bigger budget movies for the studios. Scorsese had no interest in continuing to make low-budget films like some other independents such as Jim Jarmusch and John Sayles. Because of this, Scorsese had to treat *After Hours* as a calling card to Hollywood, despite his already-established critical reputation. He needed to prove that he could be trusted to work quickly and cheaply while still producing a quality product. Scorsese's goal was to reinvent himself as a bankable director while maintaining his reputation as a prestigious auteur. *After Hours* thus proved an ideal vehicle. It marked continuity with Scorsese's previous work in being set in New York, where all of his films except *Alice Doesn't Live Here Anymore* primarily took place, and in returning to the type of lower budget filmmaking he had abandoned after *Taxi Driver*. Moreover, the film became a critical and commercial success, albeit on a more minor scale. The nature of the "success" of *After Hours* is heavily contradictory, and tells us a great deal more about filmmaking in the United States in the mid-1980s than it does about the film itself.

Despite the fact that *After Hours* is an "independent" film with connotations of art, it is more of a commercial project for Scorsese than most of his other work. Compared with other early films of the "independent" movement, not to mention the experiments of a "Hollywood" director like Coppola on *One from the Heart* and *Rumble Fish*, *After Hours* is rather conventional in both style and subject matter. But rhetorically, it worked perfectly. The reviews of the film mark an interesting contrast to the reviews of Coppola's work from the same period. Examining a Coppola film from this period without a reference to how much it cost is difficult. Economic matters were indistinguishable from aesthetic concerns. *After Hours* was looked at similarly but from a positive rather than negative perspective. The film's small budget was seen as praiseworthy. The similarities to Scorsese's first success with *Taxi Driver* were emphasized, despite the fact that the film has little in common with the earlier work other than location. The perception of *After Hours* being an authentic Scorsese work was prevalent at the time. Retrospectively, the film has been seen by most as less important from an artistic perspective. But looked at contextually, *After Hours* was a successful negotiation of both cultural and economic capital. Scorsese's next film, *The Color of Money*, would prove a much more difficult text to position and would rely even more on extratextual considerations.

"Has Martin Scorsese Gone Hollywood?" (Part Two): *The Color of Money*

The Color of Money opens with a voiceover monologue by Scorsese describing the game of nine-ball pool and philosophizing about luck. Following the credits, we are introduced, or rather reintroduced, to Eddie Felson (Paul Newman), a character originated in Robert Rossen's *The Hustler* (1961) twenty-five years earlier. The former pool hustler is now in the liquor sales business, although he marginally follows the backroom circuit. He meets a young man, Vincent (Tom Cruise), and his girlfriend Carmen (Mary Elizabeth Mastrantonio), and he is convinced Vincent has the potential to be a pool champion. Vincent also reminds Eddie of his younger self and sees the opportunity to live vicariously through his protégé. They tour various pool hall dives on their way to the big tournament in Atlantic City, with Eddie trying to teach Vincent how to properly hustle. Eventually, Eddie has the desire to start playing again himself. He gets hustled by a young man named Amos (Forest Whitaker), and the humiliation leads him to break with Vincent and try a comeback on his own. He and Vincent meet in the Atlantic City tournament, where Eddie is victorious. Later, he finds out Vincent intentionally lost for gambling purposes. Eddie pulls out of the tournament and challenges Vincent, asking for his best game. The film concludes just as the final showdown begins, on a freeze-frame of Eddie saying, "I'm back."

Of all of Scorsese's feature films, few if any are as neglected as *The Color of Money*, even including such commercial and critical failures as *New York, New York*. Unlike Scorsese's other less-appreciated films, critics have not been able to resurrect *The Color of Money* as a subversive, critical text. Commercially it was Scorsese's most successful film to date and the production proved to Hollywood that Scorsese was a "professional" director, capable of making a marketable film that was shot quickly and under budget. Given that Scorsese's critical reputation has required that he maintain his status as a director of Hollywood films that would not move him to the margins of the American industry, *The Color of Money* is a rather important film in his career and even in the advancement of his critical reputation. But it unquestionably threatened Scorsese's status at the time. As with *Alice Doesn't Live Here Anymore*, Scorsese had to deal with the accusation that he had "gone Hollywood."

Like the term "independent." "Hollywood" here is not used as an industry term, but rather as a sign of artistic regression. *The Color of Money* is often neglected because it is considered too mainstream and conventional and lacks Scorsese's usual authorial signature. Because of this, it contradicts Scorsese's image of himself as an outsider, an image he has tried to cultivate over the last few decades. For example, the conclusion of the documentary *Easy Riders, Raging Bulls* features an end-note stating, "Martin Scorsese has continued to make uncompromising personal films with Hollywood's money." Of course, the situation is not that simple. Scorsese has had to compromise a great deal to continue to work in Hollywood over the past decades. By making *The Color of Money* on time and under budget, Scorsese was able to further reestablish himself in Hollywood, where he continues to make films today. This comes at a certain cost to Scorsese's critical reputation, which is one of the reasons it is often ignored in critical overviews. For example, it is skipped over completely in the documentary *Scorsese on Scorsese*. Roger Ebert, one of Scorsese's strongest supporters, felt Scorsese was not living up to his potential with this film: "If this movie had been directed by someone else, I might have thought differently about it because I might not have expected so much."[60] Scorsese's critical reputation was in danger because of the perception that he was being assimilated into commercial filmmaking. In interviews today, Scorsese tries to talk about the film like his others, downplaying any notion that this was purely a commercial project: "In a way it was an experiment for me, to see what it would be like to make a movie with someone like Paul Newman. . . . The important idea was to make each shot fresh."[61] Scorsese has also tried to justify the happy endings of both *After Hours* and *The Color of Money*: "I do think the endings of *After Hours* and *The Color of Money* maybe have a little more hope in them than my earlier pictures. Once you make a decision at a certain point in your life that you're going to live, when you realize you've got to go on, then that glimmer of hope will show in your work."[62] Scorsese is trying to personalize what is a very industrialized, standardized product by discussing *The Color of Money* in terms of his own growth.

Ultimately, the film is very much a Hollywood product of the moment. It is both a star vehicle (for Newman and Cruise) as well as a sequel. Thus the film was marketed to fans of Newman and the original film *The Hustler* as well as to younger audiences with the presence of Cruise. It bears most of the markers of what Justin Wyatt has described as the "high concept" style of the 1980s. Wyatt argues that beginning in the late 1970s and becoming increasingly popular during the 1980s, a new group of high concept films were developed in Hollywood. This is tied to the rise of the "blockbuster" not only because of its emphasis on presold elements, but also because it includes a difference in style as compared to classical storytelling. Wyatt describes many characteristics of high concept style that distinguish these films from their predecessors. First and perhaps most important is the influence of advertising. High concept films are shot with marketing in mind, and many directors of these films began in television commercials (Adrian Lyne, Tony and Ridley Scott). These filmmakers specialize in creating a distinctive "look." Because of this, the style of high concept tends to be "excessive": the films are more about creating visually arresting images of spectacle than in creating tight, well-told narratives. This extends to the style of acting, with many star performances existing for their own spectacle, such as Jack Nicholson in *Batman* (Tim Burton, 1989), rather than to create fully rounded, believable characters. Wyatt differentiates this excessive style from auteurism, arguing that high concept differs from classical auteurs like Douglas Sirk or postclassical directors like Scorsese and their excessive styles. As Wyatt states, "Since the excess represented in the high concept is not driven by a personal vision, the logic of the marketplace is clearly the author of the style."[63] The style is excessive in order to create visuals that can be used to market the film in trailers, posters, or, increasingly in the 1980s, music videos. With the rise of MTV and music videos in youth culture and with Hollywood marketing strongly to this demographic, movies become more like commercials and music videos. Many high concept films were driven by music: *Flashdance* (Adrian Lyne, 1984), *Footloose* (Herbert Ross, 1984), *Purple Rain* (Albert Magnoli, 1984), *Staying Alive* (Sylvester Stallone, 1983), *The Bodyguard* (Mick Jackson, 1992), and many others.

Figure 3.4. *The Color of Money* (Martin Scorsese, 1986), music video sequence starring Tom Cruise.

As a result of the increased focus on the image, characters often become reduced to types. We see a greater emphasis on the look of the actor rather than developing the character, with characters often existing in a void. Hence the popularity of sequels where character development can be elided altogether. High concept films also tend to foreground their existence as films, referencing other movies, television shows, and other forms of mass culture. This is used from a marketing perspective to give the audience easy reference points and as a way of transmitting information about plot or character in a shorthand manner: "Since the core movie-going public share a common body of media knowledge, filmmakers have been able to appropriate this knowledge into the construction of narrative and character."[64] Of course, this idea of intertextuality and the foregrounding of a film's status as a film have a history within the art cinema mode of representation. This leads Wyatt to argue that aesthetically, high concept is a combination of Classical Hollywood and art cinema techniques. In spite of their similarities, a huge aesthetic difference exists between most films of the art cinema and high concept, which this is due to the economic basis of high concept films. High concept uses the art cinema style and applies it to a highly marketable and exploitable premise, fusing style with marketing. *The Color of Money* is rarely included in the list of films designated as "high concept" despite the fact that it adheres to many of its characteristics. In addition to the film's use of Cruise and Newman and its status as a sequel, *The Color of Money* is marked stylistically by its ability to be marketed. The film features a pop song written for inclusion in the film for cross-marketing purposes, "It's in the Way that You Use It" by Eric Clapton and Robbie Robertson. Scorsese directs one sequence set to Warren Zevon's "Werewolves of London" very much as if it were a music video, with Tom Cruise as the marketable star image. The "authorial expressivity" of Scorsese as director is subsumed by the "industrial expressivity" of Hollywood. But Scorsese's authorial signature is such that the film is excluded from these discussions. If the high concept nature of *The Color of Money* makes it a film marginalized within Scorsese's oeuvre, the fact that the film is still directed by "Martin Scorsese" makes it inappropriate for discussions about cinema and advertising. As Scorsese's career again makes apparent, the divide between high and low culture remains, despite postmodern attempts to bridge this distance.

Scorsese and De Palma

The question that still needs further exploration is how Scorsese's reputation remains intact despite his seeming capitulation to Hollywood and financial concerns. This extends not only to a film such as *The Color of*

Money, but also to Scorsese's other projects at the time. In contrast to the low-budget documentaries Scorsese was producing in the 1970s as a cultural supplement to working in Hollywood, his non–feature film work in the 1980s is much more economically motivated. Scorsese directed a television episode for Steven Spielberg's *Amazing Stories* in 1986 ("Mirror, Mirror), the music video *Bad* for Michael Jackson in 1987, and even commercials for Giorgio Armani in Italy. Nevertheless, his reputation continued to be secured. This is in marked contrast to his peers such as Coppola, Cimino, and Brian De Palma. The comparison with De Palma is particularly relevant here because in 1987, De Palma directs the big budget Hollywood film *The Untouchables*, an adaptation of the popular television program of the same name that ran from 1959 to 1963. Both Scorsese and De Palma had seemingly sold out to Hollywood, unable to make their signature films within the new system of the 1980s. Only De Palma's reputation would ultimately collapse, and to understand why, contextual factors need to be considered. Of particular importance is how Scorsese and De Palma respectively handled their mutual admiration for the great auteur directors of the past.

Between the late 1970s and early 1980s, Scorsese and De Palma were frequently linked in popular discourse and in various academic articles. Both were New Yorkers educated at New York universities, Scorsese at NYU and De Palma at Columbia University and later Sarah Lawrence College, as opposed to the more industry-oriented California schools where Coppola and Lucas were trained. In 1973 both had their first mainstream breakthrough, Scorsese with *Mean Streets* and De Palma with *Sisters*. Before this, De Palma was actually the more well-known and critically acclaimed director. With films such as *Greetings* (1968) and *Hi, Mom!* (1970), De Palma was regarded as an American Godard, an irreverent maverick and avant-gardist with roots in New York's underground scene. De Palma had succeeded along with filmmakers like Jim McBride (*David Holzman's Diary*, 1967) and Robert Downey (*Putney Swope*, 1969) in making independent films in New York with a subversive edge. With *Sisters*, De Palma entered into Hollywood filmmaking and quickly became one of the more critically acclaimed of his generation of filmmakers. He was often compared to the older generation of Penn, Altman, and Kubrick in his critical attitude toward the cinema of the past and was a particular favorite of the influential Pauline Kael, who compares De Palma favorably to his fellow film school graduates. As Robert Kapsis summarizes:

> On the surface, it would appear that De Palma was no different from other student filmmakers who have also shown a fascination with old movie conventions and clichés. Not according to Kael,

who argues that unlike most student filmmakers, who are "gullible," harboring a "naïve belief in the clichés they parrot." De Palma lovingly satirizes old movie conventions "for their shameless, rotten phoniness." Instead of simply "reproducing" the grotesque effects of classic horror-film sequences, he redeems their phoniness through his humor. Like the works of other filmmakers of the seventies whom Kael championed, such as Robert Altman, Arthur Penn, Sam Peckinpah, and Roman Polanski, De Palma's films, in her view, were also deliriously self-conscious and reflexive, especially with respect to old movie genres and conventions.[65]

De Palma was taken seriously as a great filmmaker, a new breed of director who, like Scorsese, was fascinated with the formal devices of the cinema and eager to revise past narrative structures.

But what De Palma gradually lost over his years of working in Hollywood was his authenticity, the ability to convince critics that he had maintained his unique individuality as an artist. The major problem he encountered was the fact that he frequently returned to the same genre of his first success, *Sisters*. The suspense thriller genre that so often attracted De Palma meant that he would always be in the shadow of Alfred Hitchcock. De Palma consistently had to deal with these comparisons with Hitchcock and the allegations that he was simply an imitator. This was especially the case with his remake of *Vertigo*, *Obsession* (1976), and his reworking of *Psycho*, *Dressed to Kill* (1980). Moreover, Hitchcock's critical reputation started to rise throughout the 1970s and peaked in 1982, when *Vertigo* was first included in the *Sight and Sound* Top Ten poll. Before this, De Palma was able to compete with Hitchcock, with many younger critics like Kael actually arguing that De Palma was superior to Hitchcock as an artist. As Kapsis argues, during the 1970s De Palma's art was often characterized positively in postmodern terms. Had postmodernism become the dominant artistic style within canonized circles, De Palma's reputation may have flourished (he remains a favorite of the postmodern auteur, Quentin Tarantino). But despite the arguments of critics like Kael, eventually auteurism became the dominant theory of film history. With this critical shift came a greater respect and admiration for the Classical Hollywood cinema, which was no longer seen as simply mass culture "trash." The cinema that came to be respected was either the classical cinema of Ford, Hawks, and other auteurs, or the modernist cinema of which Scorsese was often held up as the exemplar.

In contrast to De Palma, Scorsese came to be seen as respectful of the classical cinema, not simply a parodist or an imitator. But during the early to mid-1980s, various journal articles commented on Scorsese's and De Palma's similarities in their artistic approaches. No fewer than three pieces grouped together Scorsese and De Palma. John Mariani in *Attenzione* wrote a piece on Scorsese, De Palma, Cimino, and Coppola; Leo Braudy in *Film Quarterly* compared Scorsese, De Palma, and Coppola; and Stephen Mamber in the *Quarterly Review of Film and Video* discussed Scorsese, De Palma, and Kubrick.[66] Mamber's essay is particularly intriguing because of his claims for the postmodern characteristics of three films the respective directors made in the early 1980s: *The King of Comedy* (1983), *Body Double* (Brian De Palma, 1984), and *The Shining* (Stanley Kubrick, 1980). Mamber argues that all three films are "nearly identical in their attention to the following parody-related activities."[67] He then lists and outlines the postmodern aesthetics of the films: "intertextual overkill," "failed artists," "daring to be bad," "parodic cultural juxtaposition," "conflicted obsession," and "self-parody as signature." In addition to *The King of Comedy*, Mamber argues that Scorsese's *After Hours* also fits into this aesthetic category of the postmodern.[68] Based on the evidence of the films they were making during this period, Scorsese and De Palma seemed very much linked in their stylistic approaches. But when both filmmakers moved into making a mainstream Hollywood film, Scorsese with *The Color of Money*, De Palma with *The Untouchables*, their reputations move in very different directions. To explain this, we must return to the cultural activities Scorsese is engaging in outside of his filmmaking.

Scorsese's color preservation campaign was merely the first of his efforts within the field of film archiving. At the same time he began this campaign he forged a relationship with MoMA in New York. Later, despite his criticism of Kodak in 1980, he formed a relationship with the George Eastman House archives in Rochester. These relationships were initiated because they were mutually beneficial. Scorsese needed the facilities to preserve his extensive collection and for the prestige of being associated with these cultural institutions. MoMA and the Eastman House valued Scorsese's collection and his status as a critically acclaimed director still working within the Hollywood industry. It was in the interest of both institutions to promote Scorsese as both a great artist and a patron of the arts. Despite the fact that these were at least partially economic arrangements, they were not obviously commercial in nature. Unlike Coppola, who alienated the cultural institution supporting him through his commercial promotion of *Napoleon*, which included his own self-promotion as name brand to sell the film, Scorsese positioned himself as the respectful and modest protector of cinematic heritage.

Scorsese's work in film preservation gradually became part of his public persona during this time. For example, a 1987 article in the *New*

York Times reporting a New York City tribute party for Scorsese includes a discussion of his work in film preservation:

> As for Mr. Scorsese, the director of such distinctly New York films as "Mean Streets," "Taxi Driver" and "Raging Bull" modestly expressed pleasure at the impending tribute, diverting attention from himself to Eastman Kodak. "As you know," he said, "I'm very interested in film preservation and the new film stocks and that sort of thing." And so, he said, he looks upon the tribute to him as his reciprocal opportunity to pay tribute to Eastman Kodak. "I thought it was time to acknowledge certain advances that Kodak has made in furthering the cause of film preservation," Mr. Scorsese said. "As you know, back in 1979 and 1980 I led a campaign. Since then, in the past three years, they have made a stronger film stock available at no extra cost."[69]

Clearly, by 1987 Scorsese and Eastman Kodak had come to an amicable agreement and were both working toward furthering the prestige of each. The discussion of film preservation provides Scorsese with the opportunity to increase his cultural capital, to make further links with cultural institutions, and to appear respectful of tradition rather than as a self-promoter, and it is reiterated repeatedly by Scorsese in interviews and echoed by journalists and critics. In a piece on *GoodFellas* in 1990, David Ehrenstein states that although Scorsese is "our leading moviemaker," Scorsese himself would be "the last to admit it."[70] This is in marked contrast to both Coppola and especially De Palma, who has been hostile and critical at times when defending his own films. When *Obsession* was critiqued for being a Hitchcock rip-off, De Palma was openly critical of Hitchcock's later work, such as *Family Plot* (1976).[71] When similar criticism was directed toward *Dressed to Kill* in 1980, De Palma lashed out at the directors of "message" pictures. Echoing the sentiments of early auteur critics like Truffaut, he critiqued sociologically oriented directors for condescending to audiences of genre films. De Palma defended his own filmmaking by harshly criticizing the work of others, particularly Stanley Kubrick and his horror film *The Shining*. As Kapsis explains: "In a number of interviews conducted shortly after the release of *Dressed to Kill*, De Palma reiterated his hostile views towards certain critics and filmmakers, angering many journalists."[72] At a time when Scorsese was cementing his legacy by including himself in the cinematic tradition of the past, De Palma was alienating himself from this community.

This relationship with cultural institutions would prove especially valuable to Scorsese because of the compromises necessary to continue to work in Hollywood. For example, in September 1986, shortly before the release of the obviously commercial and in many ways industry-authored *The Color of Money*, MoMA held a tribute to Scorsese showcasing his "masterpiece" *Raging Bull* and his debut feature *Who's That Knocking at My Door*. In the press release for the event, MoMA stresses Scorsese's uniqueness as an artist and his place within cinematic tradition: "The virtuosity of his *mise-en-scène* and editing reflects Mr. Scorsese's unique style as well as his passionate knowledge of film history."[73] The intentionality of this coincidence is unlikely and irrelevant. The main point is that despite his capitulation to Hollywood, which was expressed in the lukewarm reviews of the press, Scorsese was still able to maintain his critical reputation through these museum celebrations. Another example can be seen years later with the release of *Cape Fear*, another Hollywood blockbuster that many critics reviewed unfavorably. In November 1991 Boston's Brattle Theatre held a Scorsese retrospective that "confirms" Scorsese as "a major director."[74] In 1994 the George Eastman House held a Martin Scorsese Film Festival (tellingly, the festival was missing *The Color of Money*). In Eastman House's brochure for the event, in addition to noting Scorsese's accomplishments as a filmmaker, his efforts in film preservation were given a full paragraph: "Scorsese has also spent considerable time and energy over the course of his career on film preservation and restoration. In addition, he is an avid film collector and philanthropist, having presented the Eastman House in 1991 with his personal collection of 1,600 American feature films from the 1930s to 1960s for use as a resource for researchers and public film screenings."[75] Tributes and retrospectives are vital to any reputation because as the comparisons with Coppola and De Palma show, artists constantly need to be confirmed and reaffirmed and placed within a cinematic tradition. Scorsese's work outside of his feature films in the 1980s was far more successful than his actual cinematic texts in helping to secure this prestige.

Genius by Necessity: *The Last Temptation of Christ*

The Last Temptation of Christ retells the familiar biblical story of Jesus of Nazareth, but from a psychological perspective different from that in the Gospels. The emphasis is on Jesus as a human being and with his difficulty in accepting his role as the savior. It begins with a quote from the author Nikos Kazantzakis about the dual nature of Christ, explicitly stating that the story is not based on the Gospels but on this fictional account. Jesus (Willem Dafoe) is a carpenter who makes crosses for the Romans to crucify other Jews and who is tormented by voices in his head. He is looked down on by his community, especially his friend Judas

(Harvey Keitel), who accuses him of collaboration. But what Jesus wants is to avoid his fate as the messiah, to try to spite God. He goes into the desert and begins his spiritual journey, speaking the word of God that he hears in his head. Many of the Gospel incidents are retold (for example, "he who is without sin cast the first stone"), but on a smaller scale than the typical biblical epic. Eventually, Jesus gains a following despite being unsure of himself and his mission. He preaches, but he continues to have doubts and fails to comprehend his own teachings. After a visit to John the Baptist and an extended hallucination in the desert, he begins to comprehend his power, performing miracles and defying both Roman and Judeo law. He also realizes that he must die in order for redemption to occur, and on a further twist to the Gospel story, he asks and convinces Judas to betray him. Following the Last Supper, Jesus is captured and crucified by the Romans. In this state of suffering, the devil tempts him and he comes down off the cross. He experiences an ordinary life with Mary Magdalene (Barbara Hershey) and grows an old with a family. Judas confronts him on his deathbed for betraying their cause. Realizing what he has to do, Jesus returns to the cross and accepts his place as the savior with the final words, "it is accomplished."

In 1988, following such commercial projects as *The Color of Money* and Michael Jackson's *Bad* video, Scorsese returned to his longtime project of trying to adapt Kazantzakis's novel. The previous failure to adapt the novel in 1983 was due in large part to the Christian protest against the film, but can also be at least partially attributed to the state of Hollywood at the time. Studios in 1983 were reluctant to take risks and were particularly reluctant to hire "genius" directors who had unreliable box-office results. By 1988 the situation had changed. Scorsese had proven himself to be a reliable Hollywood director by making *The Color of Money* on time and under budget. Scorsese then made a key move by signing with the powerful agent Michael Ovitz of Creative Artists Agency (CAA). Because of this, the seemingly dead project of *The Last Temptation of Christ* was suddenly viable again. As Scorsese describes it, "In a sense, the film had been the laughing stock of cocktail parties in Hollywood until the minute I signed with CAA—then it was made!"[76] Without Scorsese moving into the Hollywood mainstream, *The Last Temptation* would not have been made. Importantly, the project would not have been possible without a director of Scorsese's status.

In their defense of the film against the attacks of Christian protestors, Universal was required to place extra stress on Scorsese as a director of highest artistic distinction. Accusations were commonly being made that the studio was deliberately fueling the controversy and profiting from attacking people's religion.[77] As a result, Universal launched an advertising campaign emphasizing Scorsese as an artist motivated to make the film because of his religious convictions and not to make money. For example, Universal's newspaper advertisement reads as follows:

"MARTIN SCORSESE, AMERICA'S MOST GIFTED,
MOST DARING MOVIEMAKER,
MAY HAVE CREATED HIS MASTERPIECE"
Richard Corliss, *Time* magazine
On Friday, August 12,
one of the greatest filmmakers
of our time brings us a startling vision.
An extraordinary story,
based on the highly acclaimed
novel by Nikos Kazantzakis
THE LAST
TEMPTATION
OF CHRIST[78]

While using a director's star power to promote a film may not be unusual for studios, in this case it was an absolute necessity. In order to sell *The Last Temptation of Christ* as a serious prestige picture rather than just another for-profit commodity, Universal had to make sure that Scorsese's reputation as a great auteur was well-known and secure.

Figure 3.5. *The Last Temptation of Christ* (Martin Scorsese, 1988), Jesus and Mary Magdalene having sex.

Because of the censorship debate that surrounded the film's release, the nation's critical establishment heavily supported Universal and Scorsese. The almost overwhelming critical support for *The Last Temptation of Christ* was contingent on the criticism religious conservatives directed against the film by religious conservatives. As Robin Riley argues:

> Almost uniformly, biographers and critics speak positively about Scorsese because his films challenge the status quo of mindless Hollywood entertainment. To them, the fact that *The Last Temptation* was met by religious conservatives with great anger and retribution was evidence of his currency as a great filmmaker. These supporters identified with Scorsese's marginality and noncompliance. For them, Scorsese and his film served as vehicles by which they, as marginal figures, could ignite their creative impulse and ingenuity, and somehow, in the mundane moments of the weekly film review, become mythic figures, themselves loved or hated for their symbolic features and loyalties.[79]

The actual characteristics of the film itself had much less to do with the positive response from critics than the protests from the religious right. Evidence even suggests that this was deliberate on the part of at least one critic. After an advanced screening of the film, critic Michael Medved recounts the following story:

> I found it impossible to understand the one critic who had snorted the loudest and clucked the most derisively at the afternoon screening we both attended, but whose ultimate report to the public featured glowing praise and only the most minor reservations. . . . When I called him to ask about the contrast between his privately expressed contempt and his on-the-record admiration, he proved surprisingly candid in explaining its inconsistency. "Look, I know the picture's a dog. We both know that, and probably Scorsese knows it too. But with all Christian crazies shooting at him from every direction, I'm not going to knock him down in public."[80]

The solidarity critics felt with Scorsese ideologically meant that criticism of the film needed to be muted or ignored at least at the initial stages. Subsequently, the film has proven to be a far less acclaimed film than initial responses seemed to indicate. It is clearly not considered to be as accomplished as an aesthetic text as was initially claimed, and it ranks far below Scorsese's now canonical films.[81]

But in terms of Scorsese's overall critical reputation, one can argue that *The Last Temptation of Christ* is the most important film of his entire career because of the particular contingencies involved. Any discussion of Scorsese as a mainstream, Hollywood director was now entirely absent, despite the fact that *The Last Temptation of Christ* was a studio film and despite the fact that its very status as a Hollywood film accounts for a great deal of the controversy. The film's visibility led to the protests against it and revolved around the century-old debate about Hollywood, entertainment, and art. One of the many ironies of the reception of the film is that critics threw their support around Scorsese and Universal as the defender of free speech: "[T]heir [film critics] identification with Scorsese as an artist supports their underlying skepticism toward institutionalized power of all forms, particularly those of the Christian persuasion."[82] The institutional power that gets ignored, of course, is Hollywood itself. The debate over *The Last Temptation of Christ* was not, primarily, one of free speech. Rather, it was a battle between two rival institutions, Hollywood and the Church, over their respective powers of influence. In the popular press, the religious protestors merely replaced the studio system as the enemy of artistic freedom. If Hollywood had refused to make the film, as they already had in 1983, there would have been no criticism of the studios for suppressing artistic freedom. In fact, most of the discussions of the 1983 shutdown of *The Last Temptation* now focus on the religious protest that forced Paramount's decision, rather than the studio's refusal to invest in an unreliable director like Scorsese. Only after Scorsese had signed with CAA and proved his ability to make commercially viable films cheaply and under budget did Universal decide that he could be used as a "prestige" commodity. The film was also part of a larger deal Scorsese signed with Universal, and clearly the studio felt that even if it lost money on *The Last Temptation*, it would make money later with other films, which proved to be the case with *Cape Fear* three years later.

In his book *The New Censors: Movies and the Culture Wars*, Charles Lyons argues that the Christian protest over *The Last Temptation of Christ* was the only really successful attempt to limit the audience for a controversial film. Other such protests against films like *Dressed to Kill* (women's groups), *Cruising* (William Friedkin, 1980; gay activists), and *Basic Instinct* (Paul Verheoven, 1992; gay and lesbian groups) failed in their attempts, ultimately giving each respective film much more publicity and increasing rather than decreasing its box-office revenues.[83] The difference with *The Last Temptation* was that the protest group was much larger and it effectively targeted exhibition venues: "Although they were unable to force Universal to withdraw the film from release, religious conservatives were quite successful in pressuring a number of theaters and chains not to show the movie."[84] However, the film was still ultimately successful, both commercially and critically. According to *Variety*, *The Last Temptation* had an eventual $8.4 million domestic box office combined with $25.4 million overseas. Thus the film made $33.8 million.[85] Considering that the film's budget was an estimated $10 million, *The Last Temptation* certainly made money. The theatrical boycott may have hurt, but the controversy generated also helped at the box office. At the film's premiere engagements, "many in attendance admitted they bought tickets simply to counter the protest efforts of conservatives to prevent its release."[86] Without the controversy, it seems unlikely the film would have been as successful as it was.

In terms of Scorsese's cultural capital, it is hard to overestimate the positive impact *The Last Temptation of Christ* ultimately had. Scorsese was seen as a martyr in much of the popular press, an uncompromising artist with an authentic vision. All of the stories about the attempts by the religious protestors to censor his film only added to the impression of Scorsese as a victim of a restrictive cultural institution. The most resonant of these was the widely circulated story that a group of religious leaders led by Bill Bright offered to buy the film from the head of Universal, Lew Wasserman, with the purpose of destroying the negative.[87] For those with knowledge of film history, the similarities with *Citizen Kane* are striking. In 1941, in order to prevent an attack on the studios by the Hearst press, Louis B. Mayer and the other studio heads offered to buy the negative of *Citizen Kane* from RKO in order to destroy it. The linking of *The Last Temptation* with "the greatest film of all time" increased its prestige, and the idea of any group wanting to destroy a film contrasted with Scorsese's efforts to preserve cinema's past. Not surprisingly, Universal used this offer from the religious leaders to increase its self-image in the press: "Universal had little to gain from selling the film and did not take the offer seriously. Instead, the studio took advantage of the situation, using it to launch a publicity campaign to refute religious conservatives. Its refusal to sell might alienate some audiences, but a strong rebuttal would elevate the studio's status among its peers in the film community and reinforce a strong common bond with those who supported constitutional guarantees of free speech."[88] While religious conservatives may have won some battles in having theaters (and later the Blockbuster video chain) refuse the film, Universal, and especially Scorsese, won the long-term war, not only financially but also culturally.

Coming in 1988, *The Last Temptation of Christ* was Scorsese's last feature film of the decade (his short "Life Lessons," was a contribution to the anthology film *New York Stories* in 1989). In 1990 critics voted

Raging Bull the best of the decade.[89] The discussion of *Raging Bull* echoed many of the defenses of *The Last Temptation*, and Scorsese was praised for making an uncompromising film that defied convention. For many Scorsese's determination to make *The Last Temptation of Christ* established the idea that he was now the uncompromising artist of his generation. The praise Scorsese received just for making the film reflected back onto his previous masterpieces, especially *Raging Bull*. Without the controversy over *The Last Temptation of Christ* and the subsequent uncritical backing of the popular press that turned Scorsese into a martyred genius, he most likely would not have ascended to the post of greatest filmmaker of his generation. *The Last Temptation*, along with Scorsese's work within film preservation, allowed him to effectively mediate his move into the Hollywood mainstream.

4

Histories of Cinema and Cinematic Histories

Scorsese as Historian

[I'm going to] make my own Hitchcock film. But it has to look, it has to be the way he would have made the picture then only making it now. . . . But the way he would have made it then. If he was alive now making this now, he would make it now as if he made it back then. . . . But his film, not mine, because I couldn't. . . . It's one thing to preserve a film that has been made. It's another to preserve a film that has not been made. . . . I'm obviously not going to shoot them as I would. But, can I shoot them as Hitchcock? I don't think so. So who will I shoot them as? [long pause] This is the question.

THIS ABSURD AND HILARIOUS dialogue comes from Scorsese (as one can probably guess from the rhythmic pattern), as part of his 2007 short film/commercial *The Key to Reserva*. This extended Alfred Hitchcock parody/homage features Scorsese discovering three pages of a lost Hitchcock script and deciding to "restore" the nonexistent film. It is meant to be comedic and absurd to show how prominent Scorsese's image as a film preservation specialist has become and to comment on the whole complicated notion of the auteur within

127

cinema.[1] But it is also remarkably close to the justification film archivists Robert Harris and James Katz give in their 1996 restoration of Hitchcock's *Vertigo* (1958) that they were making alterations that Hitchcock himself would have made if he had access to newer technology. Scorsese participated in the promotion of the restored *Vertigo*, but never explicitly endorsed the preservation work itself, and he years later made this short as a subtle critique, which highlights in many ways the unique position of Scorsese within the world of Hollywood and film history.

Scorsese's move into the area of film preservation coincided with his role as a chronicler of film history through his archival efforts and the majority of his feature films. Increasingly, Scorsese presents worlds that no longer exist. Since his biblical epic *The Last Temptation of Christ*, the recent or distant past has been Scorsese's focus: the New York mob world of the 1950s, 1960s, and 1970s in *GoodFellas* (1990), the late-nineteenth-century New York of *The Age of Innocence* (1993), the 1970s Las Vegas mafia scene in *Casino* (1995), Tibet before Chinese rule in *Kundun* (1997), the mid-nineteenth-century Five Points district of *Gangs of New York* (2002), America (and Hollywood) of the 1930s and 1940s in *The Aviator* (2004), the paranoid McCarthy era 1950s in *Shutter Island* (2010), and Paris of the 1930s in *Hugo* (2011).[2] The two that are not, *Cape Fear* (1991) and *The Departed* (2007), are remakes. Scorsese also made two documentaries on cinema history, *A Personal Journey with Martin Scorsese through American Movies* (1995) and *My Voyage to Italy* (1999); appeared as an authority in numerous documentaries and shorts dedicated to the cinematic past; edited a book series for the Modern Library reprinting four texts of film literature;[3] and produced a seven-part documentary on *The Blues* for PBS. Like his work in preservation, Scorsese's role as a historian and an educator was rewarded both officially and unofficially.[4] This chapter analyzes how and why Scorsese has been presenting history and the evolution of his concern with the past.

Preserving (and Entering) Film History

Scorsese's early preservation efforts foreshadowed his eventual move into the role of film historian. Throughout the later portion of his career, Scorsese increasingly made the historical past his main concern, while his contemporaries have been criticized for a lack of concern with cinematic history as it relates to their own work. George Lucas, for example, has upset many *Star Wars* fans by reworking the original films using digital technology. Lucas was accused of revising the past and, by not making the original available, eliminating a key piece of cultural history (the versions first screened in theaters). Coppola similarly reworked his 1979 film

Apocalypse Now into a new version, *Apocalypse Now Redux* (2001). Scorsese, on the other hand, consistently associated himself with the past, with cinema's cultural heritage, and maintained an interest in film as film on the specificity of the cinematic medium. This has also aligned Scorsese with cultural institutions like the MoMA where artistic reputations are made. By having his work celebrated within the high art context of the museum, Scorsese maintains and confirms his reputation. Like any set of beliefs or ideology, the idea of Scorsese or anyone else (such as Coppola) as an artist is never permanent and static. It needs to be repeated and reconfirmed, a process that Scorsese's relationship with cultural institutions has enabled.

One of the most extensive of these programs took place at Lincoln Center in 1993, cosponsored with NYU. The program consisted of Scorsese's films on double bills with the movies that inspired them, along with two lectures, "An Evening with Martin Scorsese" and "The Art of Collaboration: Working with Martin Scorsese." This event both consecrated Scorsese's reputation and marked Scorsese's role through film preservation as a contributor to the film canon. Stephen Holden, writing about the event in the *New York Times*, stated:

> Along with the universality of Mr. Scorsese's taste, it is his passionate perceptiveness in discerning personal artistic visions and technical feats in the lowliest B movies that gives the series a genuine historic interest. . . . Mr. Scorsese, who has been a passionate advocate for the preservation of old movies, was adamant about the ultimate worth of B movies and other Hollywood throwaways. "It's a dangerous situation if you have to start making value judgments about which ones should be saved and which not," he said. "Thirty years from now, the film you destroy could have been something that influenced twenty-five people to make wonderful movies."[5]

The repeated reference here to Scorsese's "passion" of taste and preservation is somewhat contradictory. Because of Scorsese's "universal" taste, he is able to recognize the value of films otherwise felt to be artistically worthless. At the same time, he worked to downplay the fact that implicit value judgments were made through his selections. Scorsese also advocated the lack of value judgments in his 1980 preservation manifesto: "*No Value Judgments*: all film must be saved. No committees should decide which film lives or dies, whether or not TV commercials are less important than movie trailers. Preserving only commercially successful films, or Academy Award winners and nominees or film festival winners, is a step in the right direction, but far from enough.—Very often, as in the case of *The Magnificent Ambersons* or *The Searchers*, it is only time itself which lets a film's true value shine through."[6] Scorsese advocates the lack of value judgments but at the same time relies on the cultural authority of more recently canonized works such as *The Searchers*. Scorsese avoids having value judgments placed on his particular selections while making value judgments (based on his "passionate perceptiveness") through these selections.

Noteworthy is the combination of Scorsese's films appearing on double bills with the movies that inspired him. Scorsese chose the influential films himself, and they include the following pairs: *Who's That Knocking at My Door* and *Shadows*; *Boxcar Bertha* and *Guns Don't Argue* (Bill Karn and Richard C. Kahn, 1957); *Mean Streets* and *Before the Revolution* (Bernardo Bertolucci, 1964); *Alice Doesn't Live Here Anymore* and *Take Care of My Little Girl* (Jean Negulesco, 1951); *Taxi Driver* and *Murder by Contract* (Irving Lerner, 1958); *New York, New York* and *The Man I Love* (Raoul Walsh, 1946); *The Last Waltz* and *The Tales of Hoffman* (Michael Powell and Emeric Pressburger, 1951); *Raging Bull* and *Rocco and His Brothers* (Luchino Visconti, 1960); *The King of Comedy* and *Station Six Sahara* (Seth Holt, 1963); *After Hours* and *Getting Gertie's Garter* (Allan Dwan, 1945); *The Color of Money* and *Il Sorpasso* (Dino Risi, 1963); *The Last Temptation of Christ* and *Accatone!* (Pier Paolo Pasolini, 1961); *GoodFellas* and *Ocean's Eleven* (Lewis Milestone, 1960); and *Cape Fear* and *Night of the Hunter* (Charles Laughton, 1955). Scorsese's choices here were very revealing, with an eclectic mix of highbrow art films with lowbrow genre films. Scorsese positions himself, as he has in many interviews, as a liminal figure, an "outsider" to both the European art cinema and the world of Hollywood. The deliberately obscure Hollywood films serve two purposes. First, they distract from the self-promotion involved. Scorsese was not only comparing his work to established masters, but also to the ordinary genre films of Hollywood's past. Second, the obscurity of the Hollywood films establishes Scorsese's authority as an expert in American film history. The selections may be lowbrow, but their very anonymity grants Scorsese cultural status. Just as the most renowned critics (Manny Farber, Parker Tyler, Andrew Sarris, Pauline Kael, J. Hoberman, Jonathan Rosenbaum) established their brilliance by intelligently discussing lesser movies, Scorsese proves his skill by the very lowness of some of his influences. Scorsese also deliberately chose only two national cinemas, American and Italian (with the exception of the one Powell-Pressburger film). The dominance of Italian art cinema selections over other films from the European art cinema serves a clear strategic purpose. The influence of the Italian films was not simply a sign of his university education in film, but rather a product of his ethnic background. The connection with the Italian films is emotional, not intellectual. Likewise, the seemingly simple American genre films can be made into works of greater complexity by being associated with Scorsese's movies.

The sponsorship of the NYU's Tisch School of the Arts, which in conjunction with the screenings presented several panel discussions featuring film critics, academics, and artists who have worked with Scorsese, gave the program a further imprimatur. In a Lincoln Center press release, Mary Schmidt Campbell, dean of the Tisch School, stated, "Martin Scorsese's commitment to describing modern reality, combined with his reverence for films' historical past, have provided a model for aspiring filmmakers and film lovers around the world."[7] Professor William Simon, a former NYU student of Scorsese's time as an instructor, praised Scorsese as "a director uncompromising in his dedication to authentic portrayal of setting and character."[8] These comments complement the overall argument of the program, which stresses Scorsese as an "authentic" filmmaker concerned with reality and passionate about film history. Obviously, NYU as an institution and Scorsese as an individual benefit from their mutual association, with Scorsese's prestige giving NYU an advertising platform and NYU's academic capital further legitimating Scorsese's reputation. But it is worth noting that it is the cinema studies program—not the film production unit where Scorsese first studied and taught—that co-sponsored the event. Scorsese's interests in film preservation and archiving and in rediscovering works from the past perfectly timed with broader shifts within academia. This small local program at the Lincoln Center would evolve in the next several years into Scorsese's two 4-hour documentaries on American and Italian film history. These projects would be part of a broader movement within both academic and popular circles to emphasize the importance of cinema history.

In fact, this movement had already begun on a smaller scale in the 1980s as Scorsese was beginning to mount his second career as a film archivist and historian. In her discussion of the cable television channel American Movie Classics (AMC), Barbara Klinger examines the causes of the rise of a broader interest in film preservation. Rather than simply celebrating preservation efforts, Klinger seeks to analyze why this became an initiative at this time: "While few would deny film's close relationship to society or the need to preserve it as part of a culture's heritage, we should not overlook the significance of the way in which these issues are explained. The explanation allows the historical enterprise not only to stake certain claims about the importance of classic cinema but also to create a specific narrative of the nation's history."[9] During the 1980s, the rhetoric used to justify preservation was globalization and the anxieties provoked by the acquisition of U.S. media companies by foreign owners. This created, according to Klinger, a "general ideological climate of protectionism about American business and underscored the sense that the media embody the spirit of America."[10] This idea of movies being a "uniquely American art form" (as U.S. Congressman Richard Gephardt argued)[11] was pushed and led to the creation of the National Film Registry and to the various heritage narratives cable channels such as Turner Classic Movies (TCM) and AMC promote: "In preservation discourse, Hollywood maintained its cachet as the site of distinctive American products, just as it helped to recall an era when the industry reigned supreme at both home and abroad."[12]

Scorsese began his efforts into film preservation in 1980 before these nationalist anxieties influenced the larger dialogue into the importance of film to cultural heritage. Nevertheless, the increasing awareness of preservation at this time certainly helped Scorsese establish himself as a cultural figure. The arguments Scorsese used constantly stressed the "heritage narrative" that channels such as AMC promoted in its preservation festivals. As early as his first public demonstration of color fading at the 1979 New York Film Festival Scorsese stated, "we are committing cultural suicide."[13] By the early 1990s, AMC had picked up on this rhetoric and organized a Film Preservation Festival on its channel. Scorsese was the natural choice for AMC when it decided on a prominent spokesperson for this cause. AMC's second promotional brochure for the festival quoted Scorsese stating, "Film is history. With every foot of film that is lost, we lose a link to our culture, to the world around us, to each other, and to ourselves."[14] By the early 1990s, the rest of the cultural industry supported Scorsese's film heritage initiative. In 1995, on the occasion of film's centennial celebration, Scorsese would contribute to a series of national heritage films BFI commissioned. With this film Scorsese made his first explicit text in the role of a film historian.

Scorsese's American Heritage Narrative(s)

A Personal Journey with Martin Scorsese through American Movies contrasts with two types of aesthetic history, the academic and the popular. Within these two large and admittedly artificial categories are numerous approaches and with a discipline as young as film studies, a potential third category: the preacademic.[15] These would be early film histories that had academic ambitions but predate establishing of film studies as a separate entity. Among the last and most successful of the preacademic histories were the so-called great man histories such as those by Gerald Mast and Andrew

Sarris.[16] This approach receded during the early 1980s and a new, more "historical" and "objective" history began to take over. Two important publications of the mid-1980s illustrate the turn in aesthetic film history: Douglas Gomery and Robert Allen's *Film History: Theory and Practice* and, most importantly, David Bordwell, Janet Staiger, and Kristin Thompson's *The Classical Hollywood Cinema: Film Style and Mode of Production to 1960*. Bordwell, Staiger, and Thompson move away from the great man history and concentrate instead on the "average" film and its stylistic characteristics. This has become the dominant academic model with regard to Classical Hollywood despite some challenges. Popular aesthetic histories of the American cinema are mostly documentaries (particularly television documentaries), often with an accompanying book (following the pattern of Kevin Brownlow's *Hollywood* series for Thames TV), which tell the history of American film. These became particularly prevalent in the 1990s because of the 100-year anniversary of the cinema, including the American Film Institute's (AFI) "100 Years, 100 Movies" special that aired in June 1998 on the CBS and counted down the greatest 100 movies in American film history according to AFI voters. Several spin-offs followed this documentary: "100 Years, 100 Thrills" (greatest thrillers special), "100 Years, 100 Laughs" (greatest comedies special), and a variety of one-hour specials dealing with a certain theme. The prime-time network slot in which these documentaries were shown (even if it was during the less important summer schedule) gave them a great deal of exposure and influence (not to mention the promotional tie-in with Blockbuster video). A ten-part series, *The American Cinema*, which originally aired on PBS in the United States, targeted at a slightly more specialized audience. However, the fact that the documentary subsequently aired on the History Channel reveals its popular approach. Numerous other documentaries on the American cinema share roughly the same approach to American film as the AFI documentaries: multiple talking heads discussing mostly well-known films in the manner of the popular newspaper review, which resulted in very little analysis and even less history.[17]

Scorsese's documentary not only falls somewhere in between the preacademic, the academic, and the popular, but it is also different from all three in certain ways. As a way of examining this documentary as historiography, consider Michel Foucault's essay "Nietzsche, Genealogy, History." Somewhat unusually, Foucault sets up a type of binary in the piece, "traditional" history as opposed to "effective" history, or genealogy. Furthermore, it is posited as a "for-against" model that Foucault ordinarily rejects. Its more schematic and binary nature makes it a useful starting point for a discussion of *A Personal Journey*. Consider this question: Is Scorsese's film an effective history according to Foucault's definition?

Surprisingly, given the enormous differences between Foucault and Scorsese, the answer is, at least partially, yes. For instance, Scorsese's personal journey does not make any grand claims at objectivity or distance, something Foucault sees as being a trait of effective history: "It reverses the surreptitious practice of historians, their pretension to examine things furthest from themselves, the groveling manner in which they approach this promising distance."[18] This approach of examining things from a distance can be seen in the type of scientific research Bordwell, Staiger, and Thompson conducted for *The Classical Hollywood Cinema*. Robert Ray criticizes this approach in his poststructralist-influenced essay, "The Bordwell Regime and the Stakes of Knowledge": "[I]t is simultaneously modest and vain: not a personally expressive 'structuration' [Barthes' own term for *S/Z*] of film history, but the impersonally accurate *truth* about the Hollywood Cinema."[19] An example of Bordwell, Staiger, and Thompson's scientific method is their "random sample" approach to American cinema history. This involves putting every feature film made in Hollywood up to 1960 into a computer and producing 100 (that magic number again) films at random that are then taken to be an accurate representation of the classical Hollywood style. As Ray points out, this shows an uncritical belief in science to explain an aesthetic form like cinema: "[I]t is curiously blind to its own unquestioning participation in our culture's hegemonic arrangements between truth and power. . . . They have not chosen to examine their own 'scientific' methodologies."[20] This is the problem with formalist analysis in general; it concentrates too much on the text at the expense of other possible factors. In their own way, Bordwell, Staiger, and Thompson are very similar to the auteurists they criticize. They simply replace the myth of the artist with the myth of the scientist.

Scorsese's documentary moves away from this kind of objective distance that characterizes a great deal of academic historiography. This objective distance is characteristic of most "popular" documentaries as well, even though the techniques of these documentaries are much less sophisticated than Bordwell, Staiger, and Thompson's. For what is the survey of "film professionals" AFI conducted for its 100 best list if not a claim for objectivity? Likewise, the discourse of third-person narration combined with talking heads interviews typical of the AFI and countless other history of cinema documentaries is very much a discourse of objectivity. In contrast, Scorsese's documentary foregrounds his closeness to the material. This is characteristic of Foucault's final trait of effective history, the "affirmation of knowledge as perspective."[21] Scorsese's documentary, if nothing else, both reveals his passion for his subject and foregrounds his own bias: "I can't really be objective. I can only revisit what has moved or intrigued me. This is a journey inside an imaginary museum, unfortunately one too big for us to enter each room. There is too much to see, too much to remember! So I've chosen to highlight some of the films that colored my dreams, that changed my perceptions, and in some cases even my life. Films that prompted me, for better or for worse, to become a filmmaker myself."[22] Scorsese's foregrounding of his own subjectivity makes *A Personal Journey* a more effective history, according to Foucault's definition of the term, than most academic or popular histories. Others have already pointed out Bordwell, Staiger, and Thompson's false objectivity. But it can even be seen in great man preacademic histories like that of Andrew Sarris's *The American Cinema: Directors and Directions*. The book's categorization and ranking of directors ("Pantheon Directors," "The Far Side of Paradise," "Expressive Esoterica," "Fringe Benefits," "Less than Meets the Eye," "Lightly Likable," "Strained Seriousness," and so on) locates it within an objective, quasi-scientific discourse of classification. One can argue that the tone is more generally playful, but it is hierarchical in a way that Scorsese's categories are not. The popular documentaries similarly have this objective stance. For example, the AFI documentary includes many "film professionals" (actors and directors mostly, although a few critics are included) giving their personal views on certain films. However, the variety of opinions framed by the list of films gathered from a survey give the impression of consensus, something beyond merely a subjective opinion. There is an objectivity through multiple subjects framed by an unnamed master discourse: the survey list itself and the (mainly financial) interests it serves.

One particular section of Scorsese's documentary, "The Director as Smuggler," especially foregrounds and celebrates films that Foucault dubs "the successes of history," those "capable of seizing these rules, to replace those who had used them, to disguise themselves so as to pervert them, invert their meaning, and redirect them against those who had initially imposed them."[23] The rules in Scorsese's examples are those of the Hollywood studio system. While we should not overestimate the importance of the films and filmmakers Scorsese discusses, we should neither dismiss their impact nor dismiss Scorsese's self-conscious foregrounding of these transgressions. As historian Hayden White notes, "The more historically self-conscious the writer of any form of historiography, the more the question of the social system and the law that sustains it, the authority of this law and its justification, and threats to the law occupy his attention."[24] This can be seen in Scorsese's approach. An obvious identification exists with those who transgress Hollywood's rules. He is clearly not interested in the "ordinary" film or filmmaker.

Artistry is tied to the idea of inverting meaning, of breaking with the system. Scorsese makes the following comments near the beginning of the documentary: "What does it take to be a filmmaker in Hollywood? Even today I still wonder what it takes to be a professional or even an artist in Hollywood. How do you survive the constant tug of war between personal expression and commercial imperatives? What is the price you pay to work in Hollywood? Do you end up with a split personality? Do you make one movie for them, one for yourself?"[25] These are questions that would only be asked by somebody who sees the laws of the system as restrictive and in need of subversion. Plenty of directors do not feel this "tug of war" because their personal expression coincides with commercial imperatives (Spielberg being the most famous and obvious example).

A Personal Journey has another characteristic of a more poststructuralist approach to its historical material. Scorsese neither presents a linear history nor does he break his sections into historical periods, unlike popular documentaries such as *The American Cinema* or academic histories such as *The Classical Hollywood Cinema*. Instead, his approach is

Figure 4.1. *A Personal Journey with Martin Scorsese through American Movies* (Martin Scorsese and Michael Henry Wilson, 1995), Douglas Sirk as smuggler and the critique of television as mass culture.

closer to concept formation. As Robert Ray describes, "the postmodern problem is the reverse of the Middle Ages': not too little information, but too much."[26] Scorsese arranges his commentary around concepts: the Director as Storyteller, Illusionist, Smuggler, and Iconoclast. This leads to a freer and more open history than other contemporary models that have been applied to the American cinema thus far without the explicit hierarchy of Sarris. For instance, an early history like Gerald Mast's *A Short History of the Movies* follows a linear progression from "Birth" to "Griffith" to "Soviet Montage" to "Sound" up to "Today." Bordwell, Staiger, and Thompson divide their study into a similar linear progression: "The Formulation of the Classical Style, 1909–1928," "Film Style and Technology to 1930," "The Hollywood Mode of Production, 1930–1960" and "Film Style and Technology 1930–1960." Both of these academic models are unimaginative and traditional in their approach. Allen and Gomery's *Film History: Theory and Practice* does a good job critiquing the various historical approaches applied up until that point (1985), but their replacement models leave much to be desired, especially their model for aesthetic film history. Allen and Gomery rightly criticize the "masterpiece tradition" of Sarris and Mast as "a brand of film history that is not very *historical*—that is merely film criticism and aesthetic evaluation applied to films in chronological order."[27] The problem is Allen and Gomery practice an aesthetic film history that is not very aesthetic. Scorsese's approach avoids the extremes of both views and manages to focus on aesthetics without neglecting history—at least until his final section.

Scorsese follows what Foucault would describe as traditional history in other ways, however. *A Personal Journey* fits the description of what Foucault, through Nietzsche, calls "monumental history," which is "a history given to reestablishing the high points of historical development and their maintenance in a perpetual presence, given to the recovery of works, actions and creations through the monogram of their personal essence."[28] This program of recovering works through the monogram of their personal essence (that is, the "vision" of the filmmaker that is so prevalent in Scorsese's discourse) is a major project of *A Personal Journey*. Also, Foucault notes that traditional history "is given to a contemplation of distances and heights: the noblest periods, the highest forms, the most abstract ideas, the purest individualities."[29] Scorsese is distanced from the material despite his personal involvement: he is examining what he sees as a Golden Age of American Cinema (Classical Hollywood), an age in which he, as an artist, does not belong. He is unable to examine the historical period in which he is enmeshed. At the conclusion of his documentary, Scorsese states, "This is where we have got to stop. We just don't have the time and space to go any further. Also, we have reached a different era, the late sixties, the years when I started making movies myself. . . . I could not really do justice to my friends who are making films, my companions, my generation of filmmakers. Not from the inside."[30] This reluctance on Scorsese's part has to do with a traditional notion of what a historian should be; that is, outside, not inside, of his subject matter. Thus, the myth of objectivity is present here as well.

This brings up the question of Scorsese's authority. This authority comes not only from Scorsese's status as a filmmaker, but also from his role as a champion of film preservation. Scorsese has gained a great deal of cultural prestige by helping to preserve America's "film heritage," and this documentary can be seen as an extension of that project. Both the style and presentation of the documentary work to reinforce this authority. Scorsese is formally dressed and seated in an empty room talking directly to the camera. The film does not deviate from this straightforward and conventional talking-head shooting style. Throughout, Scorsese's voiceover acts as a voice of authority, and the film very much resembles a lecture with all credits and chapter titles displayed on the screen like writing on a chalkboard. In terms of objectivity, the idea of authority offered by a teacher or a professor certainly counts for more in our culture than any other subjective account. This discourse of learning is explicitly spelled out by Scorsese at the beginning of part 3:

> I am often asked by younger filmmakers: Why do I need to look at old movies? The only response I can give them is: I still consider myself a student. Yes, I have made a number of pictures in the past twenty years. But the more pictures I make, the more I realize that I don't really know. I'm always looking for something or someone that I can learn from. This is what I tell young filmmakers and students: Do what the painters used to do, and probably still do. Study the old masters. Enrich your palette. Expand the canvas. There's always so much more to learn.[31]

So while Scorsese modestly still considers himself a student, it is he as experienced filmmaker who is passing on his knowledge and advising younger would-be directors. It is also implicit that Scorsese himself will be one of the "old masters" the younger generation studies. In this way, A Personal Journey is far from subjective and is by no means outside of the discourse of objective history.

Of all the sections in the documentary, "The Director as Iconoclast" is the most problematic because the "purest individualities" that Scorsese identifies fail to be related to their social system. He notes that some iconoclasts failed (Orson Welles, Erich von Stroheim) while others succeeded (Elia Kazan). The question that is not answered or even approached is *why* did some fail and why did some succeed? With Kazan, this is particularly problematic. Kazan was able to become a great director and "forge a new acting style" in *On the Waterfront* (1954) partly because he gained industry security by "naming names" during the blacklist. Scorsese leaves this out of his account, despite the fact that he had discussed the influence of the blacklist on 1950s Hollywood earlier. The respect for Kazan's artistry blinds Scorsese in his assessment. Similarly, his discussion of Welles and *Citizen Kane* (1941) make no mention of Welles' leftist politics and his connection to the Federal Theater Project during the 1930s. Scorsese is content to see Welles as a victim of Hollywood without any further contextual factors being considered: "He actually lost all his privileges a year after *Citizen Kane* on *The Magnificent Ambersons*, which was chopped down and even partially reshot in his absence."[32] Scorsese thus repeats a familiar story of Welles losing his Hollywood privileges and *Citizen Kane* being his only untouched Hollywood masterpiece. But as Jonathan Rosenbaum has pointed out, this is not the case. *Citizen Kane* is more an independent film made with studio backing than a Hollywood film itself.[33] Scorsese's analysis repeats this received notion, and throughout the Iconoclast section he is typically very traditional, repeating the accepted industry opinion.

Scorsese's conclusion is similarly problematic. Although Scorsese says that this is a story without an end, he nevertheless provides closure: "I believe there is a spirituality in films, even if it's not one which can supplant faith. I find that over the years many films address themselves to the spiritual side of man's nature, from Griffith's *Intolerance* to John Ford's *The Grapes of Wrath*, to Hitchcock's *Vertigo*, to Kubrick's *2001* . . . and so many more. It is as though movies answered an ancient quest for the common unconscious. They fulfill a spiritual need that people have to share a common memory."[34] Thus, Scorsese provides a "moral" to the story of the American cinema. As Hayden White comments, "the demand for closure in the historical story is a demand, I suggest, for moral meaning, a demand that sequences of real events be assessed as to their significance as elements of a moral drama."[35] This is perhaps inevitable. As White asks, "Could we ever narrativize without moralizing?"[36] The form this moralizing takes at the conclusion, however, is mythical rather than social. Scorsese discusses "man's nature" as a historically unproblematic notion and even evokes the Jungian collective unconscious, the *ne plus ultra* of essentialist discourse. Movies are seen as fulfilling and answering an "ancient quest" that is presumably outside and beyond history. This conclusion is especially disappointing given the social dimension of most of the film.

Clearly, despite the presence of some of Foucault's traits of effective history, *A Personal Journey* is not Foucaultian. But it is an alternative to a great deal of both academic and popular historicizing of American cinema. The question is how much of an alternative, and is this alternative a worthy one to pursue? Although Scorsese does not completely follow a Foucaultian effective history, is this necessarily negative? The one film-maker who has followed Foucault's spirit in approaching cinema history is Jean-Luc Godard in his ten-part documentary *Histoire(s) du Cinema*. The heavily deconstructionist strategies Godard used are not really open to Scorsese in his film.[37] Scorsese operates in an area somewhere between the banality of most popular documentaries, the formalism of most academic histories, and the obscurity of the radical historians. Because of this, Scorsese the artist-historian is in an important position within both film culture and society as a whole. In short, Scorsese is in the position to synthesize several approaches and bridge the gap between certain discourses. To what extent does *A Personal Journey* do this?

Scorsese's discourse operates between two broader trends within American film historiography, the academic and the popular, without really belonging to either one. Much about Scorsese's film is academic, which should not be surprising given his university background. Certainly we find links between *A Personal Journey* and Sarris's *The American Cinema*. Of the fourteen directors in Sarris's "Pantheon," ten are discussed via a film clip by Scorsese (Chaplin, Ford, Griffith, Hawks, Keaton, Lang, Murnau, Ophuls, Sternberg, and Welles). More tellingly, fifteen of the twenty filmmakers in Sarris's second tier category, "The Far Side of Paradise," are included (Borzage, Capra, Cukor, De Mille, Fuller, Mann, Minnelli, Preminger, Ray, Sirk, Von Stroheim, Sturges, Vidor, and Walsh) and ten of the twenty-one filmmakers in the third tier and more obscure "Expressive Esoterica" receive attention (Boetticher, De Toth, Dwan, Garnett, Karlson, Lewis, Mackendrick, Penn, Stahl, Tourneur, and Ulmer). By contrast, Scorsese includes only three of the eleven directors in Sarris's dismissive "Less than Meets the Eye" category (Kazan, Wellman, and Wilder) and just one of eighteen directors of the even more damnable "Strained Seriousness" category (Kubrick). Clearly, Sarris has had a great impact on Scorsese and the formation of his taste. Compare Scorsese and Sarris to the more popular AFI list: nine of the eleven directors from the "Less than Meets the Eye" category have films in the Top 100 (Huston, Kazan, Lean, Mankiewicz, Milestone, Reed, Wilder, Wyler, and Zinnemann) and twenty-two of the one hundred films are from directors in the "Less than Meets the Eye" and "Strained

Seriousness" categories. Only six of the fourteen "Pantheon" directors are included (Chaplin, Ford, Griffith, Hawks, Hitchcock, and Welles), four of the twenty from "The Far Side of Paradise" (Capra, McCarey, Ray, and Stevens), and three of the twenty-one from "Expressive Esoterica" (Donen, Mulligan, and Penn). Scorsese is taking his cue from an academic with cultural capital like Sarris rather than the more popular and well-known classics.

However, I have been misleadingly referring to Sarris as an obvious academic. While Sarris taught courses on film at Columbia University (at roughly the same time Scorsese has attending and then teaching film classes at NYU) and certainly was influential in having film taken seriously as an object of academic study, most academics have generally dismissed his approach, especially as history. Even as a critic, many view Sarris as rather antiquated. His work lacks the rigor of most academic approaches to film analysis and is criticized as being too subjective and intuitive. Consider the following passage from Sarris's section on Jean Renoir: "Renoir's career is a river of personal expression. The waters may vary here and there in turbulence and depth, but the flow of personality is consistently directed to its final outlet in the sea of life. . . . The fact that Renoir is a warm director and Eisenstein a cold one cannot be explained entirely through forms and themes. Directorial personality is, as always, the crucial determinant of a film's temperature."[38] This type of impressionistic writing is not the type of close, formal analysis one expects from academic criticism today. Sarris too is situated somewhere between the academic and the popular.

The influence of academic writing on Scorsese is not limited to preacademics such as Andrew Sarris. *A Personal Journey* displays clear affinities to the post–1968 ideological criticism, in particular Jean-Luc Comolli and Jean Narboni's immensely influential article, "Cinema/Ideology/Criticism" (first published by *Cahiers du Cinéma* in October 1969 and translated by *Screen* in Spring 1971).[39] In this essay, Comolli and Narboni develop their "category e" to describe Hollywood films in which a sophisticated formal style (imagery) can transform conventional narrative and story material: "If he [the filmmaker] sees his film simply as a blow in favor of liberalism, it will be recuperated instantly by the ideology; if on the other hand, he conceives and realizes it on the deeper level of imagery, there is a chance that it will turn out to be more disruptive. Not, of course, that he will be able to break the ideology itself, but simply its reflection in his film. (The films of Ford, Dreyer, Rossellini, for example.)"[40] As Robert Ray perceptively notes, "the need to develop *category e* attests to the persistent appeal of movies that are aesthetically interesting."[41] The influence of "category e" can be seen in

"The Director as Smuggler" section of *A Personal Journey*. In discussing the smuggler, Scorsese argues that "[s]tyle was crucial. The first master of esoterica was Jacques Tourneur, who began making his mark in low-budget supernatural thrillers. On *Cat People*, he had a good reason not to show the creature. 'The less you see, the more you believe,' he stated. 'You must never try to impose your views on the viewer, but rather you must try to let it seep in, little by little.' This oblique approach perfectly defines the smuggler's strategy."[42] Scorsese's echoing of Sarris's use of the word "esoterica" is not accidental, and links are certainly found between "category e" and "auteurism," as Ray notes, "*Category e* promptly filled up with all the old auteurist favorites: John Ford, Howard Hawks, Hitchcock, Nicolas [*sic*] Ray."[43] What changed was the method in which the films were described and why the films were celebrated. A social dimension was added to the auteurist mix, something Scorsese is aware of in his discussion of the smuggler: "The fifties. This is a fascinating era were the subtext became as important—or sometimes more important—than the apparent subject matter."[44] The use of "subtext" by Scorsese reveals this academic influence. Films have to be read in order to gain meaning; they—the great films at least—are not reducible to their explicit subject matter.

A Personal Journey is an attempt to bring this academic education to a broader audience. The film establishes Scorsese as an authority, a film teacher lecturing to students. However, the style of the film is conventional and not at all difficult. It is a very typical talking-head with voiceover technique that many documentaries use. The style is popular, despite the academic discourse Scorsese occasionally deploys. The film is certainly aimed at a highbrow, cineliterate audience, but it is not aimed exclusively at that audience. The film was made for Channel 4 in Great Britain and played on TCM in the United States. This is a long way from primetime network television, but it is still a broader audience than most academic critical writing will receive. It has also been released on VHS and then DVD in North America. As an attempt to contribute to popular film culture, it is an admirable and needed work. As Jonathan Rosenbaum argues, "like it or not, one of the major activities of any film culture is a labeling of certain films as good and others as bad, and no academic approach can eliminate this activity entirely."[45] Scorsese effectively takes on this challenge to deliver an aesthetic film history and to try to include many filmmakers and films recognized by academic film study within a broader film culture.

But another question remains: has Scorsese crossed what Andreas Huyssen has dubbed "the great divide" between modernism and mass culture? This is where the weaknesses of Scorsese's documentary are most apparent and where his use of "traditional history" is most problematic. Initially *A Personal Journey* can be seen as bridging this gap by showing the artistic merit of a mass culture form (Hollywood cinema). But Scorsese is not really a postmodernist who is trying to erase the division between modernism and mass culture; instead, he is trying to move Hollywood cinema from one side of the divide (mass culture) to the other (modernism). This took place in the 1970s with the institutionalization of cinema in the university and the application of New Criticism to Hollywood cinema, primarily in the film journal *Movie* and with critics such as Victor Perkins and Robin Wood. This modernist discourse remains pervasive today and Scorsese's documentary can be seen as a continuation of this practice. Instead of arguing against high modernity, this discourse argues against "mass culture" despite the fact that Hollywood cinema is obviously, for better or worse, a mass culture phenomenon. The target of this discourse would be Comolli and Narboni's "category a": "The first and largest category comprises those films which are imbued through and through with the dominant ideology in pure and unadulterated form, and give no indication that their makers were even aware of the fact. . . . The *majority* of films in all categories are the unconscious instruments of ideology which produces them."[46] Replace the word "majority" with "mass" and the discourse becomes clear. Furthermore, cinema has another medium in which it can place the label of mass culture: television. It is telling that Scorsese includes a clip from *All that Heaven Allows* (Douglas Sirk, 1955) that uses television as a symbol of mass culture: "If you can't have a life, settle for its imitation—a TV set. This is what Jane Wyman receives from her children as a substitute for her lost love. Television, the movies' rival medium in the fifties, was cast as the ultimate symbol of alienation."[47] Sirk (who certainly fancied himself a high modernist) is using television to represent the repression of mass culture. Why television is an imitation of life but cinema (or anything else regarded as "art") is not is never explained explicitly, but the implication is clear: art transcends the alienation of mass culture.

This modernist basis (and bias) has broader significance and can help explain many of the absences in *A Personal Journey*. For example, the gender bias within *A Personal Journey* also exists in a great deal of modernist discourse, as Huyssen has argued: "The powerful masculinist mystique which is explicit in modernists such as Marinetti, Jünger, Benn, Wyndham Lewis, Céline et al. (not to speak of Marx, Nietzsche, and Freud), and implicit in many others, has to be somehow related to the persistent gendering of mass culture as feminine and inferior—even if, as a result, the heroism of the moderns won't look so heroic anymore."[48] This masculinist mystique is present in *A Personal Journey*: all of the filmmakers Scorsese discusses are male except for one (Ida Lupino). And while this is symptomatic of the era he is discussing, Scorsese nevertheless endorses this era as a Golden Age and does not critique or even acknowledge the male privilege. A similar unrecognized bias is with regard to race, which is also true of modernist discourse: "There is a growing awareness that other cultures, non-European, non-Western cultures must be met by means other than conquest or domination, as Paul Ricoeur put it more than twenty years ago, and that the erotic and aesthetic fascination with 'the Orient' and 'the primitive'—so prominent in Western culture, including modernism—is deeply problematic."[49] This awareness of the problem of race is strikingly absent in Scorsese's discussion of Griffith's *The Birth of a Nation* (1915) and *Broken Blossoms* (1919). Scorsese is unwilling to counter the mystique of the great artist. In fact, he quite disingenuously champions Griffith as a progressive artist in his discussion of *Intolerance* (1916), which argues that the film "was a daring attempt at interweaving stories and characters, not from the same period, but from four different centuries. Freely cross-cutting from one era to another, he blended them all together in a grand symphony devoted to one idea—a passionate plea for tolerance. Griffith's passion for history was balanced by his passion for simple people, the victims of history."[50] Scorsese does not point out that *The Birth of a Nation* was also concerned with people Griffith considered the "victims of history," that is, the "innocent" whites terrorized by the recently freed black slaves, because this would demythologize Griffith to a great extent. This is not to say that Scorsese ignores race throughout: to his credit, he includes dramatic clips from two important films that do say something about American racism: *The Phenix City Story* (Philip Karlson, 1955) and *Shock Corridor* (Samuel Fuller, 1963). But these are included mainly to show the greatest of these filmmakers. There is no hint from Scorsese that Hollywood cinema has been a tool of ideological oppression along gender and racial lines because this would interfere with his project of recognizing the greatness of American film.

The fact that Scorsese is still entrenched within this modernist discourse and that he fails to break from this privileging of "high art" over "mass culture" is symptomatic of the greater crisis facing artist-intellectuals in the United States. Jonathan Rosenbaum describes this dilemma in comments concerning Orson Welles: "[H]e was too much of an artist and intellectual to endear himself to the general public unless he mocked and derided his artistic temperament and intellectualism."[51] One cannot blame Scorsese for not wanting to parody either his own persona or American cinema as a whole, or for wanting to take American film seriously. But this very high modern seriousness is part of the bias against mass culture and in turn against gender and racial others that postmodernism rebelled against. Within an anti-intellectual climate like that in the United States, Scorsese as an artist-intellectual is in a double bind.

In his article on being a student of Scorsese's at NYU, Allan Arkush describes Scorsese as a teacher of film history in glowing terms:

> When it came to teaching film history, I have never seen his equal. Before every film, he'd pace in front of the class with Andrew Sarris's "The American Cinema" in one hand. He'd read off paragraphs or lists of pictures by a director. Then he'd act out scenes from a movie and connect all the director's movies with an analysis of theme and style. It was unlike any other film history course I'd ever taken, because it was being taught by a filmmaker, not a literature professor. Marty made me understand why as a child I had loved *Rio Bravo* and *The Horse Soldiers* and taught me how to love them over again. But best, he was entertaining.[52]

Arkush describes Scorsese in his earliest days as a teacher of film history at NYU as very nontraditional in his demeanor and style:

> The first film of the semester was Sam Fuller's *Shock Corridor*. It was a blunt, brutal, and very forceful introduction to American movies for the artsy-fartsy crowd. The thunderstorm in the corridor of Fuller's mental hospital practically knocked me out of my chair. Marty rewound the reel and we re-screened the fight scene in the kitchen between the journalist and the murderous guard. Marty jumped up and down with excitement as he talked about the camera movement that tracked the guard as he is dragged the length of the food-laden kitchen counters.[53]

This image of Scorsese as a teacher is very much at odds with how Scorsese presents himself in *A Personal Journey*. Instead of the hyperactive, frenzied persona Arkush describes, the Scorsese of *A Personal Journey* is composed, dignified, and authoritative in his presentation. At the same time, Scorsese as a historian is a "filmmaker," not a "literature professor." The graphics of the documentary are illuminating in this regard: the opening credits are written to mimic a teacher writing on a chalkboard, but at the same time produce an exaggerated outline of Scorsese's profile (à la Hitchcock) that identifies him as the celebrity director he has become. Thus the intellectualism of the enterprise is tempered by Scorsese's status as a celebrity.

Figure 4.2. *A Personal Journey with Martin Scorsese through American Movies* (Martin Scorsese and Michael Henry Wilson, 1995), Scorsese as Hitchcockian icon.

Italian or American Film History? *My Voyage to Italy*

The most striking difference between *A Personal Journey* and Scorsese's Italian cinema documentary is the anxiety over canon formation that is present in the American cinema, an anxiety that is absent from *My Voyage to Italy*. The visuals match the composed nature of Scorsese's delivery in *A Personal Journey*, which feature Scorsese sitting in a chair against a nondescript background speaking to the camera. In *My Voyage to Italy*, Scorsese is much more relaxed, certainly not the manic figure Arkush describes, but nevertheless avoiding the high seriousness with which he delivers the material in *A Personal Journey*. Instead of the empty studio setting of the previous film, Scorsese films *My Voyage to Italy* on location in his old neighborhood in New York City. *My Voyage* is the more personal of the two documentaries, with Scorsese delving deep into his own family history and relating this to the films. Despite this, *A Personal Journey* includes the disclaimer that this is a personal rather than an objective history. Scorsese's insistence on the film's personal nature is a way for him to disavow the canon formation in which he participates. The two main reasons why this anxiety is present in the American and not the Italian cinema documentary are (1) the films discussed in the Italian cinema documentary are mostly established classics by well-known auteurs—at least within cinephile circles, and (2) the films in *My Voyage to Italy* can be easily discussed within a liberal humanist vein, unlike the many problematic films present in *A Personal Journey*.

One immediately noticeable difference between the two films is that Scorsese spends a great deal more time on individual films in *My Voyage to Italy*: thirty-three films by eleven directors, compared to *A Personal Journey*, which features ninety-two films by fifty-seven directors, despite the fact that the films are of comparable length (*My Voyage* is actually 21 minutes longer, 246 minutes as opposed to 225 minutes). As opposed to the commercially based Hollywood films, the art films of Italian cinema presumably have a slower pace that needs to be respected, even within an introductory overview. Even the tone and volume of Scorsese's voice is noticeably different, speaking in a hushed and almost reverential manner.

Figure 4.3. *A Personal Journey with Martin Scorsese through American Movies* (Martin Scorsese and Michael Henry Wilson, 1995), Scorsese as lecturer.

Figure 4.4. *My Voyage to Italy* (Martin Scorsese, 1999), a personal family history, shot on location.

At the conclusion of *My Voyage*, Scorsese addresses the viewer:

> When I started to make this series, as I said earlier, I simply wanted to express my feelings for Italian cinema. I also wanted to get younger people interested in these movies. Even today, I suppose, history remains something that is handed down, that is between people. In fact, I learned that from watching these movies. So, the best way I have to keep film history alive is to try to share my own enthusiasm, my own experience. And I know that if you're young film history can seem like a chore, it's like doing homework. I mean, usually people get excited about a movie by hearing about it from somebody else. So I'm simply trying to tell you: I saw these movies, I didn't read about them or learn about them in school, and they had a powerful effect on me, and you should see them. Thank you.

Presumably, the cultural prestige that the films have already acquired allowed Scorsese to be bold enough to make such an authoritative statement as, "you should see them."

The rhetoric on display here indicates Scorsese's desire to be an intellectual with regard to the cinema. In fact, only with regard to cinema does Scorsese seem willing to engage larger issue of political and social value. The origins of *My Voyage to Italy* can be traced to 1993 when Scorsese wrote an angry letter to the *New York Times* regarding a negative piece written on Federico Fellini shortly after his death. The original article complained about Fellini's style getting in the way of his storytelling, but Scorsese extends this to the greater issue of cultural diversity:

> The issue here is not "film theory," but cultural diversity and openness. Diversity guarantees our cultural survival. When the world is fragmenting into groups of intolerance, ignorance and hatred, film is a powerful tool to knowledge and understanding. To our shame, your article was cited at length by the European press.
>
> The attitude that I've been describing celebrates ignorance. It also unfortunately confirms the worst fears of European film makers.
>
> Is this closedmindedness something we want to pass along to future generations?
>
> If you accept the answer in the commercial, why not take it to its natural progression:
>
> Why don't they make movies like ours?
> Why don't they tell stories as we do?
> Why don't they dress as we do?
> Why don't they eat as we do?
> Why don't they talk as we do?
> Why don't they think as we do?
> Why don't they worship as we do?
> Why don't they look like us?
> Ultimately, who will decide who "we" are?[54]

Scorsese's attempt at intellectual intervention on behalf of liberal humanist values of cultural diversity is nevertheless uniquely American in one respect: the anxiety over the role of being an intellectual. Scorsese's position within American popular culture is rather schizophrenic and reflects what Andrew Ross calls "the general ambivalence about, if not distrust of, the authoritative role of experts in people's lives."[55] Scorsese is a prime example of how this ambivalence reflects not only an individual's actions, but how those actions are interpreted and discussed because "the popular disrespect for experts and intellectual authorities is somehow justified, while at the same time the narrative is intent on reinforcing their authority."[56]

In both his Italian cinema documentary and in his earlier letter to the *New York Times*, Scorsese is very cautious about intellectualizing his defense of these films. The films are always seen as "emotional" experiences for Scorsese. He states that he did not "learn about these films in school" and that his defense of Fellini is not about "film theory." The cultural prestige of the Italian films allows Scorsese to recommend them without qualification, but this recommendation cannot seem like he is giving the audience an education (hence the reference to "homework"). As Alberto Pezzotta persuasively argues, the methodology of *My Voyage to Italy* reveals "a tendency to view the history of Italian cinema as a series of isolated masterpieces by auteurs, ignoring the wider context."[57] Scorsese's Italian documentary is traditional history, especially in the Italian context. But all evidence in the film points to the fact that the documentary is ultimately not concerned with Italian cinema and culture, but rather about American culture and Scorsese himself as an Italian American. It is not only Scorsese's anxiety about being an intellectual that is on display, but also his anxiety over the acceptance of Italian culture (and by extension Italians) in America. *My Voyage to Italy* opens with Scorsese explaining that he is making this film on Italian cinema because he is concerned that audiences are now only watching American films: "These days it seems as if American cinema is all there is, and that all the other cinemas are secondary, including Italian cinema, and that really worries me. In fact, it's the reason I'm making this documentary. The fact is I know that if I'd never seen the films that I'm going to be talking about here, I'd be a very different person, and of course, a very different filmmaker." Scorsese's argument concerns American culture and his desire to improve this situation with greater diversity. This would include his own films, which he has consistently positioned as outside of the Hollywood cinema, between the American and Italian cinema. Italian cinema as Scorsese discusses it is not considered in relation to Italian culture. Rather, he uses a few established, canonized classics to argue for an alternative to the Hollywood tradition. By contrast, because of the large number of films and filmmakers examined, the history of *A Personal Journey* is by necessity social and political, however much Scorsese tries to downplay these contexts.

Scorsese's Cinematic Histories

Scorsese has discussed the issue of how he makes history with Columbia University history professor Simon Schama. At one point, Schama has the following exchange with moderator Kent Jones:

K. J: In your work, Simon, are you trying to popularize history, and make it more of a narrative form?

S. S: Yes, but you know it's like reinventing the wheel. There were many hundreds of years in which history was never anything except popular. Unfortunately, though, the professors came along. [Laughter] But yes, I'm sometimes presented as being on a kind of crusade to "bring the reader back to history."[58]

Schama recognizes his pursuit of narrative as a way of making history alive, and notes the influence of narrative forms such as novels, films, and poetry on his writing, emphasizing the imaginative work necessary to any historical retelling. This connects him with Scorsese, who similarly emphasizes films that tell history through narrative. What this discussion with Schama reveals is Scorsese's awareness of himself as a historian, not only in his documentaries but also through his fiction films. As Scorsese moved into the role of film historian in the 1990s, this was reflected in his feature films, all of which have been concerned with past worlds. Throughout the decade, these cinematic histories have provided a unity to Scorsese's work on otherwise diverse and divergent material.

In this same discussion with Schama and Jones, Scorsese tries to explain his attempts to deal with historical material in his feature films, stating, "A number of the movies I've made in the past ten years have been period pieces. What I tried to do in these pictures was to show character detail. The detail reflects the civilization."[59] He wants to move away from the historical epic form and move toward a style similar to Italian filmmaker Roberto Rossellini: "I was so impressed and influenced in the late '60s or so by Rossellini's historical films, starting with *The Rise of Louis XIV*. The king's absolute power is revealed in his daily eating ceremony, not when he is attending to affairs of state. That's when I said: This is really history. It's about people. I've always been interested in the way history is recorded."[60] This can be seen in films such as *GoodFellas*, *The Age of Innocence*, *Casino*, and *Kundun*. Scorsese attempts to break away from the classical mode of history, represented by such epics as *Lawrence of Arabia*: "Audience's eyes glaze over. Too much historical information is being thrown at them."[61] Scorsese instead wants to move into a realism of character and quotidian detail. Cinema studies saw a similar move toward film history in this decade, and the next generation of younger filmmakers from the American independent cinema scene similarly took up historical concerns. This had consequences for Scorsese's critical reputation—both positive and negative—over the course of the 1990s. There was a further canonization of Scorsese's past films and a devaluation of his current work.

Scorsese's first work of the decade, *GoodFellas*, based on the true-life crime story *Wise Guy* by Nicolas Pileggi, was a return to the gangster genre. The opening scene immediately establishes the film's black comic tone. The main character, Henry Hill (Ray Liotta), is driving with friends Jimmy Conway (Robert De Niro) and Tommy DeVito (Joe Pesci) when they hear a noise coming from the car. They pull over and open the trunk, revealing a beaten, bloodied man they thought was dead. Tommy stabs him repeatedly before Jimmy draws a gun and shoots the man. Henry closes the trunk as the frame freezes on his face, drenched in a red light. As Tony Bennett's upbeat "Rags to Riches" plays on the soundtrack, Henry narrates in voiceover: "Ever since I can remember I always wanted to be a gangster." The story then flashes back to Henry's childhood and his movement from his poor, working-class family to his more affluent Mafia clan. As Henry narrates, we follow him through this criminal underworld, through his stint in prison, and eventually to his drug addiction and arrest on felony trafficking charges. To avoid jail, Henry testifies against his friends and enters the government's Witness Protection Program, where he is trapped in a suburban hell, lamenting the passing of his old glory days.

GoodFellas is the last Scorsese film to be canonized as one of his masterpieces, along with *Mean Streets*, *Taxi Driver*, and *Raging Bull*.[62] The film's critical reception at the time was the most overwhelmingly positive of Scorsese's career. *GoodFellas* swept all of the major critics' awards, from the National Society of Film Critics to the New York Film Critics Circle to the Los Angeles Critics Awards, winning by an overwhelming margin with the National Society of Film Critics in particular (voting 43–2 for the eventual Academy Award–winner, *Dances with Wolves*). The comparison with *Dances with Wolves* and its win over *GoodFellas* has become part of Scorsese lore along with *Ordinary People* (Robert Redford, 1980) defeating *Raging Bull* and *Rocky* (John Avildsen, 1976) defeating *Taxi Driver*. In particular, the treatment of history in *Dances with Wolves* looks very traditional compared to earlier revisionist Westerns, especially its obvious forerunner *Little Big Man* (Arthur Penn, 1970). While being about an earlier historical moment, *GoodFellas* is mainly antiepic in scope. Instead, it concerns itself with the small, intimate details of Mafia life, drawing heavily on its real-life source material, and this realism greatly impressed most of the film's critical supporters. Instead of looking at the film in relation to *Dances with Wolves*, a movie of a completely different genre, considering *GoodFellas* in relation to the small-scale gangster revival of 1990 that included both *The Godfather*

Part III and *Miller's Crossing* (Joel Coen, 1990) is more productive. The extreme difference in the reception of *GoodFellas* to these contemporary works is illuminating in terms of the direction Scorsese's career would take for the rest of the decade.

Chapter 3 discusses the parallels between the careers of Scorsese and Coppola throughout the 1980s. This parallel continues with both returning to the gangster film in 1990. However, they return to this genre with their critical reputations very much transformed. Through his work in film preservation, Scorsese was able to maintain a critical distinction despite taking on commercial projects like *The Color of Money*. Coppola was afforded no such luxury and was seen very much as a director in decline. In 1988, both made personal films meant to signal their artistic "comeback." The controversy over *The Last Temptation of Christ* made Scorsese into a martyr of the film critics, while Coppola's *Tucker: The Man and His Dream* was largely ignored after its lack of box-office success. Thus, we should not be surprised that the critical reception of *GoodFellas* and *The Godfather Part III* would vastly differ. How the two films were discussed and respectively praised and critiqued offers an example of how changing contexts can alter reception. The conditions for Scorsese's film to be praised were clearly much more favorable than Coppola's. That each director produced a film very much in the style of their previous work emphasizes the importance of extratextual factors. *GoodFellas*, despite its historical setting and rise-and-fall structure in detailing organized crime, follows Scorsese's interest in the quotidian aspects of his characters and their lifestyles. While not a sequel in any sense, it is connected to Scorsese's previous *Mean Streets*. *The Godfather Part III* is likewise very much in the style of Coppola's most well-known work in its epic quality and its continuation of the story of Coppola's canonized *The Godfather* and *The Godfather Part II*. In the climate of the 1970s, both of these filmmakers and their respective styles were praised and respected, Coppola even more so than Scorsese. By 1990 this situation has altered significantly.

Even the status of *The Godfather Part III* as a sequel had new connotations. In 1974, when Coppola made *The Godfather Part II*, the sense was that it was a sequel made not only for commercial purposes but also for ideological ones. The film was received not as a cheap attempt to make money, but as a legitimate artistic statement that was even superior to the initial film. John Hess, writing in the radical left film journal *Jump Cut*, calls *The Godfather Part II* "the greatest Hollywood film since *Citizen Kane*."[63] The reasons for this assessment are primarily ideological. Hess argues, "the real strength of the film is its demonstration that the benefits of the family structure and the hope for community have been destroyed by capitalism."[64] Hess supports this argument with quotations from Coppola himself on the revisionist nature of the film. He quotes Coppola as stating, "I was disturbed that people thought I had romanticized Michael," implying that the sequel allowed Coppola the ability to fix this mistake.[65] But by 1990 critics would be more cynical about Coppola's motives. Part of this is the result of a greater cynicism toward the rise of the high concept film during the 1980s, but even more relevant is the fall of Coppola's reputation by 1990. This downfall is reflected in a greater tendency to see Coppola as a more conventional filmmaker who lacks formal and stylistic rigor. Scholars Robert Ray and Robert Kolker have made this observation about even the original *Godfather* films, and the third film only reinforced this tendency within mainstream criticism. In Bourdieu's terms, Coppola's work simply lost its distinction as being uniquely cinematic. *The Godfather Part III* was seen as closer to a Classical Hollywood film like *Casablanca* rather than a truly innovative work like *Citizen Kane*.

Scorsese, on the other hand, continued to be taken seriously as a creative force, mostly because of contextual factors previously outlined. Thus, when *GoodFellas* was released, the conditions were prepared for its critical success. The film was not only overwhelmingly successful with critics on initial release, but was also taken seriously as high art by scholars. This can be seen in its high standing in the *Sight and Sound* poll and by Robert Kolker discussion of the film in the third edition of his New Hollywood study *A Cinema of Loneliness*. Kolker compares *GoodFellas* to Laurence Sterne's eighteenth-century novel *Tristram Shandy* and other modernist texts: "Why do we believe anything we see in gangster films? Scorsese seems to ask."[66] For Kolker, *GoodFellas* is not only a detailed historical fiction about gangsters; it is also a deconstruction of the whole genre, a sophisticated and knowing examination of cinema history. *GoodFellas* manages to appeal both to critics seeking traditional storytelling as well as to scholars like Kolker interested in more challenging representations.

The same could not be said of *Miller's Crossing*, the other gangster film released in 1990. In terms of the reflexivity Kolker described and celebrated, the Coen brothers in fact go much further in their creation of a world that is clearly a representation based on cinematic models. Everything about the world of *Miller's Crossing* is artificial, including its view of the historical period being recreated. This kind of radical deconstruction alienated many critics who preferred *GoodFellas* and its more balanced mix of quotidian detail and stylistic flourish. Roger Ebert's reviews of the two respective films highlight this difference. In praising *GoodFellas*, Ebert writes that "Scorsese is the right director—the only director—for this material. He knows it inside out."[67] The key to the film, for Ebert, is Scorsese's authenticity as an Italian-American director who grew up observing this gangster world. This is borne out by Scorsese's collaborator on the film, Nicolas Pileggi, who praises Scorsese's authenticity through, ironically enough, his earlier movie, *Mean Streets*: "While the wiseguys [*sic*] love *The Godfather*, seeing it as ennobling them, their favorite Mafia movie is Marty's *Mean Streets*. . . . This is a home movie to them."[68] Scorsese is thus the right director for Pileggi's nonfiction novel because the subjects themselves believed in Scorsese's accuracy in earlier depictions of their world.

By contrast, in critiquing *Miller's Crossing*, Ebert discusses its lack of realism: "*Miller's Crossing* is not quite as successful as it should be . . . it seems like a movie that is constantly aware of itself, instead of a movie that gets on with business."[69] That being "aware of itself" may be part of the "business" of *Miller's Crossing* never enters Ebert's discussion. It would, however, be the focus of debates over American narrative cinema practice over the course of the next decade. In particular, these debates centered around familiar disagreements on modernist versus postmodernist art practice, with the Coen brothers use of pastiche as the key dividing point.[70] With the widespread critical and commercial success of *Pulp Fiction* (Quentin Tarantino, 1994), this postmodernist pastiche reached the mainstream of film journalism. Even Roger Ebert was impressed with the film, although he notably placed it second in his

Figure 4.5. *GoodFellas* (Martin Scorsese, 1990), cultural authenticity: slicing garlic with a razor.

year best list behind the documentary *Hoop Dreams* (Steve James, 1994). In terms of its impact, *Pulp Fiction* has much in common with *GoodFellas*, despite the much greater box-office success of the former. *Pulp Fiction* was very popular with mainstream critics and quickly became one of the most canonized films of the decade.[71] However, unlike *GoodFellas*, *Pulp Fiction* also received a backlash due to its status as the representative of postmodernism within the context of American commercial cinema. These criticisms came from mainstream critics, from fellow filmmakers, and from academics. As Jeffrey Sconce details, the postmodern sensibility of many "independent" filmmakers began to be heavily critiqued as "nihilistic" within the popular press.[72] As the most recognizable member of this group, Tarantino in particular was often singled out. Filmmaker Paul Schrader, the screenwriter of *Taxi Driver* and other Scorsese films, has been the most vocal of other directors in their distinction between modernist and postmodernist approaches. Roger Ebert describes the difference thusly: "The existentialist hero wonders if life is worth living. The ironic hero is greatly amused by people who wonder about things like that. And there you have the difference between the work of Paul Schrader and Quentin Tarantino."[73] In the same article, Schrader describes his understanding of the ironic or postmodern view of art: "Everything in the ironic world has quotation marks around it. You don't actually kill somebody; you 'kill' them. It doesn't matter if you put the baby in front of the runaway car because it's only a 'baby.'" Ebert agrees, stating that the postmodern scene is not about the baby, it is "about scenes about babies,"[74] and this postmodern irony would be so often accused of nihilism in the following decade.

This would extend beyond the journalistic realm Sconce detailed. In the same book in which he praises the self-reflexivity of *GoodFellas*, Robert Kolker also argues against the rise of postmodern cinema. Furthermore, for Kolker, Tarantino and *Pulp Fiction* stand "as the acme of postmodern nineties filmmaking."[75] Kolker sees Tarantino as representing the worse tendencies of postmodernism and at the same time revealing more general problems with this aesthetic: "*Pulp Fiction* is without theory or consequences, or it's about laughing both off, and this itself is a great paradox within the postmodern. Postmodernism theories abound, but, unlike modernism, the works that are theorized eschew theory themselves because they deny significance. They posit only their images, sounds, or words within their closed narrative worlds, snubbing a quest for resonance, history, politics. Modernism is the enemy of complacency, postmodernism its accomplice."[76] These modernism-postmodernism debates are hardly exclusive to the American cinema, of course, but they do function here in a very specific manner. What results is the creation of a past Golden Age of American cinema represented by the 1970s and filmmakers such as Scorsese at the expense of more recent American films and filmmakers. It allows the continuation of a "great divide" between the modernism of the past and the postmodern mass culture of today. This argument relies on seeing Tarantino and *Pulp Fiction* as representatives of this aesthetic. But even an iconoclastic modern like Kolker admits Tarantino represents only one pole of postmodernism. In contrast, Kolker does see that postmodern style can be a legitimate intervention in the culture: "At its best, the postmodern is an attempt to move beyond modernism, beyond the voice of the despairing author seeking coherence of form and structure in the face of an incoherent universe and to move toward an inclusive celebration of the death of meaning in which all art, high and low, is recognized as sharing a community of images and sounds."[77] In other words, the postmodern can move beyond the great divide of modernism and mass culture. But moving beyond this distinction also has the effect of displacing evaluation as an activity considered worthy of academic attention.

The End of Evaluation(?): Canonization in the Postmodern Age

I have repeatedly referenced the *Sight and Sound* Top Ten poll, conducted once every ten years since 1952. I have relied on this poll for two reasons: (1) it is the most widely respected effort at canonization in the field of film studies; and (2) no other alternative academic canon exists. The very issue of making evaluations has become a far more contentious issue in the last two decades. Even the *Sight and Sound* poll has become more aware of the politics involved in taste formations, even referencing Bourdieu in Ian Christie's introduction to the 2002 survey: "The implications of Bourdieu's work for such exercises as the ten-yearly poll are that we will never understand its mapping of taste unless we get serious about who's being asked to vote and what image of cinema culture they're trying to project."[78] Even those organizing the canonization process now recognize that making value judgments is contingent on many factors. Because it can no longer be seen in idealized terms within the academy, evaluation is mostly ignored. Some scholars are surveyed as part of the *Sight and Sound* survey, but academic writing and publishing rarely makes evaluation the focus.

   Film critic Jonathan Rosenbaum has been very critical of the academy for this failure to evaluate. He argues that this has left the canonizing process in the hands of marketing forces rather than individuals with any knowledge of film aesthetics and history. Rosenbaum's argument is framed within a familiar modernist fear of the "dumbing down" of culture and as such can be seen as conservative and reactionary in terms of taste. But Rosenbaum's critique of the AFI's "100 Years, 100 Movies" CBS television special is more than simply an elitist backlash. Rather, it is a concern about how uncritical the AFI was of its own list, with films simply selected from the pantheon of successful Hollywood films of the past. Rosenbaum's own response was to establish an "Alternative 100" list of American films and then to publish his own canon of 1,000 great films, *Essential Cinema: On the Necessity of Film Canons*. The goal of these evaluative exercises is to prevent cinema culture from fossilizing around fewer and fewer films and to stop films that are less marketable from being ignored. This has occurred not only with popular lists like those of the AFI, but also with the *Sight and Sound* list, which in 2002 created a survey of the top films from the past twenty-five years because of the dearth of contemporary films in its poll.[79]

Rosenbaum represents one of the few liminal figures between the world of academic and critical writing, just as Scorsese is between the worlds of filmmaking and film history. We should also note that Rosenbaum's arguments around canonization differ considerably from defenders of the canon in literary studies, such as Harold Bloom. Rosenbaum does not lament challenges to the canon. To the contrary, he encourages them, often from a leftist political perspective. What he argues is that instead of having debates around notions of aesthetic value and politics, as Janet Staiger encouraged more than two decades ago in her article on the politics of film canons, film studies has ignored the questions as unimportant. Not surprisingly, Rosenbaum responded positively to Scorsese's American cinema documentary because of its esoteric choices and celebration of lesser-known figures.[80] Scorsese discusses eighteen of the one hundred films on Rosenbaum's list as opposed to only ten on the AFI's survey. Of course, these choices corresponded with those of Andrew Sarris, the most influential taste maker on the baby boomer generation to which both Scorsese and Rosenbaum belong. Thus the choices were not surprising to cinephiles, but were nevertheless very much at odds with the AFI. Like Scorsese, Rosenbaum challenged the official "traditional" history of the industry to try to promote a more "effective" historical engagement with American film culture. But ultimately, Rosenbaum's challenge is more radical because he is explicit about his evaluative stance. Scorsese may acknowledge his personal investment, but uses this to disavow the evaluation that is taking place. Because Scorsese is an acclaimed filmmaker, all of the selections are subsumed under his authorship. The importance of the films becomes partially reliant on their significance to Scorsese's work rather than to the culture as a whole, which is where Rosenbaum's concern always remains.

The combination of the lack of evaluation and the turn to history in film studies has led to the lack of current cinema featured prominently in the *Sight and Sound* poll, which had a detrimental effect on the critical reception of Scorsese's work during the 1990s. While *The Age of Innocence*, *Casino*, and *Kundun* all received some positive and at times lavish reviews, none of these films have entered the Scorsese pantheon. Even *GoodFellas*, the last acknowledged Scorsese masterpiece, has not received the prominence of either *Taxi Driver* or *Raging Bull*. But this is not to suggest that Scorsese's 1990s films and their mostly positive reception have not been beneficial to Scorsese's critical reputation. They have allowed Scorsese to accumulated increasingly more cultural prestige and reinforce his status as a great, if no longer innovative, filmmaker. This has subsequently allowed his "masterpieces" from the last Hollywood Golden Age only to grow in stature. No matter what the aesthetic quality of Scorsese's films of the 1990s, clearly they would not be canonized to the same degree as his earlier work. There was a critical consensus that the most exciting work to come out of the American cinema happened prior to the 1980s, and that the contemporary climate was simply not capable of producing films as distinguished.

Furthermore, cinema itself was now seen as reaching its end, and many "death of cinema" declarations appeared in the popular media.[81] This was reflected in the crisis within film criticism and evaluation, as both Greg Taylor and Raymond Haberski have detail. Taylor argues that the tradition of vanguard criticism popularized in the 1950s and 1960s led to the "retreat into theory" of the next decades and eventually to the contemporary situation: "Today's highbrow film critic does not presume to evaluate; he merely explicates and interprets. . . . The serious critic can now assume difficult judgment questions to be 'beside the point,' and best left for those common journalists still beholden to readers who insist on getting their money's worth. Vanguard criticism does not allow the bar to be lowered so much as thrown away—or, rather, disavowed—by those who have cultivated a preference for the aesthetically incomplete, fractured, uncontrolled."[82] The golden ages of the various New Wave youth movement cinemas, including the brief Hollywood Renaissance, also included a critical apparatus shifting away from traditional notions of what constituted film criticism. As Haberski writes in the conclusion to his study of films and critics in American culture, "although movies had accumulated cultural capital, that development had happened at the expense of more traditional notions of art and criticism."[83] One of these traditional notions of art and criticism is evaluation and canon making. As a result, the canonization process was left to middlebrow magazines such as *Sight and Sound* in England and *Film Comment* in the United States. The *Sight and Sound* poll thus remains the closest to an academic canon we have with the presence of scholars such as David Bordwell. In academia, canon making remains largely an implicit activity.

The implicit nature of evaluation within film studies has become even more pronounced with the move away from theory and toward history. Theory may have attempted to overturn past notions of evaluation, but it still retained a certain prescriptive basis in terms of what should be valued in films. The shift that occurs is from the principles of auteurship to the standards of ideological criticism. Film theory tended either to praise alternative practices for their emancipation of the spectator or reconsider mainstream films in terms of their ideology. As chapter 2 argues, ideological critics were very important to the establishment of Scorsese's reputation. With the move to film history, however, the issue of evaluation has become much more implicit. Scorsese's own work as a film historian and archivist can serve as an example. Scorsese does not position his histories as evaluative, but rather as "personal" favorites that have shaped him as a filmmaker. This is especially the case with the American documentary because of the less canonical status of the films compared those established classics in *My Voyage to Italy*. Scorsese has no interest in overtly challenging any established taste distinctions, favoring instead a policy of inclusion. This philosophy extends to his archival work and his call for "no value judgments."[84]

But canonization is still very much in evidence here. Scorsese's cultural status enables the films he admires to be featured in his documentary as well as in retrospectives organized around Scorsese and his influences. The result is the canonization of Scorsese and his films as the organizing principle of these projects. Despite the focus on celebrating the past, no films benefit more from Scorsese's historical interests than his own. They are the central texts. This involves doing history in reverse. It matters more to trace the various influences on Scorsese films than to take a past work and examine how it influenced many subsequent directors. While not explicit, this is hardly work that is free of value judgments.

In the conclusion to his study *Artists in the Audience*, Greg Taylor makes an argument for the reintegration of evaluation into the film studies discipline: "Contextualizing (and rethinking) their aversion to judicious judgment would afford highbrow film scholars the opportunity to confront some of their prized distinction from middlebrow journalists. More important, it would encourage an acknowledgement and interrogations of those stubbornly modernist aesthetic biases which underlie their appreciation of movies yet also discourage analysis and promotion of elusive and difficult works not illustrative of theory."[85] While Taylor's prescriptive call for an acknowledgement, contextualization, and interrogation of the process of evaluation may be useful or even needed within academic film studies, it certainly would not benefit Scorsese and his critical reputation. The modernist aesthetic biases Taylor mentions have made a distinction between Scorsese and the current postmodern filmmaking styles. The move toward history and away from evaluation have allowed for a perpetuation of the canon, and Scorsese's status as an artist-historian has subsequently ensured that his earlier canonized films will continue. As a Hollywood filmmaker, his works continue to be discussed as examples of ideology and theory, unlike more elusive and difficult art that Taylor suggests would be more prominent in a different context. Scorsese's own nonevaluative stance toward film history and preservation is understandable given that the field of film production as it has evolved has been so beneficial to Scorsese's cultural prestige.

Case Study: Scorsese and the Presentation of the *Vertigo* "Restoration"

I return to the chapter opening and briefly analyze an example of film history and preservation in which Scorsese was indirectly involved: Universal's 1996 restoration of *Vertigo*. Neither Scorsese nor the Film Foundation undertook this project. The role Scorsese played was one of validation, using his cultural prestige in the field of film heritage to legitimate the work done on Hitchcock's original.

The archival work on *Vertigo*, which Robert Harris and James Katz did, both preserved and restored the film. The preservation met with little controversy because it involved copying the film as faithfully as possible as well as treating and storing the original components. The restoration of the film, however, was far more contentious because it involved making changes to the original decisions Hitchcock made. As a result, Harris, Katz, and Universal were forced to justify their alterations to the text. When *Vertigo* was first released in its new format, it was accompanied by the documentary *Obsessed with "Vertigo"* (Harrison Engle, 1997), which originally aired on AMC and has subsequently been included on home VHS and DVD releases of the film. At the beginning of the documentary, Harris and Katz explain why they undertook restoring *Vertigo*, citing three reasons: (1) the greatness of the film; (2) the need of archival work to preserve the film's original elements; and (3) the desire to rerelease the film into theaters. Throughout the documentary, which is essentially a promotional piece for the new version, these three reasons are intertwined into a single argument. Thus the changes that were made to the film for commercial purposes (theatrical release) are justified by reference to Hitchcock as auteur (the greatness of the film) and the deterioration of the original print (the need for the restoration).

The interconnection between these elements can be seen in the structure of the documentary, which alternates between a typical production history of the making of the film and the details of the preservation and restoration process. The production history centers on the figure of Hitchcock as auteur, an artistic genius whose work needs to be preserved for future generations. The details of the preservation and restoration use similar rhetoric, admiring the technical skill of Hitchcock and stating that they want to preserve the "precise visual texture Hitchcock intended." But paradoxically, the restoration preserves Hitchcock by making changes to the original. This is especially the case with the film's soundtrack. Leo Enticknap argues that this is part of a general concession to commercial interests in sound design: "Whereas many public-sector film archivists would not advocate the approach taken in this instance, restoration work carried out on a commercial basis will often be geared to a very different set of priorities."[86] Because of these alternations, Harris and Katz place extra emphasis on authenticity. They state that they obtained contemporary recordings of a 1950s police revolver and of the exact cars used in the film.[87] And they emphasize that they were trying to honor Hitchcock's intentions, making the film he would have made today if he had access to current technology. This has commercial motivations as well. Universal believed it could not present the film without modern "enhancement," but it knew that *Vertigo* could not be sold without Hitchcock's name. This is why the documentary/promotional film is structured the way it is, cross-cutting between selling Hitchcock as an artist and selling the technological process as enhancing that artistry.

The role of Scorsese in the documentary is largely symbolic, and like the rest of the film works at reconciling the different goals of the restoration: the celebration of Hitchcock as auteur and the alternation of Hitchcock's original vision for commercial purposes. When Scorsese appears as a talking head in the film, the caption below his name does not read "Film Director," as one may expect. Instead, he is introduced as "Martin Scorsese, The Film Foundation." Scorsese is selected not because he is a critically acclaimed and well-known filmmaker, but because he is known for his work in film preservation. He thus helps to legitimate the preservation and restoration work done by the studio for its theatrical rerelease. But what is especially curious is that although Scorsese is identified by his preservation work, he is completely silent on the actual restoration itself. Instead, Scorsese praises the film for being so "unabashedly personal" in nature and for its "disturbing" qualities. In other words, Scorsese focuses on the film's authorial signature and its ideological subversion, the two main canonical approaches. Scorsese's actual words are used to prove the film's greatness, and his symbolic power and cultural prestige as a film preserver are used to prove the legitimacy of the restoration.

That Scorsese is quiet on the actual restoration itself is telling, and this is not simply accidental. In this situation, Scorsese found himself in a familiar liminal position. At the time of the *Vertigo* restoration, Scorsese had a contract with Universal Studios. He completed *Casino* for the studio in 1995 and had earlier made *Cape Fear* in 1991 and *The Last Temptation of Christ* in 1988. As David Thompson and Ian Christie argue, "[w]hen Universal backed *The Last Temptation of Christ*, there was an understanding that Scorsese would go on to make more commercial film[s] for them."[88] One can view Scorsese's participation in the documentary as similar to his making of *Cape Fear* for the studio as a back payment for *The Last Temptation*. However, while Scorsese does participate

MARTIN SCORSESE
The Film Foundation

Figure 4.6. *Obsessed with "Vertigo"* (Harrison Engle, 1997), Scorsese as cultural authority.

in praising Hitchcock and his work, he does not make any comments on the restoration itself. We must remember that Scorsese has for many years been an active advocate for "artists' rights." On March 15, 1995, Scorsese made a pitch on Capitol Hill for legislation that would grant filmmakers the right to warn viewers of their objections to films that have been altered for commercial purposes (such as viewings on airlines, home video, and broadcast television).[89] The *Vertigo* restoration clearly contradicts this proposed legislation and shows how the studios often use (or abuse) Scorsese's prestige for commercial purposes. But Scorsese is also in a powerful enough position that he can use that same prestige to question the legitimacy of the studios and their actions as he does with *The Key to Reserva*. The liminal position of Scorsese as both Hollywood director and Hollywood outsider has meant that Scorsese plays a key role in a remarkably high number of issues within the contemporary culture as a whole. This chapter focuses specifically on the issues of film history and preservation, but Scorsese is important to several other areas in the culture as well, which is the subject of the final chapter.

5

What Is Scorsese?

Scorsese's Role in Contemporary Postmodern Culture

There is no more suitable or potent image or symbol for our time than the image of the blind art collector. I think that sums it up. If you were going to write a history of the era, you should call it The Blind Art Collector, and Other Stories.

❈

THE 2010 HBO DOCUMENTARY *Public Speaking*, a profile of New York writer-intellectual Fran Lebowitz, initially seems an odd project for Scorsese to direct. Other than the commonality of New York itself, no connection is apparent between the Italian-American male filmmaker and the Jewish-American female writer. But from Lebowitz's opening remarks quoted above, the attraction becomes clear, especially since Lebowitz has become known less as a writer and more as an intellectual commenting on the cultural scene. Much of Lebowitz's commentary is an argument against postmodernism and what she views as the disaster of culture's "democratization." She rants about the terrible effect of television, which has replaced the world itself, and argues that much of Andy Warhol's notion of "fame" was meant as a joke that, unfortunately, most of the culture did not understand. The dwindling standards that have occurred in the past decades seem self-evident to Lebowitz and her commanding presence and intelligence dominate the picture. Scorsese himself is mostly seen in the corner of the frame, laughing and responding to Lebowitz's remarks. The one oddity of the otherwise conventional talking-head profile is the inclusion of two sequences using clips from Scorsese's own *Taxi Driver*. They illustrate Lebowitz's discussion of New York in the 1970s, as well as her driving a Checker cab. They are entirely apt for the illustrative purpose they serve, but because Scorsese is quoting himself, it causes a certain dissonance. Why does Scorsese include these seemingly self-aggrandizing allusions? Perhaps to make a personal connection to Lebowitz, to make the link between them in the viewer's mind. But I would argue that it relates more to Scorsese's status as an artist-intellectual. Certainly, Scorsese does not want to be the "blind art collector" of the postmodern era. The allusions to his masterpiece *Taxi Driver* emphasize that however much he may be a historian, critic, and even collector himself, he is first and foremost an artist. Furthermore, he is an artist who was established by high modernist criticism, freed from the postmodern label that often stigmatizes contemporary artists.

Distinctions between high art and mass culture were breaking down in the 1960s, resulting in movies (particularly Hollywood movies) being taken more seriously than before. But this does not mean that distinctions went away. The rise of postmodernism in the 1970s challenged the modernist idea that high art has to be separated from the contamination of mass culture, but this attempt did not have any lasting effect as Lebowitz's remarks demonstrate. Thus, while Scorsese as a Hollywood figure has benefited from the acceptance of popular film as a legitimate art form, the great divide remains. Furthermore, Scorsese has come to represent the last Golden Age of American film (from which *Taxi Driver* comes), which has been implicitly or even at times explicitly linked with modernist high art. Scorsese is often positioned in opposition to postmodern culture, not only by academics like Robert Kolker but also by fellow filmmakers like Paul Schrader. Scorsese's work outside of his feature films has undoubtedly contributed to his reputation as a serious, modernist alternative by critics who view postmodern culture as a negative, "contaminating" force.

However, what makes Scorsese an intriguing figure is that he continues to circulate within this culture and thus cannot avoid being "contaminated" in some way. *Taxi Driver* may be something of a canonized museum piece, but it is also a part of the popular culture. While the text itself continues to be the subject of critique and debate, it has also been transformed by its status as a popular cultural object. Many critics continue to treat *Taxi Driver* simply as an autonomous art object and deal with its internal features, but its textual meaning is constantly being negotiated through its status as an iconic film (even by Scorsese himself in *Public Speaking*). The film's meaning can no longer (if it ever could be) be judged outside of these mediating influences (cartoons, posters, and advertisements). Likewise, Scorsese himself has to be seen not only as a person but also as a text, continually being evaluated and reevaluated by film critics as well as within contemporary postmodern culture as a whole.

Too Smart, Too Soon: *The King of Comedy* as Predecessor of American Independent Cinema Sensibility

> *The King of Comedy* puzzled many people, including many of Scorsese's [*sic*] admirers. Yes, the end more or less recapitulated the end of *Taxi Driver*, but otherwise, how does it relate to the previous films? An anomaly, a dead end, a new departure?
>
> —Robin Wood[1]

> *The King of Comedy* was right on the edge for us; we couldn't go any further at that time.
>
> —Martin Scorsese[2]

Released in 1983 to both box-office indifference and occasional critical befuddlement, *The King of Comedy* has been one of Scorsese's most neglected films, and this neglect has little connection to the film's lack of quality; rather, it is intimately related to the contingencies of its reception. Many years after the initial release of *The King of Comedy*, a whole group of films Jeffrey Sconce identified as "the new American smart film"[3] were being celebrated as among the greatest American films of our time. Not surprisingly, in recent years, the reputation of *The King of Comedy* has begun to grow.[4] Tracing the connections between Scorsese's work and these later films of the American Independent Cinema will resituate *The King of Comedy* as a key text in the evolution of American commercial art cinema over the past decades.

As a filmmaker, Scorsese is most strongly associated with the era of the New Hollywood. Since the fall of this movement, Scorsese has been seen as one of its most uncompromising survivors, being able to work within the system while maintaining his artistic integrity. Scorsese's relationship with the American Independent Cinema movement, beginning roughly as the New Hollywood era ends, is often ignored.[5] This is despite *After Hours* winning the prize for Best Feature at the first annual Independent Spirit Awards in 1986 and Scorsese and the New Hollywood in general often being regarded as major influences on independent directors.[6] In fact, the myth of Scorsese as an outsider, despite his working within Hollywood on large budget features, mirrors the place of American Independent Cinema as being outside the Hollywood system even as it is increasingly coopted by the major studios. Scorsese's Hollywood films, such as *GoodFellas*, *The Age of Innocence*, *Casino*, and *Bringing Out the Dead*, air on the Independent Film Channel (IFC), suggesting that "independent" film is often an aesthetic category rather than a strictly commercial one.[7] But Scorsese's film with the most direct influence on this movement is not any of these more well-known commercial films or his canonized classics. Instead, the relatively unknown *The King of Comedy* is closest to an American Independent Cinema sensibility.

This sensibility, according to Jeffrey Sconce, emerged in particular force in the mid- to late 1990s, with films such as *Welcome to the Dollhouse* (Todd Solondz, 1995), *Safe* (Todd Haynes, 1995), *Citizen Ruth* (Alexander Payne, 1996), *The Ice Storm* (Ang Lee, 1997), *In the Company of Men* (Neil LaBute, 1997), *Happiness* (Todd Solondz, 1998), *Rushmore* (Wes Anderson, 1998), *Election* (Alexander Payne, 1999), and *Your Friends and Neighbors* (Neil LaBute, 1999), to name just some of the most telling examples. Sconce notes that in the ten years from 1991 to 2001, this "New Smart Cinema" emerged to the point that it became a marketing strategy.[8] Released within this particular climate, one could expect *The King of Comedy* to have fared very well, certainly critically if not commercially.[9] But there was no such identified group to target back in 1982, which led to the Fox Studios actually shelving the film for a period, eventually releasing it in February 1983.[10] Fox had marketing difficulties because the film's audience had not yet been targeted as a demographic. Because there was not yet a "smart aesthetic" (a shared set of stylistic and thematic practices), there was also not a "smart set" (a sociocultural formation informing the circulation of such films).[11]

The King of Comedy can be seen as the dividing point between the New Hollywood out of which Scorsese emerges and the soon-to-develop Independent sensibility. The film marks a striking stylistic departure for Scorsese: both the documentary style realism of Method performances and locations and the expressive use of the mobile camera, lighting, editing, and sound of his earlier work are almost entirely absent.[12] In addition, at the level of character and performance, the creative vigor also seems to be missing. Instead of the tormented, anguished, violent, yet energetic characters of previous De Niro/Scorsese creations like Johnny Boy of *Mean Streets*, Travis Bickle of *Taxi Driver*, Jimmy Doyle of *New York, New York*, or Jake LaMotta of *Raging Bull*, in *The King of Comedy* we have Rupert Pupkin, a rather ordinary, untalented would-be comedian with none of the self-destructive talent of Doyle or LaMotta, nor the inner anguish of Bickle. The picture also confused Roger Ebert, normally a staunch Scorsese supporter.[13] In addition to stylistic differences, Ebert mentions both the lack of release and the lack of a "satisfying" conclusion. These comments are intriguing because in many ways *The King of Comedy* is similar to Scorsese's previous films, *Taxi Driver* and *Raging Bull*, both of which can also be described as "painful, wounded" movies about "lonely, angry people." The difference is the sense of release (or entertainment) these films give to the audiences. *Raging Bull*, for example, features the highly expressive, violent fight scenes that act as a catharsis for the audience, allowing for an emotional release (the scene of the audience getting splattered with blood during LaMotta's final fight is a good example of this). Similarly, *Taxi Driver* ends with a violent climactic shootout in which Travis Bickle slaughters a pimp and his associates in order to save Iris from prostitution, however ironic the film may be about his "heroism."

Scorsese reworks the classic tale of the ending of *The King of Comedy* is similarly ironic, but we are not given the element of spectacle in this film that we are given at the end of *Taxi Driver*. Thus the film is even more uncomfortable for the audience, primarily due to its heavy use of the emotion of embarrassment, a theme that both Timothy Corrigan and William Ian Miller discuss.[14] Scorsese has used embarrassment before, most effectively in *Taxi Driver* during the now-famous shot in which Scorsese moves his camera away from the protagonist as he is getting rejected on the phone, unable or unwilling to watch the humiliation.

Figure 5.1. *The King of Comedy* (Martin Scorsese, 1983), a rare moment of expressionism within an otherwise blank (or mature) style.

In *The King of Comedy*, however, Scorsese stays and watches, forcing the viewer to witness a multitude of embarrassing situations. Scorsese is using the emotion of embarrassment as an assault or attack on the audience, in much the same way as the violence of his earlier films assaulted the viewer. But this emotion is even more of a confrontation with the spectator than violence. In *Taxi Driver*, Scorsese moved away from Travis Bickle's embarrassment, not his violence. The film was a box-office success, partly, as Robert Ray argues, because it was able to appeal to the "naïve" audience, who could read the film as another in the *Death Wish* (Michael Winner, 1974) cycle of vigilante films.[15] With *The King of Comedy*, this "double" reading is not really possible, leading to its commercial failure. It is impossible because embarrassment, as opposed to the spectacle of violence, is not something an audience looking for traditional Hollywood entertainment wants to experience.

It is, however, an emotion common to many of the films of the American Independent Cinema movement. Many of these auteurs, from Alexander Payne to Wes Anderson to Neil LaBute, seem to deliberately construct moments in which the audience may cringe and even turn away while watching their films. The master of this type of comedy (if that is even the appropriate term) is Todd Solondz, whose work is designed to produce discomfort: "Solondz makes feel-bad films. In the indie coal mine, Solondz is the canary. So long as someone whose voice is as dystopian as his can continue to be heard, there's still hope."[16] His first film to receive a wide distribution, *Welcome to the Dollhouse*, presents the various humiliations of an unpopular junior high school student, shown in a blank, matter-of-fact style that adds to the disturbance. Solondz takes this to an extreme in his next film, *Happiness*, which most critics consider his masterpiece to date. Not only does Solondz deal with issues such as pedophilia, he also films this pedophiliac relationship using the most conventional of cinematic techniques.[17] Because of the importance of this ironic tone that puts audience discomfort at the core of the viewing experience, Solondz and many others of the indie movement are difficult filmmakers to discuss and appreciate in purely formalist terms. Their films need to be placed relationally within the culture because so much of their impact relies on an oppositional sensibility rather than an obviously oppositional style.

This tone helps define this "smart aesthetic" that emerges from indie films. "The new smart cinema has for the most part re-embraced classical narrative strategies, instead experimenting with *tone* as a means of critiquing 'bourgeois' taste and culture."[18] Crucial to this tone is the notion of irony, of a distance from characters and events that expresses itself as stylistically distinct from the New Hollywood:

Figure 5.2. *Taxi Driver* (Martin Scorsese, 1976), Scorsese looks away from the lead character's rejection.

A centerpiece of the 1990s smart film might best be termed 'blank' style . . . a series of stylistic choices mobilized to signify dispassion, disengagement and disinterest. Often this stylistic strategy is manifested most basically through framing and editing patterns. Surveying these films, one cannot help but be struck by the frequent (even dominant) use of long-shots, static composition and sparse

Figure 5.3. *The King of Comedy* (Martin Scorsese, 1983), Scorsese stays and watches the humiliation.

cutting. Vibrant editing and camera movement, so pivotal to 1970s American art cinema, would seem to have been usurped in 1990s smart cinema by a preference for static mise-en-scène and longer shot lengths.[19]

This lack of "vibrancy" is precisely what many felt *The King of Comedy* was missing when it first appeared on the cultural scene; retrospectively, however, the film is a key transitional text, marking a move away from the stylistic cinematic excess of the New Hollywood Renaissance toward the greater minimalism of the independent movement.

At the most obvious level, *The King of Comedy* has grown in reputation as its vision of the madness of America's obsession with celebrity has seemed less like an exaggeration and more like a reality, not unlike that of another noted satire of television, *Network* (Sidney Lumet, 1976), although it lacks this film's histrionics. It has also benefited from its oppositional relationship with the growing development of high concept style, which connected the products of the New Hollywood art cinema with a disreputable and critically disparaged style. This can be seen as influencing independent filmmakers toward a more "blank," ironic approach as a means of differentiating themselves.

The shifting nature of cinematic style and the notion of art during this period of transition are both evident in the following comments Scorsese made about the film:

> When it [*The King of Comedy*] was shown on the first night at the Cannes Festival, I went backstage with Sergio Leone and he looked at me and said, "Martin, that's your most mature film." I don't know if it was his way of saying he didn't like it. I guess that comes to mind because over the years my friends and I have had a running joke about slow movies, where the camera doesn't move, as being "mature." I read in the *Village Voice* that Jim Jarmusch, who made *Stranger than Paradise* and *Down by Law* said something like, "I'm not interested in taking people by the hair and telling them where to look." Well, I *do* want them to see the way I see. Walking down the street, looking quickly about, tracking, panning, zooming, cutting and all that sort of thing. I like it when two images go together and they move. I guess it may not be considered "mature," but I enjoy it.[20]

These comments are compelling for several reasons. First, the fact that Leone, hardly the most subdued filmmaker, praises the film along these lines points to a certain movement within the cultural field away from the expressionist impulse of 1960s and 1970s art cinema. Second, this shift can be seen personified in the figure of Jarmusch, one of the first indie directors and the one closest to defining a new ironic, postmodern indie sensibility that would eventually emerge. Finally, and most importantly, Scorsese's comments link *The King of Comedy* to this new style while also noting how different he normally is as a filmmaker from the movement as a whole. In terms of position taking, Scorsese has aligned himself with the New Hollywood style, thus leaving *The King of Comedy* in a state of limbo, neither in the style of the New Hollywood but also not made by an independent director. This accounts for the film's original neglect as well as its reconsideration once independent cinema had defined its own position against that of the high concept Hollywood style. As Sconce argues, "The choice to trade in blank irony—a move made by so many filmmakers in the 1990s—exemplifies Pierre Bourdieu's concept of 'position-taking,' a means of distinguishing one's work in relation to a larger aesthetic and cultural field of production. For 'smart' cinema to exist, after all, someone or something else must be perceived and portrayed as 'stupid,' a demarcation that can understandably lead to conflict."[21] The advantage current films entering this marketplace have is that this position has been defined and its audience now well established if still marginal. The films are occasionally controversial, but they nevertheless can find an audience and even use this controversy within the marketplace. There is cultural conflict, but that conflict has now been structured into both the text and the marketing of these movies. It is also mitigated, as Sconce notes, by the popularity of this sensibility on television with such programs as *Beavis and Butthead* (1992–1997), *Seinfeld* (1989–1999), and *The Simpsons* (1989–).[22]

The conflict these ironic films and television shows created resulted in the culture wars of the 1990s in which works made in this ironic style were heavily criticized for a moral relativism. This echoes the response to *The King of Comedy* by Pauline Kael, who felt the film was a sick joke by Scorsese on his own experience with *Taxi Driver* and the resulting assassination attempt on President Ronald Reagan in 1981 by John Hinckley.[23] This added context of the film being in possible bad taste added to the film's level of discomfort, especially because the film subjects this material to comedy. For a recent example, one can cite Gilbert Gottfried's joke about the tragedy of 9/11 a few months after the events, in which an audience member shouts "too soon" after Gottfried's intentionally distasteful remark, "My flight made an unexpected stop at the Empire State Building." In fact, as Sconce notes, many commentators cited 9/11 as the end of the age of irony that so characterized the 1990s. In the case of *The King of Comedy*, taking place at the outset of the conservative 1980s, the age of irony had not yet begun.

Sconce notes two major themes running through smart cinema: "interpersonal alienation within the white middle class (usually focused on the family) and alienation within contemporary consumer culture,"[24] which are also the major points of emphasis in *The King of Comedy*. Robin Wood wrote an extensive analysis of the film's use of irony as a critique of the family and its repressiveness and has related this to the film's alternative vision in comparison to the mainstream of American film.[25] As Wood argued, *The King of Comedy* succinctly combined the two dominant themes of 1990s indie cinema: the film exposed the banality of both the middle-class family and the media culture in which the simulacrum of identity counts for more than reality. But it was also one of the only films to question the dominant values of what Andrew Britton, writing in 1986, dubbed "Reaganite entertainment."[26] By the 1990s an independent cinema sensibility emerged precisely because of the conventionality of Hollywood at this period in history. Without a space available within this system, unconventional films moved into the low-budget Independent arena. The aesthetic changes from a heightened expressionism to a blank irony were not only because of budgetary concerns, but were also a reaction to the coopting of art cinema techniques by the market-driven stylistic of high concept. *The King of Comedy* predated and anticipated these changes; thus, although it remains a stylistic anomaly in Scorsese's career, the film was a part of a cultural shift in contemporary art cinema. The film remains an important signpost for the future as well as a commentary on the movies of its time.

Unlike Scorsese's earlier films, by the time of *The King of Comedy* there was no longer an American film culture that encouraged or even allowed for challenging work. As a result, *The King of Comedy* offered no sense of aesthetic release: the audience was not only trapped with obnoxious, unappealing, and empty characters, it was also given a style that turns the motion picture into a television screen. One almost expects the final credit to read, like Jean-Luc Godard's *Weekend* (1967), "Fin du Cinéma." This sense of American cinema's dead end was borne out by Scorsese's following films, *After Hours* and *The Color of Money*. To return to the quote from Scorsese that begins this section, the "we" that could not go any further at that time was not only himself and his collaborators, but the New Hollywood as well. At the same time, while *The King of Comedy* might have represented an "anomaly" and a "dead end" for Scorsese personally, it also represented a new "departure" for American cinema as well, a departure that would be explored fully with the rise of the American independent film movement.

Scorsese and New Technology

Scorsese's relationship with American Independent Cinema is a micro-cosm for his other interactions with postmodern culture. Scorsese not only has clear affinities with American indie filmmakers, but he also needs to make himself distinct from them and align himself with the previous modernist Golden Age of the New Hollywood. This is similar to Scorsese's relationship with technological changes in the film industry. Scorsese's attitude to the various media through which cinema circulates shifted as his career progressed. In fact, examining Scorsese's relationship to technology can be causally explained by his particular status within the industry at various historical moments, up to and including his use of 3-D in 2011's *Hugo*.

Scorsese is often regarded as a cinema purist, someone with a pas-sion for the medium of celluloid film. This is juxtaposed with others of his generation, such as Francis Ford Coppola and George Lucas, who are more associated with the rise of digital technology. Scorsese is seen as someone who still cares passionately about the "film as film,"[27] and this can be traced to his campaign for color preservation in the early 1980s and his growing reputation as an obsessive cinephile constantly screen-ing the masterpieces of the past. Scorsese's films seemed to support this reading with their many references to the materiality of the cinematic image: the opening credits of *Mean Streets* with its home movie projector; the obsessive cinema-going of Charlie in *Mean Streets* and Travis in *Taxi Driver*; the Classical Hollywood homage of *Alice Doesn't Live Here Any-more* (shot in the old Academy ratio of 1.37:1, as opposed to the 1.85:1 ratio of the rest of the film); the musical *New York, New York*, with its deliberately artificial look (and a film Scorsese also wanted to shoot in the old academy ratio); and *Raging Bull*, with both its black-and-white cinematography and color 8mm home movie footage (which Scorsese deliberately scratched and faded to suggest decay). When Scorsese did deal with television with *The King of Comedy*, it was in the form of a satirical critique of the medium. Of all the filmmakers of his generation, Scorsese has associated himself most with cinema as a specific form, and this has been an important influence on his growing reputation.

However, other technologies have played a huge factor in Scors-ese's moviemaking and in his extrafilmic activity. Scorsese has stated that he consciously avoided the widescreen format during the 1980s because he knew the films would be "panned and scanned" (the image reduced for the 4:3 aspect ratio of television screens) for video and television.[28] Scorsese thus acknowledged that films no longer circulated exclusively or even primarily in movie theatres. Scorsese switched to the widescreen aspect ratio (2.35:1) in 1991 for *Cape Fear*. Scorsese argued that widescreen television technology was imminent and would make panning and scanning less of a problem, and that laser disc players would allow home viewers the opportunity to watch the films in the correct format. Scorsese was mistaken by about a decade in how long this transition to widescreen televisions and video formats would take. Whether this was the only reason for Scorsese's decision is also debatable. By 1991 Scorsese returned to big-budget Hollywood films. An action thriller such as *Cape Fear* is typically shot in the widescreen format, and any resistance Scorsese made to this may well have caused problems with Universal Studios, which supported Scorsese on *The Last Temptation of Christ*. Furthermore, Scorsese would make historical films for most of the next decade and would have had trouble securing the funding needed if he had insisted on not using widescreen. Scorsese justified this decision by turning his attention toward home video technology as a complement to his advocacy of the medium of celluloid.

The same year that Scorsese switched to widescreen filmmaking with 1991's *Cape Fear*, he participated in the laser disc releases of *Taxi Driver* and *Raging Bull*. Scorsese recorded an audio commentary for both films and each disc included a wealth of "supplementary material." This was still an unusual phenomenon within the mainstream industry at the time, leading to an *Entertainment Weekly* article that included an interview with Scorsese in which he calls tape "antiquated."[29] Steve Daly's piece on the two films amounts to an advertisement for the laser disc format, and the choice of Scorsese as the figure to promote this was another demonstration of Scorsese's unique position. Scorsese's films were familiar enough with mainstream audiences for a popular entertainment magazine to use them as an example. The Criterion Collection at that time released many critically acclaimed films, but none with the mainstream crossover appeal of a figure like Scorsese (the article even mentioned that Scorsese was shooting the remake of *Cape Fear* at the time). But Scorsese's prestige was such that the laser disc format could still be promoted as an elite technology aimed at serious fans of the cinema. Scorsese himself argued that the laser discs are "an invaluable tool for learning"[30] due to the amount of supplementary material provided, citing the Criterion Collection's *The Magnificent Ambersons* as an exemplar. But *The Magnificent Ambersons* was an example of an academic approach to a classic film that had little chance of crossing over into the mainstream.[31] The Criterion versions of *Taxi Driver* and *Raging Bull* were very different and have all the material that would eventually become standard on today's DVD editions: audio commentary with the director and other members of the creative team; storyboards of sequences; shooting scripts; and interviews with individuals involved with the production.

Also prefiguring DVD is the way in which these Scorsese laser discs are offered as something more than a lesser reproduction of the original cinematic experience. With videotape and the programming of movies on television or cable, one could always argue that one was watching something different or inferior to the filmic event. Home technology was more convenient, but even casual viewers would not argue that it was superior in any other way. By contrast, the Criterion home video releases of *Taxi Driver* and *Raging Bull* offer something different that, as Steve Daly maintains, can be seen as superior to the experience of a theatrical rerelease: "Each of these laser discs offers a more richly rewarding way to watch and re-watch Scorsese's work than any theatrical reissue could. By lending his voice and archival materials to Voyager's efforts and convincing several key collaborators to contribute as well, Scorsese has helped transform two movies about violent, unsympathetic characters into engaging, thought-provoking, and intensely pleasurable experiences."[32] The rhetoric here moved away from looking at home video as an inferior technology to cinema and signaled the move toward a new kind of "home film culture."[33] Earlier I discussed the emergence of what Barbara Klinger dubbed the "hardware aesthetic" in which films become valued for their capacity to fully display home theatre technology. This has become more prominent as DVD has become more widespread and can be seen in the DVD release of *Raging Bull*, as mentioned in chapter 3. But Scorsese generally was used to promote a different home video culture that focused both on technological improvement and cultural prestige.

Klinger used the term "new media aristocrats" to describe the transformation of a low-brow technology like television into the high-brow idea of "home theater." As Klinger states, "public discourse on home theater define its machines of reproduction as possessing special qualities that bestow 'titles of cultural nobility' on the viewers who use them."[34] This takes place at multiple levels involving both economic and cultural capital, and these levels merge effectively with a figure like Scorsese. As early as 1988, Scorsese's cultural prestige was used in advertisements for high-end home theater equipment. The advertisement for Mitsubishi, "Martin Scorsese on Television," began by establishing Scorsese's reputation as an artist: "Martin Scorsese is challenging. Like his pictures."[35] The advertisement then focuses on Scorsese's preservation efforts, using Scorsese's quotes on preservation he first made during the color campaign against Kodak. This idea of preservation was linked to television as a medium. Scorsese is quoted:

I have TV on all the time, in every room. I have a library, American directors, obscure films, maybe 4,000 titles. It appears that my own films may have more of life on home video than in the theater. This means that composition, lighting, size of people in the frame will be affected, as will the choice of black and white or color, mono or stereo. You have to be sure what you want to say will have as full an impact on the small screen as on the big screen.

Scorsese's role as a preserver and his role as a collector were transferred from the medium of cinema to the medium of television as an attempt to increase the cultural prestige of the later. Mitsubishi used this as a means of promoting its ability to convert the cinematic vision of great directors to the small screen: "The cinematic visions of filmmakers like Martin Scorsese challenge the manufacturer to offer video equipment capable of capturing the totality of their art in all its subtlety and nuance. Mitsubishi accepts that challenge." The discourse here is similar to marketing the Criterion laser discs, and using Scorsese to fulfill this role shows what Scorsese had already come to represent by 1988: the Hollywood director most associated with film art, and thus ironically an icon with a niche marketability.

Not surprisingly, this made Scorsese a key figure in the promotion of movie cable channels, including classical movie channels like TCM and AMC. Scorsese also actively joined the advisory board for IFC and was featured on a prominent advertisement for the channel with the tagline, "He defined new cinema. Now he's shaping new television." Scorsese ended up playing a prominent role in IFC's attempt to promote itself. He wrote a letter to "film enthusiasts" in New York City encouraging people to call or write Time Warner and request that IFC be included in its cable package. This included writing to cultural institutions to which Scorsese was affiliated, such as MoMA.[36] The very existence of channels like TCM, AMC, and IFC emphasizes the interdependent relationship of film as a medium to other technology that both enables and threatens its survival. Scorsese's iconicity served these particular channels so well because he remained a director associated with the film medium through his preservation efforts and his role as a film historian. Recall, however, the opening of *My Voyage to Italy* as an important reminder of how film culture has always had an intimate connection to the private sphere. Scorsese first sees the masterpieces of Italian neorealism on television. After the opening credits, the film opens with a shot of a television and Scorsese stating, "This is a sixteen-inch Victor television set." Scorsese then describes the experience of seeing the films in this home environment. He emphasizes the inferior quality, but argues that this did not completely dull the impact. Instead they acted as an incentive to see more of the films. He also describes the viewing circumstances, in which many members of the family and the community would gather around the single television set and watch these films from the old country. The private and the public were thus intertwined. What these examples show is that Scorsese's relationship to new technology, like his relationship to Hollywood, is contradictory. Just as Scorsese has a reputation for being outside of the Hollywood system, he is likewise seen as being devoted to the celluloid tradition. In truth, Scorsese needed to remain a Hollywood filmmaker in order to maintain his critical reputation (with delicate negotiation of course). And his devotion to film as a medium entails being interested and concerned with home film cultures that so define how films are mass distributed in today's world.

In 2007 Scorsese began an association with the digital movie supplier Direct TV by writing a column for its magazine and website.[37] Scorsese's introduction to the feature offered a justification for the digital service while paradoxically reinforcing his commitment to the medium of film: "I love movies. That's why I wanted to write this column. I also love to see them presented as well as possible. Obviously, there's no substitute for a good 35mm print, but the reality is that most people don't have access to the archives, museums and film societies in the major cities that show them." Digital services like Direct TV offer a viable substitute by presenting the films "under the best possible conditions." This includes digital remastering, the correct aspect ratio, a clean soundtrack, and no commercials. The column, titled "The Scorsese Selection," consists of Scorsese choosing a film to recommend to Direct TV suppliers. Scorsese began by choosing four films for appreciation: *Colorado Territory* (Raoul Walsh, 1949), *The Asphalt Jungle* (John Huston, 1950), *The Shining* (Stanley Kubrick, 1980), and *Sweet and Lowdown* (Woody Allen, 1999). Two of these films are from the era of Classical Hollywood that Scorsese has covered in his documentary, but two are more recent films by directors who are Scorsese's contemporaries. What these brief critiques show is how Scorsese used his cultural prestige and his interest in new ways in which film is disseminated not only to become a film historian but also a film critic. Like his dual role as filmmaker-archivist, Scorsese's current position in the culture as artist-critic presents him with a rare amount of power over the field.

Scorsese as Film Critic

Scorsese's work as a film historian culminated with his two documentaries on American and Italian cinema, both of which downplay their evaluative aspects in favor of historical perspective. Nevertheless, they are examples of Scorsese's increasing role as a film critic in which he displays not only his knowledge of film history but also his ability to discuss aesthetics in an intellectually respectable manner. His cinema histories were collaborations with noted film critics. In *A Personal Journey with Martin Scorsese through American Movies* he worked with the long-time critic for *Positif,* Michael Henry Wilson (formerly Michael Henry), and *My Voyage to Italy* was cowritten with the prominent critic Kent Jones (with whom Scorsese would often work in the coming decade). These critics positioned these histories as more than a simple retelling of historical content. Rather, these documentaries are highly interpretative readings of both individual films as well as these two national cinemas as a whole. This lead to Scorsese being taken seriously as a critical authority, which raises issues because of his simultaneous position as an active filmmaker and film critic. One way Scorsese negotiates this conflict is to avoid being critical of films. His role is rather to offer appreciation of films and filmmakers, especially the cinema of the past. Nevertheless, Scorsese inserts his voice into the contemporary film scene as well as debates within film criticism.

The notion of the "guilty pleasure" has now become a commonplace idea in film culture, but the film journal *Film Comment* initiated it as a concept in 1978. Long-time Scorsese enthusiast Roger Ebert wrote the first "Guilty Pleasures" piece published in the journal.[38] Scorsese wrote the second,[39] which can be seen as a prequel to Scorsese's American cinema documentary as well as his preservation work. He begins stating, "This is a film lover's list," thus establishing that he is arguing not for culturally reputable films but rather for movies that he loves. He admits that some of the films are "bad," such as *The Silver Chalice* (Victor Saville, 1954), but nevertheless have some aspect that recommends them (for *The Silver Chalice* it is the work of Boris Leven, whom Scorsese hired for *New York, New York*). Often, Scorsese links these movies to his own. He concludes by discussing the obscure film *The Magic Box* (John Boulting, 1951) in relation to its influence on him as a director: "It was *the* film that taught me a lot about the magic of movies. . . . When you're eight years old, it makes you want to be a filmmaker."[40] Scorsese as critic is, like in his American cinema documentary but even more blatantly, placing his own films as the central organizing principle. But he is also aligning himself with films outside of the critical establishment, often made within the Hollywood genre system or on the fringes of independent B film production. In terms of film preservation, it foreshadows Scorsese's contention in his "Outline for a Preservation Strategy" that film preservation cannot have "value judgments" because great movies of the past are not always immediately recognized. Coming in the late 1970s, Scorsese's critical stance is echoing many of the developments of the previous decade, especially the attempt to collapse the boundaries between high and low taste distinctions. The place of Scorsese himself as a great filmmaker is nevertheless a central concern of the piece.

In 1984 Scorsese contributed a short piece on director David Cronenberg.[41] Scorsese began his essay by describing the context of seeing Cronenberg's first feature film, *Shivers* (1975), at the opening of the 1975 Edinburgh Film Festival. Scorsese recalls his initial hesitation about the screening: "I never look forward to opening nights at film festivals. They're like fund-raising rallies, and the movies they show on those occasions usually have titles like 'How Tasty Was My Little Frenchman.' They're usually movies that almost everyone can like, at least a little bit."[42] In other words, for Scorsese, most festivals include films that are middle-brow in their aim and Cronenberg's film is the low-brow cult horror antidote to this good taste. He follows this by comparing Cronenberg to high-art icons: "Cronenberg's best movies still have the capacity to cause a Jungian culture shock. They're like Buñuel, or Francis Bacon: wit and trauma, savagery and pity."[43] The comparison of Cronenberg with Bacon recalls Michael Powell's comparison of Scorsese to Goya. In both cases, a more critically established director attempts to legitimate the work of a director working in a violent and disreputable genre (the horror film for Cronenberg, the crime film for Scorsese) by comparing him to a great artist (specifically, an artist from the field of painting, a more legitimate and established art than film). By this point, Scorsese was becoming familiar and comfortable with the discourse of artistic criticism and how to position himself and his tastes within it.

In 1987 the popular film magazine *Premiere* asked Scorsese to contribute his home viewing recommendations. In this context, Scorsese avoids more mainstream and contemporary films and selects three films that had acquired a great deal of cultural prestige over the preceding decades: *Citizen Kane*, *The Searchers*, and *The Red Shoes* (Michael Powell and Emeric Pressburger, 1948). A decade earlier, in the more respected film journal *Film Comment*, Scorsese made a point of avoiding the canon. Here, with a less cinema-literate readership, Scorsese introduced the masterpieces of the past to a larger audience. There is also the differing context of Scorsese's career. In 1978 Scorsese was near the height of his artistic reputation, coming off his previous critical success of *Taxi Driver*. Not needing to establish his high-art credentials, Scorsese could write about "guilty pleasures" at this time to show his enthusiasm for popular cinema. By 1987 Scorsese was rebuilding his commercial career and had just made his most mainstream project, *The Color of Money*. By discussing classics made such as *Citizen Kane*, *The Searchers*, and *The Red Shoes*, all made within studio filmmaking, Scorsese tried to position his own career as a Hollywood director. The introduction to the article made this link explicit: "The characters that populate Martin Scorsese's movies (*Mean Streets, Taxi Driver, Raging Bull, The Color of Money*) are bombs waiting to go off, and they frequently do, erupting with a torrent of emotion. Each of the movies Scorsese recommends for home-viewing focus on characters who are driven by their passions."[44]

As Scorsese moves back into Hollywood and has to make concessions to commercial interests to do so, his work as a film critic aims at reconciling the tension between art and entertainment.

After director John Cassavetes's death in 1989, Scorsese wrote a tribute piece that was also a work of art appreciation and taste distinction. The brief article included the familiar discussion of Cassavetes as an "independent" filmmaker and shared stories from Scorsese's personal history. Not surprisingly, he recalled Cassavetes encouraging him to abandon genre filmmaking following *Boxcar Bertha* and pursue more personal projects. But Scorsese also defined what he believes an independent filmmaker to be: "The question, 'What is an independent filmmaker?' has nothing to do with being inside or outside the industry or whether you live in New York or Los Angeles. It's about determination and strength, having the passion to say something that's so strong that no one or nothing can stop you."[45] This definition was obviously self-serving for Scorsese, designating "independent" in aesthetic rather than industrial terms. It also foretold the eventual fate of "independent" cinema over the course of the next decade. Increasingly, definitions of "independent" cinema had less connection to industrial conditions. This peaked in 1994, the year in which *Pulp Fiction* becomes a blockbuster success for Miramax. This turns "independent" filmmaking into a bigger business venture that involves more capital investment from studios. Independent studios frequently became a subsidiary of larger studios and removed any actual financial independence from many of the independent films in circulation.[46] As a result, the meaning of an independent film shifted to matters of textual differences from Hollywood, and these textual differences could be argued and debated according to more subjective criteria. Thus a filmmaker like Scorsese, despite his big-budget studio filmmaking, could be claimed as continuing to have an independent sensibility. It is important to note the context of this article, written in 1989, shortly after controversy over *The Last Temptation of Christ*. When Scorsese wrote about having "determination and strength" and "the passion to say something that's so strong that no one or nothing can stop you," the connotations are about himself as much as Cassavetes.

Scorsese's film histories showed the influence of his background in the discourse of film criticism and canon formation, and his film criticism is no different. Many of his pieces emphasize spiritual and transcendent concerns similar to the auteurist approach. On the occasion of a Fellini retrospective at the Film Forum in New York, Scorsese wrote an appreciation piece in the *New York Times* Film section. The title of the article, "Amid Clowns and Brutes Fellini Found the Divine," indicates the direction of Scorsese's criticism, in which he emphasizes Fellini's uniqueness and spirituality: "By the early 50's neorealism had become a noun, codified and limited in scope, if not in style. Most of all, Marxist critics had politicized it. By contrast, Fellini's autobiographical, spiritual and magical world did not fit easily into an ideology or code."[47] In order to praise Fellini's artistry, Scorsese contrasts him with the limitations of neorealism ideology as "codified" by "Marxist critics." Scorsese clearly sees this as an appropriation of the films by ideological critics, not something that is inherent in the "style" of the films. Scorsese's brief analysis of Roberto Rossellini's *Europa '51* shows an interpretation of neorealist style very much at odds with the Marxist approach. Scorsese writes:

> *Europa '51* is a picture of almost no style. Every aspect of Rossellini's artistry is at the service of exploring this question of modern sainthood. As Ingrid Bergman's Irene goes step by step on her journey to a life of selfless devotion—from the death of her child, to a need to reach out and help others, to an ideological and then on to a spiritual commitment—Rossellini's calm concentration, the sense that he's merely (but always closely) observing this woman and the people around her, never wavers.[48]

Scorsese's description of the character's journey, from ideological to spiritual commitment, implies a similar journey critics should take with regard to neorealism as a whole. The emphasis in Scorsese's work on Italian cinema focuses on the spiritual dimensions of the work and downplays the political.

A similar attention to spiritual concerns can be detected in Scorsese's critical introductions to the work of Jean Renoir, featured on the Criterion Collection DVDs of *The River* (1951) and *The Golden Coach* (1953). The fact that Scorsese chooses to discuss these particular Renoir texts, which are far less political in nature than his 1930s work, is telling. Scorsese discusses the aesthetic value of the films, particularly the use of color in *The River*, and he stresses the emotional impact of watching these cinematic experiences. Scorsese admits to not fully understanding Renoir's most political film, *The Rules of the Game* (1939), and thus chooses to concentrate on the work that he can more immediately understand. This strategy of stressing the emotional impact of foreign art cinema classics was present in his Italian cinema documentary as well.[49]

The idea is for the films to be seen as primarily aesthetic experiences that offer something unique to the viewer, but at the same time do not alienate the potential audience with discussions of politics and social context. This is not an "art for art's sake" argument, but it does prioritize aesthetic and spiritual readings that celebrate the auteur as a defining, even transcendental agent of meaning.

In addition to this mode of aesthetic justification, Scorsese was also familiar with the mode of ideological critique in his criticism. One example is an obituary written for actress and director Ida Lupino. Scorsese discusses Lupino's acting career but devoted more space to her accomplishments as a director. Scorsese makes a case for Lupino as a "pioneer" who made films critical of the typical middle-class patriarchy of the time: "Her heroines were young women whose middle-class security was shattered by trauma—unwanted pregnancy, polio, rape, bigamy, parental abuse. There's a sense of pain, panic and cruelty that colors every frame. In 'Outrage,' she portrayed rape not in melodramatic terms but in a cool behavioral study of evil in the most ordinary setting. . . . [F]ar in advance of the feminist movement, she challenged the passive, often decorative images of women then common in Hollywood."[50] This ideological justification for celebrating Lupino's work is a common characteristic of Scorsese's critical perspective on American film. It even extends to Scorsese's discussion of film actors Robert Mitchum and James Stewart. When both actors died within a day of each other in 1997 (July 1 and July 2, respectively), many articles were written celebrating their careers. Scorsese wrote an appreciation in *Premiere* magazine[51] that differed significantly from most other accounts, as James Cole Potter notes: "Scorsese's article focused on how both Stewart and Mitchum embodied aspects of postwar American malaise. For example, Scorsese's appreciation of Stewart leans more toward the actor's obsessive work with Anthony Mann than to his more optimistic films with Frank Capra. Scorsese seems to have used this opportunity to address *Premiere's* broad readership by offering some genuine sociological film history, rather than another in a series of tributes to Stewart's famously earnest star persona."[52] Borrowing from ideological work on directors like Anthony Mann and Alfred Hitchcock, as well as more general reconsiderations of postwar masculinity, Scorsese distinguishes his work from other journalistic accounts and reconfirms himself as an authority on film history.

Scorsese's more critical and academic approach to the analysis of cinema also serves to differentiate his work from other prestigious filmmaker-intellectuals within American culture. On July 30, 2007, both Michelangelo Antonioni and Ingmar Bergman, two of the most prestigious directors of European cinema, died. Five days later, film critic

Jonathan Rosenbaum published an opinion piece in the *New York Times* that provoked controversy by claiming Bergman's cinematic genius was below other true cinematic masters such as Antonioni.[53] A week later in the same newspaper, Scorsese wrote an appreciation of Antonioni, and Woody Allen, a defense of Bergman.[54] Scorsese's analysis of Antonioni, particularly the landmark film *L'Avventura* (1960), concentrated on Antonioni's stylistic "challenge" to the audience, arguing that "our attention was drawn away from the mechanics of the search, by the camera and the way it moved. You never knew where it was going to go, who or what it was going to follow." Scorsese's discussion of Antonioni seemed to align him with Rosenbaum's previous article on Bergman. Instead of concentrating on aspects of story, Scorsese concerned himself with the cinematic specificity of Antonioni's greatness rather than the theatrical storytelling skills that Rosenbaum claimed led to Bergman's prestige. Allen's appreciation of Bergman did not rebut Rosenbaum's claims but rather seemed to support them. Allen concentrated on Bergman's gifts as a storyteller and entertainer rather than his challenging of cinematic form. He devoted space to discussions of his friendship with Bergman and to descriptions of Bergman's personality. Allen's examination never moved beyond the surface of the typical memorial appreciation. Scorsese limits his personal comments to a short paragraph about a dinner he had with Antonioni, and the rest of his article describes Antonioni's filmmaking and the "possibilities" it opened. Scorsese concludes stating, "it was his images that I knew, much better than the man himself. Images that continue to haunt me, inspire me. To expand my sense of what it is to be alive in the world." Through their respective associations with two past directors, Scorsese and Allen reconfirmed their place within American culture: Scorsese as the innovative cinematic genius, Allen as the talented writer-director who lacks distinction in regards to film form.

Scorsese's work as a film critic, like his interest in film history, plays an important role in how his work is received within the culture. An example of this can be seen in his remake of the Hong Kong film *Infernal Affairs* (Andy Lau and Alan Mak, 2002). Scorsese's well-known appreciation of all world cinema, including the films of East Asia, helped to mitigate the fact that this is Hollywood coopting another national cinema.[55] The rather typical Scorsese appreciation of world cinema also served as a justification for the Hollywood remake. Scorsese was not simply a Hollywood director stealing from Hong Kong cinema, but rather a great artist reworking and reinterpreting a cinema that he appreciates and respects. Furthermore, given the amount of influence that Scorsese has had on directors such as John Woo and Wong Kar-Wai, *The Departed* is positioned as Scorsese going back to his filmmaking roots rather than pillaging world cinema to further his own reputation. Scorsese's status as respected film intellectual allows any negative criticism of cultural imperialism common in the discourse on Hollywood remakes of foreign films to be downplayed.[56] Film criticism has provided Scorsese with another method of mediating his reception in the cultural field.

Scorsese as Cultural Historian

Scorsese's emergence as a film critic was one further activity related to his emergence as a film historian. In the opposite direction, Scorsese emerged as a cultural historian beyond the realm of filmmaking. Like his other cultural activities, this role as cultural historian did not emerge suddenly. It has a genealogy that can be traced to previous projects and also has to be considered in relation to Scorsese's status within the Hollywood industry over the past decades. The most obvious and extensive field that Scorsese has expanded into is music, making numerous documentaries on the history of both genres and individuals. In 2003, Scorsese produced the seven-part series *The Blues* for PBS, directing the first episode, "Feel Like Going Home," himself. The documentary *No Direction Home: Bob Dylan* (2005), the Rolling Stones' concert film *Shine a Light* (2008), and *George Harrison: Living in the Material World* followed. Scorsese's connections to popular music can be traced to his first films made at NYU. This includes the soundtrack for his first feature, *Who's That Knocking at My Door*, as well as his avant-garde short *The Big Shave* and his decision to use rock music to score the collective student documentary *Street Scenes 1970*. Scorsese played an important creative role as editor of the seminal *Woodstock*, and continued this interest in using popular music rather than a traditional score in *Mean Streets* and even, to a lesser extent, with his first mainstream Hollywood product, *Alice Doesn't Live Here Anymore*. In 1978 Scorsese made his first documentary about rock and roll, *The Last Waltz*, which as its title suggests was self-consciously designed to be an elegy for that period. While *The Last Waltz* was to a great extent a concert film, it was also a work of cultural history with a very specific image-making agenda.

In relation to Scorsese's own image, *The Last Waltz* is an important text. Two details about the shooting of the film illuminate two aspects of Scorsese's persona that were established in this time period and which remain prominent in his biographical legend today. First, unlike most other concert films that came before it, *The Last Waltz* featured a polished and professional look. Scorsese created elaborate storyboards for each sequence and song number, producing a concert film that had many of the aesthetics of a Hollywood feature rather than a low-budget documentary. Scorsese's artistry as a director is thus still very much on display, even in a documentary project. Second, Scorsese made this film while still completing postproduction on his big-budget Hollywood musical, *New York, New York*. The very act of taking on this project was seen as an irresponsible act by an egocentric director, and would hurt Scorsese's reputation within Hollywood for years to come. But the decision to make *The Last Waltz* also shaped Scorsese's image as a risk-taker, a passionate artist determined to make the films he wanted despite working under studio control. With the publication of Peter Biskind's *Easy Riders, Raging Bulls* in 1998, Scorsese's extensive drug use during this period was documented and linked particularly to his irrational decision to make *The Last Waltz* before completing his studio project. Metaphorically, this associated Scorsese with the "sex, drugs and rock and roll" lifestyle the interviews with members of The Band detailed throughout the documentary. Although this certainly affected Scorsese negatively at the time within the industry, by 1998 it was ironically beneficial to his reputation as a romantic artist. Despite the fact that Scorsese was now firmly entrenched as a Hollywood director and respected elder statesman, tales of his previous days as a tortured rebel genius allowed the myth of his "outsider" status to continue unabated.

The Last Waltz as a documentary appears to be about the idea of collectivity. The concert itself, of The Band's farewell concert, features several important rock musicians in guest appearances: Van Morrison, Neil Young, the Staple Singers, Bob Dylan, and others. The emphasis is on the communal aspect of rock music as represented by The Band as a seemingly anonymous collection of great musicians. But as Stephen E. Savern has argued, the documentary is very much an attempt to promote guitarist Robbie Robertson as the star figure of the collective. As Savern states, "*The Last Waltz* does not simply capture an event, it constructs one."[57] This construction is all about fostering the idea of the individual over that of the collective: "*The Last Waltz* represents an exercise in self-mythologizing—through the interviews with their distinctive camerawork and settings and the on-stage footage of the actual concert—for Robertson, and the deconstruction/destruction of the group as a whole."[58] Savern relates *The Last Waltz* forward to later films in Scorsese's career, seeing this as "his first exploration of the manner by which image may be manipulated."[59] For Savern, this thematic obsession would continue with later films such as *The King of Comedy*, *The Color of Money*, and *Casino*. While I agree with Savern's overall argument, I would add that *The Last Waltz* looks back as well as forward in Scorsese's career. Specifically, in its denial of the collective and concentration on the individual, the film looks back to Scorsese's involvement in his first documentary experience, *Street Scenes 1970*. The elimination of the collective in the earlier film was largely the consequence of entering the festival circuit in which the auteur was valued. Earlier Scorsese was the figure being manipulated, whereas with *The Last Waltz* Scorsese is in control of the process—at least at the level of production. The difference between the films is also one of exposure. With *The Last Waltz* the other members of The Band, notably Levon Helm, have been able to counter the representations Scorsese and Robertson put forth.[60] In contrast, *Street Scenes 1970* remains largely anonymous due to Scorsese's control over the film's accessibility. This is a part of Scorsese's growing prominence as a cultural historian. He not only makes culture but also has a voice in deciding what culture gets exposure.

Following his work in film history and preservation, we should not be surprised that Scorsese would turn his attention to music as a cultural form. As Bourdieu has argued, "Music is the 'pure' art par excellence. It says nothing and has *nothing to say*. . . . Music represents the most radical and most absolute form of the negation of the world, and especially the social world, which the bourgeois ethos tends to demand of all forms of art."[61] Bourdieu's arguments here refer primarily to classical music and its class associations. One can argue, however, that they do not apply to the context of American popular music, which is the cultural history Scorsese has been in the process of telling over the past decade. Arguing that musical genres such as folk, blues, and rock have no social meaning is difficult: On the contrary, this music seems impossible to comprehend without this social context, and Scorsese's series on *The Blues* and his documentary on Bob Dylan are not lacking in historical context. They reflect his general fixation on historical material that has obsessed even his feature film production. Bourdieu's comments on music as a "pure" art nevertheless apply to Scorsese's work on music culture. The notion of music's purity works to downplay the social as much as possible, and instead becomes one of the "countless variations on the soul of music and the music of the soul."[62]

Scorsese only directed one episode of the seven-part *The Blues*. The films include Scorsese's "Feel Like Going Home"; Wim Wenders's "The Soul of a Man"; Marc Levin's "Godfathers and Sons"; Mike Figgis's "Red, White and Blues"; Clint Eastwood's "Piano Blues"; Richard Pearce and Robert Kenner's "The Road to Memphis"; and Charles Burnett's "Warming by the Devil's Fire." Seeing all the films as identical in approach or arguing that the social dimension is always downplayed in praise of the spirituality of the blues would be unfair. Charles Burnett's film (the only one directed by an African American), for example, is a brilliant piece about the spiritual and physical contradiction many African Americans feel toward blues music. As Burnett explains, "I wanted to put the music in context, too. The blues came out of the South, and the South has its history of struggles, and it seemed to me you can't really separate the blues from their historical context: how people lived, the hardships they experienced, the texture of their daily lives—it was all related."[63] But Scorsese's "Feel Like Going Home" avoids any serious discussion of the social and political significance of the blues in favor of a familiar "origins" narrative of attempting to find genealogical roots. The social context remains on the surface and any discussion of politics is generally elided. For example, musician Willie King interprets the obsession with cruel women in the blues tradition as a metaphor for criticizing the white boss who mistreated African-American workers under Jim Crow laws. Other such instances can be found in the film, but they remain underdeveloped and subordinate to the main theme. Scorsese begins the film with his own voiceover stating, "I can't imagine my life or anyone else's without music. It's like a light in the darkness that never goes out." This is an illustration of the bourgeois attitude toward music that Bourdieu describes. Insensitivity to music is literally unimaginable. This commences Scorsese's search for the roots of this light, which is metaphorically linked to the birth of civilization itself through its eventual return to Africa.

Because the "home" and "roots" Scorsese is exploring are not his own, he makes the journey through an on-screen surrogate, the African-American musician Corey Harris. Throughout the film, Scorsese uses both his own and Harris's voice to weave a particular narrative out of this material. On closer inspection, this interweaving of voices is deliberate and rhetorical. After the opening discussion of music and the work of archivists John and Alan Lomax, Scorsese retreats and gives the narrative to Harris. Harris conducts all of the interviews and interactions in the film, both with blues musicians in the United States and musicians in Africa (Scorsese only appears on-screen very briefly in a group shot). The story becomes one of a personal journey, much like Scorsese's cinema histories, as he himself acknowledges: "I've made two documentaries on the history of cinema—one on American movies, then another on Italian cinema. And I decided early on that I wanted them to be personal, rather than strictly historical surveys. . . . For the blues series, I decided to do something similar."[64] The difference with the blues documentary is that it revolves around issues of authenticity. Scorsese is a filmmaker, an American, and has Italian heritage, all of which legitimate his voice in his cinema documentaries. With an African-American musical genre, Scorsese lacks this cultural sanction. Harris, as a young African-American blues musician, is required to fill this gap. Harris states at the beginning of the film that "to know your self [*sic*] you need to know the past," and the narrative becomes his movement through the history of blues music. Scorsese reinserts his voiceover when blues legends such as Robert Johnson are recalled, associating himself with their rebel genius. When the setting switches to Africa, Scorsese establishes the presence of African music in the blues, but then allows Harris's voice to continue the personal journey narrative line. Harris notes how "many people have gone to Africa searching for musical links with the blues" because Africa is "where everything began." This specific journey is ultimately at the service of a universalizing narrative. When Harris states "if you lose the past, you lose yourself." the message is intended to resonate beyond his particular situation and circumstance.

At the conclusion, Scorsese once again evokes John and Alan Lomax and their work as preservationists. Anyone familiar with Scorsese's work in the field of film preservation will note the obvious self-promotion at work here. Earlier in the film, Scorsese claims that John and Alan Lomax were performing "one of the most important things anyone can do. They were preserving the past before it disappeared completely." Scorsese sees himself operating in this same tradition. He also claims that Alan Lomax was interested in preserving all music, from all over the world. Again, this is at the service of a universalizing discourse made explicit at the conclusion of the film in a conversation between Corey

Figure 5.4. "Feel Like Going Home" (Martin Scorsese, 2003), Corey Harris as Scorsese surrogate.

Harris and Mali musician Ali Farka Toure. Discussing African Americans and Americans, Farka Toure argues, "our souls, our spirits are the same . . . there is no difference." The only difference he acknowledges is the commercial demands of America, the need to play to make a living. That this is the final conversation in the film is significant. It plays into another discourse around the blues that is related to the issue of cultural legitimacy. As Andrew Ross argues, "because of the fundamental contribution of Afro-American music to popular taste, any cultural historian of that relationship cannot avoid commenting on the ways in which a discourse about color ('whitened' music) is spliced with a discourse about commercialization ('alienated' music)."[65] Scorsese's film is no different. The idea of a "pure" music free of commercial interests that can be traced back to the "roots" is an important myth that structures the film's conclusion. Scorsese quotes Alan Lomax and his warning about preserving folk music: "When the whole world is bored with automated, mass distributed video music, our descendents will despise us for having thrown away the best of our culture." Mass culture is positioned here as inauthentic, echoing Theodor Adorno's account of the culture industry. This is a very modernist account and would seem contradictory coming from a Hollywood filmmaker such as Scorsese. But it is a very common strategy for Scorsese. Even as he moves further into high-budget filmmaking designed to appeal to as large an audience as possible, Scorsese simultaneously validates folk art and his quest to preserve it. This division between high art and mass culture is a false one, as even a cursory glance at the context of the documentary shows. In addition to airing on PBS, the series was packaged in a DVD box set and the music from the documentaries was released in several CD compilations. The modernist influence on cultural legitimacy, however, has never completely vanished, and Scorsese used it to maintain his symbolic capital even as he mediates his position within postmodern culture.

Scorsese's documentary on Bob Dylan, *No Direction Home*, focuses on Dylan's early career, ending with his last tour before his 1967 motorcycle accident. The film explores, through interviews with Dylan and many other contemporaries, the rise of Dylan as the most important political voice in the culture and Dylan's subsequent rejection of this label. It is a conventional work, using talking heads to offer viewers a history of the time period through one of its most important figures. Its main distinction, like in *The Blues* series, is the access Scorsese had to archival material. It is markedly different from every other Scorsese documentary in that Scorsese himself is almost entirely absent. In "Feel Like Going Home," Scorsese is forced to downplay his role and provide

Figure 5.5. "Feel Like Going Home" (Martin Scorsese, 2003), Alan Lomax as Scorsese parallel.

an appropriate surrogate in Corey Harris. In *No Direction Home*, the personal voice is given primarily to Dylan himself. Even while presenting other voices and perspectives, such as that of Joan Baez, the film accepts Dylan's position that he is primarily an artist and only secondarily a social being. This mythology is one Scorsese embraces, and the reason that Scorsese does not conduct the interviews with Dylan himself (Michael B. Borofsky produced and filmed the interviews in the film). Scorsese wants to position himself with Dylan, not as any type of an antagonist. At one point in the film, Dylan has the following exchange with the off-screen interviewer:

> Interviewer: What about the scene were you sick of?
>
> Dylan: People like you. [Laughs] You know, just being pressed and hammered and expected to answer questions. It's enough to make anyone sick really.

Scorsese clearly does not want to be in this position. Despite his role as cultural critic, Scorsese wants to align himself with Dylan, not with Dylan's critics.

Scorsese inserts his own voice into the film only once. In voiceover, Scorsese reads the speech Dylan gave on receiving Thomas Paine Freedom Award from the Emergency Civil Liberties Union. It reads as follows:

> I haven't got any guitar, but I can talk though. I want to thank you for the Tom Paine Award on behalf of everyone who went down to Cuba. First of all, because they were all young and it took me a long time to get young. And now I consider myself young and I am proud of it. I'm proud that I'm young. And I only wish that all of you people who are sitting out here tonight weren't here, and I could see all kinds of faces with hair on their head and everything like that, everything leading to youngness. Old people, when their hair grows out, they should go out. I look down to see the people who are governing me and making my rules and they haven't got any hair on their head. I get very uptight about it. There's no black and white, left and right to me anymore. There's only up and down, and down is very close to the ground, and I'm trying to go up, without thinking about anything trivial, such as politics.

This speech is given special importance in the film as one of the first signs of Dylan's rejection of the label of protest singer. Scorsese's use of his own voice at this point acts as an indicator, once again, of his sympathies for Dylan's rejection of politics in favor of art. Despite the presence of other more political artists in the film, the overall function is to support the rights of the artist above all other values.

A final area in which Scorsese's status as a cultural historian can be seen is in the publishing field. Like his work in film preservation, this takes a primarily symbolic form. When the Modern Library reissued a series of early film publications, Scorsese lent his name to the project. Like his "presentations" of restored films, Scorsese provided the right balance of artistic respectability and commercial potential. More intriguing is Scorsese's undertaking as "celebrity guest editor" of *Civilization*, the magazine of the Library of Congress. It is not surprising, given the amount of cultural prestige that Scorsese has amassed, that *Civilization* would choose Scorsese for this assignment. But it is notable that he was the first selection in the magazine's "guest-editor" project. The justification of Scorsese as celebrity guest editor is worth quoting:

> His fans have their own reasons for helping make him a celebrity. My own is that he's a model modern hero. I might say that he deserves celebrity for directing beautiful, unsettling movies that subvert our fondest assumptions about ourselves, yet leave us with some hope for redemption. But I'd like to claim for him something more—a

general sort of heroism, one that we must all strive for now as we leave (or are expelled from) one safe "traditonal" [*sic*] culture/home/occupation/job/style after another. Now we must all become what Scorsese is: a hero (an *auteur!*) of the experimental life.[66]

A close examination of this explanation reveals its lack of validity. However experimental Scorsese may have been at various points in his career, this has no relation to his celebrity status. Yet as logically incoherent as this paragraph may be, its argument is now familiar. Scorsese has been able to establish the discourse about his own career. Projects that would otherwise seem completely commercial in nature, such as the television episode he directs for Steven Spielberg's "Amazing Stories," are now regarded by commentators like Aldrich as proof of Scorsese's constant experimentation.

In his introduction to the issue, Scorsese explains that each article and subject "inevitably refers to the movies."[67] Despite choosing articles dealing with different areas of culture, the overall structuring principle is cinema. Scorsese argues that this is prompted by film's interdisciplinary character: "Cinema uses multiple artistic elements simultaneously. In each sequence of frames, there is movement, color, sound, performance. If it was film that led me to literature, history and the visual and performing arts, these elements brought me again to the movies—and expanded my horizons."[68] Beyond the subject of film, the real focus of the issue is Scorsese himself. Scorsese contributes a piece on religious art, which he relates to his own works, *The Last Temptation of Christ* and *Kundun*.[69] The subject of literature spotlights Herman Melville, recalling Scorsese's earlier dedication in *The Big Shave*. The discussion of history has Scorsese in conversation with historian Simon Schama about how they both "make history." A list of "Essential Italian Movies" foreshadows Scorsese's eventual documentary while working to perpetuate the canon. Political writer Garry Wills has an article on the antiwar film *All Quiet on the Western Front* (Lewis Milestone, 1930), but its focus is on the restoration of the film the Library of Congress undertook.[70] The film's ideology is mostly ignored. The more important point is the issue of film preservation and Scorsese's continuing devotion to this cause. Terry Teachout's analysis of Hitchcock's *North by Northwest* and its omission from the canon in favor of *Vertigo* makes the argument of aesthetics over politics most explicit.[71] The title of Teachout's brief appreciation, "The Genius of Pure Effect," is near parodic in its explicit rejection of any notion of the social in artistic evaluation. The overall design of the issue is marked by Scorsese's authorship as cultural historian. There is an admirable concern with history combined with a discourse that emphasizes the spiritual and purely artistic gaze.

"Has Martin Scorsese Gone Hollywood?" (Part Three): Cultural versus Economic Capital in Contemporary Hollywood

All of Scorsese's work as a cultural historian over the past decades has provided him with an enormous amount of cultural capital. This highbrow reputation as artistic genius allowed Scorsese to attempt to exchange some of this surplus symbolic capital in order to solidify his place economically within the industry. This took the form of Scorsese's continuous attempt to secure his first Academy Award for Best Director. This began with *Gangs of New York*, followed by *The Aviator*, and eventually to final success with *The Departed*. For a filmmaker such as Scorsese, an Academy Award is not needed to cement his reputation. On the contrary, with the lack of an Academy Award, he joined other previously acknowledged masters of American film: Stanley Kubrick, Alfred Hitchcock, and Orson Welles. In discussing Scorsese's lack of industry recognition circa 1996, actor Harvey Keitel stated, "Maybe he is getting what he deserves, exclusion from mediocrity."[72] Keitel's comment effectively summarizes the general attitude even those in the industry have toward the Academy Awards. Film critics and especially film scholars have learned to regard the Academy Awards with a great deal of suspicion as an evaluating body. The list of Academy Award winning directors who have little or no cultural prestige is enormous. Winners from the past three decades include: Ron Howard, Sam Mendes, James Cameron, Mel Gibson, Robert Zemeckis, Kevin Costner, Sydney Pollack, Richard Attenborough, Warren Beatty, and Robert Redford. That Scorsese himself lost the Best Director Award to two actors, Redford and Costner, has been consistently used as a reason why the Academy Awards lack taste distinction. The desire for Academy acceptance was Scorsese's attempt to fully solidify his place as a Hollywood insider. To achieve this, Scorsese willingly risked his reputation as an uncompromising artist.

The first film Scorsese directs that was widely perceived as an attempt to win a Best Director Oscar is *Gangs of New York*. Starring box-office star Leonardo DiCaprio and the highly respected Daniel Day-Lewis and based on a historical fiction about nineteenth-century New York, it seemed to have the necessary pedigree. In addition, Scorsese was working for the first time with producer Harvey Weinstein and Miramax. Weinstein had earned a reputation as a master lobbyist for his pictures, famously earning a Best Picture award for *Shakespeare in Love* (John Madden, 1998) over the heavily favored *Saving Private Ryan* (Steven Spielberg, 1998). However, the Oscar bid failed to work. The film's release was delayed more than a year after the events of September 11, 2001. *Gangs of New York* was now considered too sensitive a topic because it dealt with American tribal violence in New York City. The film also included a final dissolve to a modern New York skyline featuring the now fallen World Trade Center towers.[73] Over the course of the delay, rumors circulated that Scorsese and Weinstein were arguing over the length of the film, especially given that Weinstein had a reputation for taking control of a film away from a director and producing his own cut. When the film was finally released, the reviews were decidedly mixed. Major critics like J. Hoberman at the *Village Voice*, David Denby at the *New Yorker*, Stanley Kauffmann at the *New Republic*, and Jonathan Rosenbaum at the *Chicago Reader* were negative in their overall assessment.[74] This combined with a lukewarm box office (a $77 million domestic gross on an estimated $97 million budget)[75] to damage the film's Oscar chances. It lost the Best Picture award to *Chicago* (Rob Marshall, 2002) with Scorsese losing Best Director to Roman Polanski for *The Pianist* (2002). Most of the blame for the film's shortcomings was given to Weinstein. Despite Scorsese insisting he had final cut, the press continued to believe that there was dispute over the final form of the work. Peter Biskind, who had already made Scorsese the artistic hero of the Hollywood Renaissance in his book *Easy Riders, Raging Bulls*, argued that Weinstein had "humiliated" Scorsese by making him cooperate in the sabotaging of his own film.[76] Even the backlash for the perceived overhyping of Scorsese as Best Director was interpreted as Weinstein's usual underhanded marketing strategy. *Gangs of New York* may have failed, but Scorsese was able to escape with his reputation relatively undamaged. Weinstein had provided a convenient scapegoat for the commercial crassness of the enterprise.

Scorsese's next Oscar bid, *The Aviator*, was a more difficult film to position within the Scorsese canon. *Gangs of New York*, despite its flaws, was considered a personal film that Scorsese had been trying to make since the 1970s. *The Aviator*, despite its Hollywood connections and obsessive protagonist, was a far more commercial project. It was primarily a star vehicle and personal project for DiCaprio, who had an intense interest in the Howard Hughes story. Working with a prestigious director like Scorsese allowed DiCaprio to gain cultural capital that he desired as a "serious" actor. The association with DiCaprio was more problematic for Scorsese. It allowed him to make films on large budgets and become part of the Hollywood establishment, but it also took away from Scorsese's reputation as an uncompromising artist. Not since *Cape Fear* and *The Color of Money* had Scorsese delivered as conventional a film. As a bio-pic, a Hollywood subgenre that was always popular with Academy voters, *The Aviator* was utterly conventional. Unlike *Raging Bull*, Scorsese included an early scene with Hughes's mother that helped explain his behavior, not unlike most other biographical films. A similar scene occurs in *Ray* (Taylor Hackford, 2004), released the same year. In fact, *The Aviator* and *Ray* received almost identical reception from critics.[77] For a director like Scorsese to be received similarly to a purely commercial director like Hackford was evidence that his search for industry power had the potential to reduce his cultural prestige, which was one of his most marketable traits. His loss of the Academy Award in 2004 to Clint Eastwood was indicative of Scorsese's dilemma. Because Eastwood had always been firmly inside Hollywood as first a movie star and then an auteur, he could make "classical" (or conventional) films like *Million Dollar Baby* and receive nearly universal praise for his craftsmanship. Scorsese could not make the transition as easily. Having built his reputation on his outsider status, Scorsese risked being labeled as merely conventional for making films in a style similar to Eastwood and other Hollywood directors. To argue that *Million Dollar Baby* is simply a greater film than *The Aviator* is to ignore the contingencies of reception, especially as they revolve around the figure of the auteur.

With his next feature film, *The Departed*, Scorsese was finally able to win the Academy Award and enter into the inside of Hollywood. *The Departed* appeared to have the same problems as Scorsese's previous films. It was a big-budget remake of a Hong Kong crime film, *Infernal Affairs*, featuring DiCaprio and Matt Damon in the leads. Scorsese openly acknowledged the limitations of the film in an interview with *Entertainment Weekly*: "The question is how close to a personal film can I make in the Hollywood system today—and this is as close as I can get. I don't know if there's room for me and the kind of picture I'd like to make anymore. I may have to do them independently because I like to take risks, and how can you do that when a picture costs $200 million? There's a lot of money involved and you have a responsibility to the studio."[78] Despite the film's conventionality, *The Departed* was successful critically and financially, leading to its industry success with both a Best Picture and Best Director Oscar.[79] The title of the *Entertainment Weekly* interview, "Back to the Mean Streets," provides a succinct explanation for this success. Scorsese was returning to the modern-day crime drama that made his reputation. Stylistically, *The Departed* conformed to the Hollywood style of "intensified continuity" as much as Scorsese's other recent Hollywood films.[80] The major difference was simply content. *The Departed* could not only be marketed as a "Martin Scorsese" film, but it also could be discussed as such by film critics. The "authenticity" of Scorsese's earlier work transformed *The Departed* into something beyond its generic and stylistic conventions. To win the Best Director award, Scorsese needed the crime genre of *The Departed*. To win the Best Picture award, *The Departed* needed the prestige of Scorsese's authorship.

Scorsese and Kazan

Although the Oscar win for *The Departed* marked the culmination of Scorsese's relationship with Hollywood, another Oscar telecast from eight years earlier perhaps best crystallizes Scorsese and his role in American culture. On March 21, 1999, Scorsese and Robert De Niro presented an Honorary Award to director Elia Kazan at the 1998 Academy Awards ceremony in Los Angeles. Because Kazan had "named names" during the 1950s Hollywood blacklist period, many vehemently opposed honoring Kazan's artistic achievements. The controversy made at least one thing clear to Scorsese: "presenting" is not always a neutral, philanthropic enterprise as it was with presenting work done in the field of film archiving. "Presenting" Kazan was more difficult (and potentially harmful to Scorsese's image) because it required engaging with a rather ugly and unpleasant history that was at once both a part of film culture and the postwar culture as a whole. And while this presentation was the subject of much controversy at the time, it was not an event about which Scorsese was willing to speak. Although Scorsese grants several interviews in rather diverse publications, he chose to not address the subject. This was clearly a deliberate refusal on Scorsese's part, avoiding the question of the Academy's decision and his role in symbolically justifying the industry. Like Kazan, Scorsese made the decision to cooperate with the Hollywood studios even if it meant alienating some of his fellow workers. Almost a decade later, Scorsese was rewarded by the Academy and joined directors like Kazan as Oscar winners.

This Oscar telecast was not the first time in which Scorsese symbolically presented Kazan to the public and praised his artistry while ignoring his politics, and it would not be the last. In *A Personal Journey*, Scorsese listed and discussed Kazan as one of the directors in his section, "The Director as Iconoclast." In other words, for Scorsese, Kazan was not a man who saved his highly valued Hollywood career by betraying members of his community; rather, he was a defiant rebel against the system. This reading can only be made coherent by stressing the aesthetic and ignoring the social. The final scene of *A Personal Journey* includes a clip of Kazan's *America, America* (1963) during which Scorsese related the film to his personal experience:

> When we talk about personal expression, I'm often reminded of Kazan's *America, America*, the story of his uncle's journey from Anatolia to America, the story of so many immigrants who came to this country from a distant foreign land. I kind of identified with it. I was very moved by it. Actually, I later saw myself mak-

ing the same journey, not from Anatolia, but rather from my own neighborhood in New York, which was in a sense a very foreign land. My journey took me from that land to moviemaking—which was something unimaginable!"[81]

The rhetoric here is that both Scorsese and Kazan are outsiders to Hollywood because of their ethnic New York background.[82] Scorsese's New Yorkness has been used to distinguish him as an artist since his days at NYU and is something of an illusion and manipulation, just as Scorsese's presenting Kazan as an opponent to the studio system is false and misleading.

Not until 2010 did Scorsese directly confronted Kazan and his politics while also addressing the presentation of the honorary Oscar. *A Letter to Elia* (Martin Scorsese and Kent Jones, 2010) is an hour-long dedication to Kazan, although mostly, as Scorsese repeatedly claims, to Kazan's films, and Scorsese's relationship to *them*. He acknowledges Kazan's naming of names to the House Committee on Un-American Activities (HUAC), although how he discusses this is telling. He begins by stating that Kazan was at the top of his chosen field, both in the theater and in Hollywood, when "something happened," a phrasing already meant to take away some of Kazan's responsibility (in contrast to "he did something"). He describes the situation in Kazan's own words, as an impossible choice, where "either way you go, you lose." Scorsese

Figure 5.6. *Letter to Elia* (Martin Scorsese and Kent Jones, 2010), "And then something happened."

states that the "consequences were tragic for everyone" and that Kazan had become a "pariah" in Hollywood. This is a rather ridiculous claim, of course, although one Richard Schickel already firmly established.[83] The whole idea of everyone suffering equally, those who cooperated and those who did not, is simply false in the material sense. Kazan continued to make movies (and money) while those blacklisted were prevented from doing either.[84] The only thing that suffered for Kazan was his reputation, something Scorsese has been at pains to restore. After this brief HUAC discussion, Scorsese quickly moves on to the films made after the testimony, claiming that the experience changed Kazan for the better: "If you're talking about the art, the work, this is when a director became a filmmaker." This is backed up by the familiar logic that the films had now become more "personal," starting with the HUAC apologia *On the Waterfront*. With regard to the presentation of the honorary Oscar, Scorsese simply claims "he had to be there for him" because of how much the films meant to him. Thus all of the issues around Kazan and his naming names are avoided, with the basic implication that the films themselves are more important than anything else. The documentary concludes with Scorsese stating that it "had to stay between me and the movies."

      This is Scorsese the critic-historian at his most solipsistic, an approach that ironically has often been used to analyze his own work and career. It places the aesthetic above the social and political, in a higher and purer realm, like much modernist discourse. And given the generally favorable reaction to *A Letter to Elia*, it is an approach many film critics are fine with embracing.[85] Fortunately, not all of Scorsese's cultural work is this myopic. At his best, Scorsese is a film and cultural historian who deals with the past and its impact on the present. Perhaps the final irony is that the very personal quality of Scorsese's best films does not always serve him best when he analyzes culture himself. What fascinates most about Scorsese and what continues to make him an intriguing figure moving forward is his liminal status between Hollywood insider and rebel outsider, visionary artist and cultural commentator. Even within the contemporary film world, he is both praised for his lack of similarity to the postmodern era and yet seen as a representative of this point in history.

Conclusion

The Next Scorsese (?): The Future of
Artistic Reputations in American Cinema

I N MARCH 2000, *ESQUIRE* MAGAZINE ran the feature "The Next Scorsese" inviting film critics to pick the greatest filmmaker of the new generation of American auteurs. The rise of American independent filmmakers, who had emerged in the industry over the preceding decade, peaking in late 1999 and early 2000 with several critically acclaimed films that were compared to the Hollywood Renaissance of the 1970s, was the inspiration for this article. The tagline for the piece ran parallel with half of Scorsese's face and read, "The most talented new generation of film directors since the auteurs of the '70s is upon us. They won't all last. They won't all leave a great body of work. And they won't all continue making ambitious movies. Which one of them will become . . . The Next Scorsese."[1] The criteria for generational greatness, of which Scorsese exemplifies, are longevity, productivity, and integrity. Within the popular entertainment industry, Scorsese had come to represent the industry's best possible vision of itself and the artistic quality it is capable of delivering. Rather than polling film critics, Esquire asked several individuals writing for popular outlets to give and briefly justify their choices (they did, however, allow readers to voice their opinion in an online poll). *New York Times* film critic Elvis Mitchell chose the Wachowski brothers; *Esquire* critic Tom Carson selected Alexander Payne; *Variety's* Todd McCarthy chose Paul Thomas Anderson; *Los Angeles Times* critic Kenneth Turan selected David O. Russell; *New York Observer* critic and auteur founder Andrew Sarris chose Kevin Smith; and, finally, Scorsese himself (Scorsese's byline humorously reads "Martin Scorsese is, well, Martin Scorsese") selected Wes Anderson.

Nearly all of the critics concentrate on the question from a purely aesthetic position, trying to determine which current director will keep

producing high-quality artistic films into the future. This is not a sur-
prise. Contextual concerns are often ignored in writings on Scorsese.
Intriguingly, the only exception to this is Andrew Sarris, the long-time
auteurist. In defending his choice of Kevin Smith, Sarris writes, "Smith's
flair for merchandising and recycling the fruits of his labor is one of the
reasons I am betting on him to break out of the low-budget ghetto and
into the movie mainstream."[2] Perhaps unwittingly, Sarris is acknowledg-
ing here that being considered the "next Scorsese" means mainstream
acceptance and exposure, not simply artistic quality and integrity. But
the other critics choose to ignore industrial factors and view "Scorsese"
as solely an artistic entity.

These choices and their critical defenses provide a microcosm of
the now popularly held discourse on Scorsese and his aesthetic distinction. Tom Carson, in his discussion of Alexander Payne, argues that "he's
already gone as far as he can go with the poignancy of drabness; it may
be time for him to give Omaha a rest."[3] This can be seen as a reference
to Scorsese's own previous need to move away from his particular milieu.
Todd McCarthy makes explicit reference to "Scorsese's visual style" and
its influence on Paul Thomas Anderson, and one can see similar connections with his argument that Anderson "has demonstrated a natural
filmmaking flair, a bent for risk taking, and a predilection for taking
actors where they might otherwise never get to go."[4] Kenneth Turan's
comments on his selection of David O. Russell are nearly identical: "Russell wants to be both playing by the rules and bending them further
than anyone thought to before. His films are audacious and entertaining,
Hollywood with a twist, able to deliver traditional satisfactions while
precariously far out on a limb. No matter what challenges Russell sets
for himself, he seems to have no difficulty carrying them off."[5] This
insider-outsider dynamic that Turan praises in Russell is exactly what has
allowed Scorsese to earn his own reputation. Scorsese's critical appraisal
of his own choice, Wes Anderson, follows this same discourse. He compares Anderson to both renowned Hollywood director Leo McCarey and
French auteur Jean Renoir, echoing his and others strategy of placing
Scorsese in the pantheon alongside his influences and idols. He notes that
Anderson "has a fine sense of how music works against an image," much
like the reputation Scorsese has gained from his use of popular music
in modern cinema. Scorsese ends his appreciation of Anderson with the
following remark about a scene in *Bottle Rocket* (Wes Anderson, 1996):
"For me, it's a transcendent moment. And transcendent moments are in
short supply these days."[6] The importance of "transcendence" to Scorsese's own reputation is echoed here in his explanation of why Anderson
has the potential to be the most critically renowned filmmaker of next

generation. Subtly, Scorsese also indicates that this generation is not as accomplished as those of the past with his comment that transcendence is in "short supply."

Of course, this question of the "next Scorsese" is a false one. There will never be another Scorsese. I do not mean this in the liberal humanist tradition of individual subjects (especially heroic male artists) being completely unique. The argument of this study has been explicitly against this type of reading. There will never be another Scorsese not because of Scorsese's distinctiveness as an artist, but because of the particular context in which he was situated. The question of the "next Scorsese" presupposes that the next generation of filmmakers will be evaluated in a manner similar to previous eras. This cannot be presumed because not only has the criteria changed but also the very legitimacy of evaluation itself mutates. Scorsese recognized this and the security of his reputation lies not in the transcendental quality of his films, but in the concrete relationships he has formed with cultural institutions. Thus, when asking who the "next Scorsese" will be, the major factor will not be aesthetics or even economics. Rather, it will be the ability of filmmakers to forge the appropriate alliances that will allow their cultural capital to be secured.

Notes

Introduction. Martin Scorsese and Film Culture

1. By as early as 1985, two book-length studies of American cinema appeared that challenged this notion of New Hollywood as radical departure: Robert B. Ray, *A Certain Tendency of the Hollywood Cinema 1930–1980* (Princeton, NJ: Princeton University Press, 1985); and David Bordwell, Kristin Thompson, and Janet Staiger, *Classical Hollywood Cinema: Film Style and Mode of Production to 1960* (New York: Columbia University Press, 1985).

2. Robert Philip Kolker, *A Cinema of Loneliness: Penn, Stone, Kubrick, Scorsese, Spielberg, Altman* (New York: Oxford University Press, 2000), xiii.

3. Ibid., 14.

4. Ibid., x.

5. Randal Johnson usefully summarizes the concept of "habitus" as follows: "The habitus is sometimes described as a 'feel for the game,' a 'practical sense,' . . . that inclines agents to act and react in specific situations in a manner that is not always calculated and that is not simply a question of conscious obedience to rules." Pierre Bourdieu, *The Field of Cultural Production*, ed. and intro. by Randal Johnson (New York: Columbia University Press, 1993), 5.

6. Pierre Bourdieu, *Distinction: A Social Critique of the Judgment of Taste*, trans. Richard Nice (Cambridge, MA: Harvard University Press, 1984), 485.

7. Ibid., 485.

8. Bourdieu, 1993, 9.

9. See Barbara Klinger, *Beyond the Multiplex: Cinema, New Technologies, and the Home* (Berkeley: University of California Press, 2006); Karen Frances Gracy, *Film Preservation: Competing Definitions of Value, Use, and Practice* (Chicago, IL: Society of American Archivists, 2007); and Michael Z. Newman, *Indie: An American Film Culture* (New York: Columbia University Press, 2011).

10. Howard S. Becker, *Art Worlds* (Berkeley: University of California Press, 1982); and Herbert J. Gans, *Popular Culture and High Culture: An Analysis and Evaluation of Taste* (New York: Basic Books, 1974).

Chapter 1. Scorsese and the University

1. David Thompson and Ian Christie, eds., *Scorsese on Scorsese* (London: Faber and Faber, 1996), 13–14.

2. Pierre Bourdieu, "The Field of Cultural Production, or: The Economic Field Reversed," in *The Field of Cultural Production*, 39.

3. James Cole Potter, "Martin Scorsese and the Poetics of Post–Classical Authorship" (PhD diss., Northwestern University, 1998), 58–59.

4. Allan Arkush, "I Remember Film School," *Film Comment* 19, no. 11 (Nov. 1983), 57.

5. Ibid., 57. This description of the poor state of equipment in the early years of NYU is supported by the comments of Peter Rea (author's interview, Sept. 10, 2004).

6. Michael Zyrd notes that this was a broader trend in curriculum reform all across the country. See Zyrd, "Experimental Film and the Development of Film Study in America," in *Inventing Film Studies*, ed. Lee Grieveson and Haidee Wasson (Durham, NC: Duke University Press, 2008), 186–187.

7. Arkush, 58.

8. Even Michael Zyrd, who argues that experimental film played a major role in the development of film study in American universities, admits University of Southern California, University of California (Los Angeles), and New York University were exceptions because they "cultivated relationships with Hollywood." See Zyrd, 211–212.

9. Thomas Fensch, *Films on the Campus* (New York: Barnes, 1970), 310–311.

10. Thompson and Christie, 14.

11. Ibid., 18.

12. Bourdieu, *The Field of Cultural Production*, 39.

13. Jonas Mekas, "Where Are We—The Underground?" in *The New American Cinema: A Critical Anthology*, 20.

14. Peter Decherney, *Hollywood and the Culture Elite: How the Movies became American* (New York: Columbia University Press, 2005), 162.

15. Ibid., 165.

16. Greg Taylor, *Artists in the Audience: Cults, Camp, and American Film Criticism* (Princeton, NJ: Princeton University Press, 1999), 35.

17. Andrew Sarris, "Avant–Garde Films Are More Boring than Ever," in *Politics and Cinema* (New York: Oxford University Press, 1978), 196–206.

18. Raymond Haberski, *It's Only a Movie!: Films and Critics in American Culture* (Lexington: University Press of Kentucky, 2001), 83.

19. Andreas Huyssen, *After the Great Divide: Modernism, Mass Culture, Postmodernism* (Bloomington: Indiana University Press, 1986), vii.

20. Andrew Sarris, "The Independent Cinema," in *The New American Cinema: A Critical Anthology*, ed. Gregory Battcock (New York: Dutton, 1967). Quoted in *Scorsese on Scorsese*, 22.

21. Jill McGreal, "*It's Not Just You, Murray!*" in *Scorsese: A Journey through the American Psyche*, ed. Paul A. Woods (London: Plexus, 2005), 17.

22. Jonathan Romney, *"What's a Nice Girl Like You Doing in a Place Like This?" Sight and Sound*, no. 6 (June 1992): 57; in *Scorsese: A Journey through the American Psyche*, ed. Paul Woods (London: Plexus, 2005), 15–16.

23. Leighton Grist, *The Films of Martin Scorsese, 1963–77: Authorship and Context* (Basingstoke, Eng.: Macmillan, 2000), 20, 22.

24. Herbert Gans, "Chapter 1: The Critique of Mass Culture," in *Popular Culture and High Culture: An Analysis and Evaluation of Taste* (New York: Basic Books, 1974), 17–64.

25. Grist, 24.

26. Ibid., 31. For a contemporary review that echoes these sentiments on the film as overindulgent, see "Almost Making It," *Time*, Sept. 19, 1969, 95–96.

27. Roger Ebert, *"I Call First," Chicago Sun–Times*, Nov. 17, 1967, in Roger Ebert, *Scorsese by Ebert* (Chicago: University of Chicago Press, 2008), 16–17.

28. Ibid., 17.

29. Grist, 32.

30. Ibid., 40.

31. Ibid., 31.

32. Ibid., 61.

33. Author interview with Peter Rea, Sept. 10, 2004. All subsequent quotes from Rea come from this interview.

34. Howard Becker, *Art Worlds* (Berkeley: University of California Press, 1982), 94.

35. For a full discussion of the two versions of *Shadows*, see George Kouvaros, *Where Does It Happen? John Cassavetes and Cinema at the Breaking Point* (Minneapolis: University of Minnesota, 2004). As Decherney points out, in one of the ironies typical of this period of film culture, "the popularity of this second version (of *Shadows*) gave Mekas the momentum he needed to turn his call for a new generation of filmmakers into an organized movement," 177.

36. Mary Pat Kelly, *Martin Scorsese: A Journey* (New York: Thunder's Mouth Press, 2004), 57.

37. Peter Wollen, "The Two Avant–Gardes," in *Readings and Writings: Semiotic Counter–Strategies* (London: Verso, 1982), 92–104.

38. Lawrence S. Friedman, *The Cinema of Martin Scorsese* (New York: Continuum, 1997), 41.

39. Kelly, 2004, 56. This anecdote is related in Keyser, 30.

40. Friedman, 44.

41. James Monaco, *American Film Now* (New York: Zoetrope, 1984), 153.

42. Becker, 22.

43. Ibid., 77.

44. Howard Thompson, *"Street Scenes 1970," New York Times* (Sept. 15, 1970), 52. This review is reprinted in Mary Pat Kelly, *Martin Scorsese: The First Decade* (Pleasantville, NY: Redgrave, 1980), 163.

45. Friedman, 44.

46. Les Keyser, *Martin Scorsese* (New York: Twayne, 1992), 31.

47. Keyser, 32.

48. Raffaele Donato, "Docufictions: An Interview with Martin Scorsese on Documentary Film," *Film History* 19, no. 2 (2007): 204.

49. Michael Henry Wilson, "J'ai dû prendre une autre voie pour survivre: Des premiers courts métrages à *Alice n'est plus ici* (Paris/Cannes, May 1974)," reprinted in *Martin Scorsese: Entretiens avec Michael Henry Wilson*, trans. Nick Nguyen (Paris: Centre Pompidou/Cahiers du Cinéma, 2006), 29–31; originally published in *Positif* no. 170 (June 1975): 8–23.

50. Bella Taylor, "Martin Scorsese," in *Closeup: The Contemporary Director*, ed. Jon Tuska (Metuchen, NJ: Scarecrow Press, 1981), 293–368.

51. Ibid., 315.

52. Ibid., 315.

53. Author's interview with John Butman, Oct. 18, 2006.

54. Author's interview with Harry Bolles, Nov. 11, 2006. All subsequent quotes from Bolles come from this interview.

55. Lesley Oelsner, "Two Indicted in Raid on N.Y.U. Center," *New York Times*, July 30, 1970, 1, 54.

56. Martin Scorsese, "Confessions of a Movie Brat," in *Anatomy of the Movies*, ed. David Pirie (New York: Macmillan, 1981), 135.

57. Howard Smith, "Notes" *Village Voice*, May 21, 1970, 21.

58. Author's interview with Ed Summer, Aug. 2, 2009.

59. Bill Nichols, *Representing Reality: Issues and Concepts in Documentary* (Bloomington: Indiana University Press, 1991), 44.

60. Author's interview with Don Lenzer, Dec. 15, 2006. All subsequent quotes from Lenzer come from this interview.

61. The Philharmonic Hall Program (New York: Saturday Review, Aug. 1970). These are early program notes for the upcoming New York Film Festival, Sept. 10–20, 1970. Lenzer attributes these notes to the festival director, Richard Roud, but technically there is no official author credited. Nevertheless, we may reasonably assume Roud was responsible for the content.

62. See festival advertisement in the *New York Times*, Sept. 6, 1970, D5; and the *Village Voice*, Sept. 3, 1970, 40. This is also the note that appears in the official 1970 New York Film Festival program. A later advertisement in the *New York Times* during the week of the festival (Sept. 13, 1970) eliminates mention of Scorsese altogether.

63. In June 2005, I wrote a letter forwarded to Scorsese's office through MoMA requesting to screen the film for research purposes. In April 2007 I sent a follow up letter. The eventual response from Scorsese's office stated that the film is restricted and not to be shown.

64. Discussion of the controversy over the relative merits of the two versions of *Shadows* can be found in Ray Carney, *Cassavetes on Cassavetes* (New York: Faber and Faber, 2001). On the recent controversy involving Carney and Rowlands, see Marshall Fine, *Accidental Genius: How John Cassavetes Invented the American Independent Film* (New York: Miramax Books, 2006), 225–229.

65. For discussions of this situation within the field of archiving, see Karen Frances Gracy, *Film Preservation: Competing Definitions of Value, Use, and Practice*

(Chicago, IL: Society of American Archivists, 2007); and Caroline Frick, *Saving Cinema: The Politics of Preservation* (New York: Oxford University Press, 2011).

Chapter 2. The Formation of Scorsese's Critical Reputation

1. Stephen Farber, "Has Martin Scorsese Gone Hollywood?" *New York Times*, Mar. 30, 1975, C1.

2. Ibid., C13.

3. *Godard on Godard*, trans. and ed. Tom Milne (New York: Da Capo Press, 1972), 134–139.

4. Ibid., 171.

5. John Hess, "*La Politique des Auteurs* (Part 1), World View as Aesthetics," *Jump Cut* no. 1 (1974): 19.

6. Peter Biskind, "American Film Criticism (Postwar)," in *Gods and Monsters: Thirty Years of Writing on Film and Culture from One of America's Most Incisive Writers* (New York: Nation Books, 2004), 106–107.

7. Hess, 19.

8. Ibid., 19.

9. Andrew Sarris, "Notes on the Auteur Theory in 1962," in *The Primal Screen* (New York: Simon and Schuster, 1973), 46; reprinted from *Film Culture*, no. 27 (Winter 1962–1963): 1–8.

10. Biskind, 2004, 109.

11. Ibid., 110.

12. Barbara Herrnstein–Smith, "Contingencies of Value," *Critical Inquiry* 10 (Sept. 1983), 22.

13. Ibid., 29.

14. Janet Staiger, "The Politics of Film Canons," *Cinema Journal* 24, no. 3 (Spring 1985), 11.

15. Ibid., 13.

16. Jean-Luc Comolli and Jean Narboni, "Cinema/Ideology/Criticism," in *Movies and Methods*, ed. Bill Nichols (Berkeley: University of California Press, 1976), 23–24.

17. Ibid., 27.

18. Thompson and Christie, 34.

19. Ibid., 38. The anecdote also appears in Kelly, 2004, 68.

20. Scarcely any account of *Boxcar Bertha* fails to retell this story. For examples, see Keyser, 37, and Grist, 61–62.

21. *Cassavetes on Cassavetes*, ed. Ray Carney (London: Faber and Faber, 2001), 80.

22. Cassavetes scholar George Kouvaros discusses this explicitly:

A personalized approach to filmmaking, such as the one advocated by Cassavetes, was held up as the mark of an alternative independent vision that could challenge the operations and products of the major studios. In the

three decades following, the privileging of the "people" over the film itself
or filmmaking came to take on more negative connotations, highlighting
both the difficulty of trying to position Cassavetes's work and the director's own stubborn refusal to engage in critical discussion of his films. His
apparent disregard for film also seemed to place his work at odds with the
emerging discipline of film studies, which during the '60s and '70s spread
across university campuses and led to the rise of a number of specialized
film journals. (3)

23. For a detailed discussion of this breakdown, see Eric Schaefer, "Conclusion: The End of Classical Exploitation," in *Bold! Daring! Shocking! True! A
History of Exploitation Films, 1919–1959* (Durham, NC: Duke University Press,
1999), 325–342.

24. Geoff King, "New Hollywood Version I: The Hollywood Renaissance,"
in *New Hollywood: An Introduction* (New York: Columbia University Press, 2002),
11–48.

25. Roger Ebert, *"Boxcar Bertha," Chicago Sun–Times,* July 19, 1972; reprinted
in *Scorsese by Ebert,* 32–33.

26. Jeremy James, "A Director Whose Violence Has Depth," *Chicago
Sun–Times,* Nov. 19, 1972, sect. 3, p. 8; reprinted from the *Los Angeles Times.*
Curiously, James compares the film to Jean–Luc Godard's *Vivre Sa Vie,* a rather
odd comparison to say the least, indicating that James was familiar with Scorsese's
previous work, *Who's That Knocking at My Door,* and its New Wave stylistics.

27. Ebert, 2008, 33.

28. The American films that have appeared in the *Sight and Sound* Top Ten
polls are all Hollywood productions: *Citizen Kane* (Orson Welles, 1941); *Vertigo,
The Searchers, The General* (Buster Keaton, 1927); *Greed* (Erich Von Stroheim,
1924); *The Magnificent Ambersons* (Orson Welles, 1942); *Singin' in the Rain* (Stanley
Donen and Gene Kelly, 1952); *2001: A Space Odyssey* (Stanley Kubrick, 1968);
City Lights (Charlie Chaplin, 1931); *The Gold Rush* (Charlie Chaplin, 1925); *The
Godfather* (Francis Ford Coppola, 1972); *The Godfather: Part II* (Francis Ford
Coppola, 1974); *Intolerance* (D. W. Griffith, 1916); *Sunrise* (F. W. Murnau, 1927);
Dr. Strangelove (Stanley Kubrick, 1963); and *Raging Bull* (Martin Scorsese, 1980).

29. See Pauline Kael, "Raising Kane," *New Yorker,* Feb. 20, 1971, and
Feb. 27, 1971; reprinted in *For Keeps* (New York: Dutton, 1994), 232–325; and
Robert Carringer, *The Making of "Citizen Kane"* (Berkeley: University of Cali-
fornia Press, 1985).

30. Jonathan Rosenbaum, "Chapter 10: Orson Welles as Ideological Challenge," in *Movie Wars: How Hollywood and the Media Conspire to Limit What Films
We Can See* (Chicago: A Cappella Press, 2000), 178–179.

31. Thompson and Christie, 38.

32. Robert Casillo, *Gangster Priest: The Italian American Cinema of Martin
Scorsese* (Toronto: University of Toronto Press, 2006), 486, 491.

33. Thompson and Christie, 43–45.

34. Ibid., 39–41.

35. Pauline Kael, "The Current Cinema: Everyday Inferno," *New Yorker*, Oct. 8, 1973, 157.

36. Kael, 160.

37. Ibid., 162.

38. James Naremore, "Chapter 2: Modernism and Blood Melodrama: Three Case Studies," in *More than Night: Film Noir and Its Contexts* (Berkeley: University of California Press, 1998), 40–95.

39. Paul Schrader, "Notes on Film Noir," *Film Comment* 8, no. 1 (Spring 1972): 8–13.

40. Richard Schickel, "A Closed Circle," *Time*, Nov. 5, 1973, 102.

41. John Simon, "Films," in *Esquire*, Jan. 1974, 18.

42. Kelly, 2004, 80.

43. For an extended analysis of the film as a text of the period, see Grist, "Into the Mainstream: *Alice Doesn't Live Here Anymore*," 98–122.

44. Thompson and Christie, 49.

45. Anthony DeCurtis, "The *Rolling Stone* Interview: Martin Scorsese," *Rolling Stone* no. 590 (1990): 108; quoted in Grist, 103.

46. Karyn Kay and Gerald Peary, "*Alice Doesn't Live Here Anymore*: Waitressing for Warner's," *Jump Cut* no. 7 (1975): 7.

47. Christine Geraghty, "American Cinema in the 70s: *Alice Doesn't Live Here Anymore*," *Movie* no. 22 (Spring 1976): 42.

48. Marjorie Rosen, "New Hollywood: Martin Scorsese Interviewed," *Film Comment* 11, no. 2 (Mar.–Apr. 1975): 42–46.

49. See Kay and Peary, 5.

50. *Taxi Driver* cost $1.3 million and grossed $21.1 million; *Alice Doesn't Live Here Anymore* cost $1.8 million and grossed $17.6 million, making them roughly equivalent in financial terms.

51. Arthur Bremer attempted to assassinate presidential candidate George Wallace on May 15, 1972. Afterward, his diary was discovered and published. Amy Taubin eloquently discusses Bremer's connection to the film, as well as his distance from the character of Travis Bickle in *Taxi Driver* (London: British Film Institute, 2000), 38–40.

52. Taubin, 1999, 16–19.

53. "*Taxi Driver* Named Best Film at Cannes Film Festival Amid Booing," *New York Times*, May 29, 1976.

54. A useful (although not exhaustive) list of both popular and academic contemporary reviews of the film can be found in Weiss, 96–100.

55. Richard Thompson, "Screen Writer: *Taxi Driver*'s Paul Schrader," *Film Comment* 12, no. 2 (Mar.–Apr. 1976): 7–19.

56. Schrader, 17.

57. Thompson, 10.

58. Hess, 22.

59. Thompson and Christie, 63.

60. Richard Goldstein and Mark Jacobson, "Martin Scorsese Tells All: Blood and Guts Turn Me On!" *Village Voice*, Apr. 5, 1976; reprinted in *Martin*

Scorsese: Interviews, 68.

61. Patricia Patterson and Manny Farber, "The Power and the Gory," *Film Comment* 12, no. 3 (May–June 1976): 27.

62. Patterson and Farber, 30.

63. Jonathan Rosenbaum, "Journals," *Film Comment* 12, no. 4 (July–Aug. 1976): 2.

64. Michael Dempsey, "*Taxi Driver*," *Film Quarterly* 29, no. 4 (Summer 1976): 37–41.

65. Robin Wood, "The Incoherent Text: Narrative in the '70s," *Hollywood from Vietnam to Reagan* (New York: Columbia University Press, 1986), 50–55; originally published in *Movie* 27–28 (Winter 1980–Spring 1981): 24–42.

66. Wood, 51.

67. Grist, 129.

68. See, for example, John Hess, "*Godfather II*: A Deal Coppola Couldn't Refuse," *Jump Cut* no. 7 (1975): 1, 10–11; reprinted in *Movies and Methods*, vol. 1, ed. Bill Nichols (Berkeley: University of California Press, 1976), 81–90.

69. Robert B. Ray, *A Certain Tendency of the Hollywood Cinema, 1930–1980* (Princeton, NJ: Princeton University Press, 1985), 351.

70. Ibid., 344.

71. For a partial listing of reviews of the film, see Weiss, 100–105.

72. Vincent Canby, "Let's Call It the Accountant's Theory of Filmmaking," *New York Times*, July 10, 1977, 11.

73. Keyser, 97.

74. Peter Biskind, "Extract from *Easy Riders, Raging Bulls*," in *Scorsese: A Journey through the American Psyche*, ed. Paul A. Woods (London: Plexus, 2005), 94.

75. See Keyser, 97–99, for a detailed consideration of this period in Scorsese's personal life.

76. Kelly, 2004, 111.

77. Grist, 163.

78. Andrew Britton, "Blissing Out: The Politics of Reaganite Entertainment," *Movie* 31/32 (Winter 1986): 1–42.

79. Richard Lippe, "*New York, New York* and the Hollywood Musical," *Movie* 31–32 (Winter 1986): 97.

80. Susan Morrison, "Sirk, Scorsese, and Hysteria: A Double(d) Reading," *CineAction!* no. 6 (Summer–Fall 1986): 24.

81. This leads, decades later, to the publication of a cookbook with the same name as the film: Catherine Scorsese, *Italianamerican: The Scorsese Family Cookbook* (New York: Random House, 1996).

82. This connection is made explicitly in *Scorsese on Scorsese* when the editors write: "*American Boy* [is] something of an objective correlative to *Taxi Driver*, just as *Italianamerican* had been to *Mean Streets*" (76).

83. Best exemplified by Bill Nichols and his modes of documentary practice. See Nichols, 1991.

84. William Rothman, "Looking Back and Turning Inward: American Documentary Films of the Seventies," in *Lost Illusions: American Cinema in the*

Shadow of Watergate and Vietnam, 1970–1979, ed. David A. Cook (New York: Scribner's, 2000), 419.

85. Monaco, 1984, 153.

86. Ibid., 161.

87. Kelly, 1980, 3.

88. Ibid., 73.

89. Ibid., 78.

90. Ibid., 80.

Chapter 3. Scorsese and the Fall of the Hollywood Renaissance

1. Stanley Kauffmann, "On Film," *New Republic*, Dec. 6, 1980, 26–27; Andrew Sarris, "Mean Fighter from Mean Streets," *Village Voice*, Nov. 19, 1980, 55; David Denby, "Brute Force," *New York*, Dec. 1, 1980, 61–63; Pauline Kael, "Religious Pulp or the Incredible Hulk," *New Yorker*, Dec. 8, 1980, 217–218, 220, 222, 225.

2. Janet Maslin, "When Puzzles become Provocative," *New York Times*, Feb. 8, 1981, 21, 23.

3. Kelly, 2004, 119.

4. Michael Henry, "Un Patrimoine Spirituel," *Positif* no. 229 (Apr. 1980): 2–13.

5. Pascal Bonitzer, "La Solitude Sans Fond," *Cahiers du Cinéma* no. 321 (Mar. 1981): 4–9.

6. Emile Bickerton, "Adieu to Cahiers: Life Cycle of a Cinema Journal," *New Left Review* 42 (Nov.–Dec. 2006): 92.

7. Wood, 1986/2003, 222.

8. Ibid., 232.

9. Pam Cook, "Masculinity in Crisis?" *Screen* 23, no. 3/4 (1982): 39–40.

10. Biskind, 1999, 399.

11. Cook, 40.

12. Klinger, 2006, 75.

13. Ibid., 83.

14. Http://old.bfi.org.uk/sightandsound/polls/topten/ (accessed July 20, 2012).

15. Potter briefly mentions Scorsese's work in preservation as part of a broader discussion of Scorsese's position as a cinephile-historian-arbiter of taste (375–376).

16. The examples on this subject are numerous. The following are a sampling of articles within the mainstream press: Matthew Flamm, "Raging Scorsese: Director's Obsession Saves Films," *New York Post*, June 10, 1992, 23; Henry Sheehan, "Scorsese Presents: *The Proud Ones* Is the Latest Fruit of His Effort to Help Preserve Classic Films," *Boston Globe*, June 21, 1992, 101, 103; David Handelman, "Score One for Scorsese," *TV Guide*, Sept. 27, 1997, 32–36.

The caption to the article reads, "AMC [American Movie Classics] and the famous director team up to make a case for film preservation with a marathon of suspense classics."

17. Frick, 9.

18. Kelly, 2004, 277.

19. R. M. M. Wiener, "Scorsese Asks Industry Help to Save Films," *Box Office*, May 12, 1980, 1, 4; Richard Harrington, "Old Movies Never Die—They're Just Fading Away," *Washington Post*, July 20, 1980, 1, 8–9; and Robert Lindsay, "Martin Scorsese's Campaign to Save a Film Heritage," *New York Times*, Oct. 5, 1980, 19–20.

20. The petition included more than 100 names from the industry as well as representatives of cultural institutions such as the New York University, University of Southern California, University of California (Los Angeles), and University of California (Berkeley) film departments, among many others.

21. Martin Scorsese, "À mes amis et collègues: Au sujet de nos film," *Positif* no. 232–233 (July–Aug. 1980): 126–127.

22. Serge Le Péron and Serge Toubiana, "Le Journaldes: Auviala fait le point," *Cahiers du Cinéma* no. 316 (Oct. 1980), i–iii; Lorenzo Codelli, "Fade out de Martin Scorsese," *Positif* no. 237 (Dec. 1980): 54.

23. Kelly, 1980, 204.

24. Thompson and Christie, 20.

25. See Howard Feinstein, "The Newest Film Fad: the Presenter," *Los Angeles Times*, Mar. 6, 1996, F3.

26. In addition, Scorsese's desire to preserve on film, the Italian–American community of his youth in his early work can be seen as an extension of his interest in preservation which is discussed in chap. 4, "Scorsese and the Presentation of History."

27. Author's interview with Mark Del Costello, Aug. 20, 2008.

28. Decherney, 205.

29. Ibid., 209.

30. Ibid., 211.

31. Ted Perry went from teaching at NYU to being the head of the film department at MoMA.

32. Thompson and Christie, 80.

33. "I decided to go on tour with the film around the whole world. At the same time, we decided to take on the film preservation programme about fading colour. I would do two nights on the film, and one on film preservation with Thelma." Thompson and Christie, 84.

34. Ibid., 80.

35. For example, critic Vincent Canby, normally a huge Allen supporter, critiqued the film stating, "It's almost as if Mr. Allen had set out to make someone else's movie, say in the manner of Mr. Bergman, without having any grasp of the material, of first–hand, gut feelings about the characters." See Vincent Canby, "Culture Shock," *New York Times*, Aug. 2, 1978, C15.

36. Taubin, 2000, 22.

37. Leonard Quart, "Woody Allen's New York," in *The Films of Woody Allen: Critical Essays*, ed. Charles L. P. Silet (Lanham, MD: Scarecrow Press, 2006), 16.

38. Following *Stardust Memories*, Allen made the following films over the rest of the decade: *A Midsummer Night's Sex Comedy* (1982), *Zelig* (1983), *Broadway Danny Rose* (1984), *The Purple Rose of Cairo* (1985), *Hannah and Her Sisters* (1986), *Radio Days* (1987), *September* (1987), *Another Woman* (1988), and *Crimes and Misdemeanors* (1989). Scorsese's output over this same period, by almost all standards of evaluative criteria, is far less accomplished.

39. Michael Powell, "Introduction," in Kelly, 1980, 1–2. Powell also contributed Forewords to *Scorsese on Scorsese*, xiii–xiv, and *Martin Scorsese: A Journey*, x.

40. Maureen Dowd, "The Impact on Scorsese of a British Film Team," *New York Times*, May 18, 1991, 16.

41. See Kouvaros for a detailing of these critiques.

42. An objection may be raised here with regard to Stanley Kubrick, the other filmmaker active during the era of the Hollywood Renaissance of the 1970s as having a comparable reputation to that of Scorsese and Coppola. However, Kubrick is usually seen as being of a different generation than those of the "film school generation." Kubrick, like Arthur Penn and Robert Altman, began his career in the 1950s before the fall of the studio system but after the so-called Golden Age of the 1940s. He is very much part of a transitional generation of filmmakers, certainly post–Classical (unlike Ford, Hawks, Hitchcock, and others) but at the same time distinct from the New Hollywood. And unlike Penn and Altman, Kubrick had great success prior to 1967 with films such as *The Killing* (1956), *Paths of Glory* (1957), *Spartacus* (1960), *Lolita* (1962), and, most famously, *Dr. Strangelove: Or, How I Learned to Stop Worrying and Love the Bomb* (1963). Both Scorsese and Spielberg view Kubrick much more as a mentor than as a contemporary. To give an example, Scorsese discusses both Kubrick's *2001: A Space Odyssey* (1968) and *Barry Lyndon* (1975) in his documentary *A Personal Journey with Martin Scorsese through American Movies* (1995), despite his statement that he does not feel comfortable talking about the films of his contemporaries. This indicates that Scorsese sees Kubrick as belonging to a different generation. Likewise, when Steven Spielberg took over the project *A.I.* from Kubrick, it was very much in the role of a disciple taking over for a master.

43. Lynda Myles, "The Zoetrope Saga," *Sight and Sound* 51, no.2 (Spring 1982): 92; quoted in Lewis, 11.

44. Lewis, 51.

45. Ibid., 81.

46. Ibid., 80.

47. Ibid., 83.

48. Ibid., 82.

49. Jack Kroll, "Coppola's Apocalypse Again," *Newsweek*, Feb. 16, 1981, 79; quoted in Lewis, 9.

50. Lewis, 89.

51. Robert Philip Kolker. *A Cinema of Loneliness: Penn, Kubrick, Scorsese, Spielberg, Altman* (New York: Oxford University Press, 1988), xii.

52. Ibid., 235.

53. Lewis, 47.

54. *The King of Comedy* is beginning to be seen as an exception to this, as discussed in chap. 5.

55. An account of this incident can be found in Andy Dougan, *Martin Scorsese: The Making of His Movies* (London: Orion, 1997), 73–75; for a longer discussion involving interviews with the key players involved, see Kelly, 2004, 161–180.

56. Thompson and Christie, 97.

57. Kelly, 2004, 181.

58. Dougan, 78.

59. Ibid., 77–78.

60. Roger Ebert, "*The Color of Money*," *Chicago Sun Times*, Oct. 17, 1986; in *Scorsese by Ebert*, 89–92.

61. Thompson and Christie, 108–110.

62. Ibid., 111.

63. Justin Wyatt, *High Concept: Movies and Marketing in Hollywood* (Austin: University of Texas Press, 1994), 61.

64. Ibid., 58.

65. Robert Kapsis, *Hitchcock: The Making of a Reputation* (Chicago: Chicago University Press, 1992), 195.

66. John Mariani, "The Four Horseman and the Apocalypse," *Attenzione* (July 1979): 40–44; Leo Braudy, "The Sacraments of Genre: Coppola, DePalma, Scorsese," *Film Quarterly* 39, no. 3 (Spring 1986): 17–28; and Stephen Mamber, "Parody, Intertextuality, Signature: Kubrick, DePalma, and Scorsese," *Quarterly Review of Film and Video* 12, no. 1–2 (1990): 29–35.

67. Mamber, 29.

68. Ibid., 32.

69. Lawrence Van Gelder, "At the Movies," *New York Times*, June 19, 1987, C10.

70. David Ehrenstein, "Wise Guy," *Image*, Sept. 23, 1990, 9.

71. Kapsis, 198–199.

73. Ibid., 208.

73. News release, "Martin Scorsese Recipient of Directors Guild of America: Fiftieth Anniversary Tribute at MoMA September 15," Museum of Modern Art, August 1986, (Scorsese File, Museum of Modern Art, New York).

74. Gregory Flaxman, "Auteur? Auteur? The Brattle's Scorsese Retro Confirms a Major Director," *Boston Phoenix*, Nov. 15, 1991, sect. 3, p. 7.

75. "Martin Scorsese: A Film Festival," Sept. 22–Dec. 8, 1994, George Eastman House (George Eastman House brochure, Scorsese File, Museum of Modern Art, New York).

76. Thompson and Christie, 123.

77. Robin Riley, *Film, Faith, and Cultural Conflict: The Case of Martin Scorsese's "The Last Temptation of Christ"* (London: Praeger, 2003), 26.

78. Universal advertisement, quoted in Riley, 27.

79. Riley, 83.

80. Michael Medved, *Hollywood vs. America* (New York: HarperCollins, 1992), 49; quoted in Riley, 84.

81. For example, the 2002 *Sight and Sound* poll did not feature a single vote, from either a critic or a filmmaker, for *The Last Temptation of Christ.*

82. Riley, 85.

83. See Charles Lyons, *The New Censors: Movies and the Culture Wars* (Philadelphia: Temple University Press, 1997).

84. Riley, 25.

85. "A Director's Journey: Martin Scorsese's Worldwide B. O. Track Record," comp. Anthony D'Alessandro, *Variety*, Dec. 9–15, 2002, A10.

86. Riley, 28.

87. Ibid., 66–67.

88. Ibid., 68.

89. The film topped the following polls: "The Decade's Best" *Premiere* 3 (Nov. 1989): 106–107; and "The Best of the Decade," *Time*, Jan. 1, 1990, 101.

Chapter 4. Histories of Cinema and Cinematic Histories: Scorsese as Historian

1. For a fine discussion in relation to auteurism and the "aura" in film, see Kartik Nair, "Aura, Auteurism and *The Key to Reserva*," *Wide Screen* 1, no. 2 (June 2010), 1–19.

2. The only feature films set in contemporary times in Scorsese's filmography over the past 20 years are the remakes *Cape Fear* and *The Departed* and the New York drama *Bringing Out the Dead* (which itself was about a past world because the New York of the film's setting, early to mid-1990s, was by then obsolete following the reforms of mayor Rudolph Giuliani). One could argue that the very fact that they are remakes means they are concerned with re–creating a past world, even if that world is fictitious. This fascination with past worlds can also be seen in earlier Scorsese films: *Raging Bull*; *New York, New York*; the opening of *Alice Doesn't Live Here Anymore*; and *Boxcar Bertha*. However, since *The Last Temptation of Christ* this interest in past worlds has almost exclusively dominated Scorsese's output.

3. The four titles reprinted are: James Agee, *Agee on Film: Criticism and Comment on the Movies*, intro. David Denby (New York: Modern Library, 2000); Rudy Behlmer, ed., *Memo from David O. Selznick*, intro. Roger Ebert (New York: Modern Library, 2000); Stephanie Schwam, ed., *The Making of 2001: A Space Odyssey*, intro. Jay Cocks, afterword Alexander Walker (New York: Modern Library, 2000); and Vachel Lindsay, *The Art of the Moving Picture*, intro. Stanley Kauffmann, afterword Kent Jones (New York: Modern Library, 2000).

4. For example, Scorsese received the William K. Everson Film History Award in 2002 from the National Board of Review as well as the Film Heritage Special Award from the National Society of Film Critics for his documentary *My Voyage to Italy* (1999).

5. Stephen Holden, "The Movies that Inspired Martin Scorsese," *New York Times*, May 21, 1993, C1, C22–23.

6. Martin Scorsese, "Outline for a Preservation Strategy," 1980 10 Scorsese File, Museum of Modern Art, New York).

7. Film Society at Lincoln Center, "The Film Society at Lincoln Center's Walter Reade Theater and the Department of Cinema Studies, Tisch School of the Arts at New York University Present 'Mean Screens: Martin Scorsese at the Movies' May 21–June 27," May 1993. Scorsese File, Museum of Modern Art, New York.

8. Film Society at Lincoln Center, "The Film Society at Lincoln Center's Walter Reade Theater and the Department of Cinema Studies, Tisch School of the Arts at New York University Present 'Mean Screens: Martin Scorsese at the Movies' May 21–June 27," May 1993. Scorsese File, Museum of Modern Art, New York.

9. Klinger, 2006, 104.

10. Ibid., 129.

11. Ibid., 129.

12. Ibid., 131.

13. Kelly, 2004, 277.

14. Klinger, 2006, 104.

15. For a discussion of this transition period, see Mark Betz, "Little Books," in *Inventing Film Studies*, ed. Lee Grieveson and Haidee Wasson (Durham, NC: Duke University Press, 2008), 319–349.

16. Gerald Mast, *A Short History of the Movies* (New York: Pegasus, 1971), and Andrew Sarris, *The American Cinema: Directors and Directions 1929–1968* (New York: Dutton, 1968). Among the earliest of these histories include Terry Ramsaye, *A Million and One Nights; A History of the Motion Picture* (New York: Simon and Schuster, 1926), and Paul Rotha, *The Film till Now: A Survey of World Cinema* (London: Cape, 1930).

17. For a critique of the AFI approach, see Jonathan Rosenbaum, "The AFI's Contribution to Movie Hell or, How I Learned to Stop Worrying and Love American Movies," in *Movie Wars: How Hollywood and the Media Conspire to Limit What Movies We Can See* (Chicago: A Capella Press, 2000), 91–106.

18. Michel Foucault, "Nietzsche, Genealogy, History," in *Language, Counter-Memory, Practice: Selected Essays and Interviews*, ed. Donald F. Bouchard, trans. Donald F. Bouchard and Sherry Simon (Ithaca, NY: Cornell University Press, 1977), 156.

19. Ray, 2001, 39.

20. Ibid., 45.

21. Foucault, 156–157.

22. Martin Scorsese and Michael Henry Wilson, *A Personal Journey with Martin Scorsese through American Movies* (New York: Hyperion, 1997), 17.

23. Foucault, 151.

24. Hayden White, "The Value of Narrativity in the Representation of Reality," in *The Content of the Form: Narrative Discourse and Historical Representation* (Baltimore, ME: John Hopkins University Press, 1978), 13.

25. Scorsese and Wilson, 17.

26. Ray, 54.

27. Allen and Gomery, 76.

28. Foucault, 161.

29. Ibid., 155.

30. Scorsese and Wilson, 165.

31. Ibid., 120.

32. Ibid., 147.

33. Rosenbaum, 2000, 178–179.

34. Scorsese and Wilson, 166.

35. White, 21.

36. Ibid., 25.

37. Interestingly, the British Film Institute (BFI) hired Godard to complete the history of French cinema as part of the same series as Scorsese's documentary, but, Godard subverted the whole project. Although they were hired for similar projects, the BFI clearly expected a more conventional and package–able film from Scorsese and most likely would not have accepted otherwise. This is not to say, however, that Scorsese could not have varied significantly from the format he did choose.

38. Sarris, 73.

39. While this article is roughly contemporaneous with Sarris, its influence on later academic writing is much more pronounced. In fact, the essay had such an impact that a whole article is devoted to its legacy. See Barbara Klinger, " 'Cinema/Ideology/Criticism' Revisited: The Progressive Genre," in *Film Genre Reader III*, ed. Barry Keith Grant (Austin: University of Texas Press, 2003), 75–91.

40. Comolli and Narboni, 27.

41. Ray, 2000, 92.

42. Scorsese and Wilson, 98.

43. Ray, 2000, 92.

44. Scorsese and Wilson, 120.

45. Rosenbaum, 2000, 90.

46. Comolli and Narboni, 25.

47. Scorsese and Wilson, 122.

48. Huyssen, 55.

49. Huyssen, 220.

50. Scorsese and Wilson, 71.

51. Rosenbaum, 2000, 185.

52. Arkush, 58–59.

53. Ibid., 59.

54. Martin Scorsese, "Why Make Fellini the Scapegoat for New Cultural Intolerance?" *New York Times* (Nov. 25, 1993), A26.

55. Andrew Ross, *No Respect: Intellectuals and Popular Culture* (New York: Routledge, 1989), 2.

56. Ibid., 3.

57. Alberto Pezzotta, "A Journey through Italian Cinema," Senses of Cinema (Jan. 2003) http://sensesofcinema.com/2003/feature-articles/journey_italian/ (assessed July 20, 2012).

58. Kent Jones, "Roughing Up the Surface: Simon Schama and Martin Scorsese Talk about How They Make History," *Civilization*, Feb.-Mar. 1998, 88.

59. Ibid., 82.

60. Ibid., 88.

61. Ibid., 83.

62. It received six votes in the 2002 *Sight and Sound* poll, three from critics and three from directors.

63. John Hess, "*The Godfather Part II*: A Deal Coppola Couldn't Refuse," *Jump Cut* no. 7 (1975), 1.

64. Hess, 1975, 1.

65. Hess, 1975, 1.

66. Kolker, 2000, 201.

67. Roger Ebert, "*GoodFellas*," *Chicago Sun–Times* (Sept. 2, 1990); in *Scorsese by Ebert*, 120–123.

68. Kelly, 2004, 268.

69. Roger Ebert, "*Miller's Crossing*," *Chicago Sun–Times* (Oct. 5, 1990).

70. For a discussion of the Coen brothers and growing legitimacy of postmodern pastiche as an artistic style, see Michael Z. Newman, "Pastiche as Play: The Coen Brothers," chap. 4 in *Indie: An American Film Culture*, ed. Michael Z. Newman (New York: Columbia University Press, 2011), 141–181. While I agree with most of Newman's points, throughout this study postmodern film practice still lacks the same degree of legitimacy of cinematic modernism, which is one of the reasons Scorsese keeps a distance from this indie culture.

71. Like *GoodFellas*, *Pulp Fiction* overwhelmingly won the Best Film prize from the National Society of Film Critics as well as the top prize at a major European film festival (Berlin for *GoodFellas*, Cannes for *Pulp Fiction*). In the 2002 *Sight and Sound* poll, *Pulp Fiction* received seven votes, compared to six for *GoodFellas*.

72. Jeffrey Sconce, "Irony, Nihilism and the New American 'Smart' Film," *Screen* 43, no. 4 (Winter 2002), 349–369.

73. Roger Ebert, "When *Taxi Driver* meets *Pulp Fiction*," *Chicago Sun–Times* (Feb. 9, 1997).

74. Ebert, 1997.

75. Kolker, 2000, 249.

76. Ibid., 250–251.

77. Ibid., 248.

78. Ian Christie, "The Rules of the Game," *Sight and Sound* 12, no. 9 (Sept. 2002), 27.

79. Nick James, "Modern Times," *Sight and Sound* 12, no. 12 (Dec. 2002), 20–23.

80. Rosenbaum, 2004, 210–216.

81. For example: Susan Sontag, "The Decay of Cinema," *New York Times* (Feb. 25, 1996); "The Moviegoers: Why Don't People Love the Right Movies Anymore?" *New Yorker* (Apr. 6, 1998), 94–101.

82. Taylor, 151.

83. Haberski, 183.

84. Martin Scorsese, "Outline for a Preservation Strategy," 1980 (Scorsese File, Museum of Modern Art, New York).

85. Taylor, 157.

86. Leo Enticknap, "Some Bald Assertion by an Ignorant and Badly Educated Frenchman: Technology, Film Criticism, and the 'Restoration' of *Vertigo*," *Moving Image* 4, no. 1 (Spring 2004): 137.

87. Ibid., 137.

88. Thompson and Christie, 165.

89. Dennis Wharton, "Scorsese Plugs for Artists' Rights on Hill," *Variety*, Mar. 20, 1995, 20.

Chapter 5. What Is Scorsese? Scorsese's Role in Contemporary Postmodern Culture

1. Robin Wood, *Hollywood from Vietnam to Reagan* (New York: Columbia University Press, 1986), 260.

2. Thompson and Christie, 92.

3. Jeffrey Sconce, "Irony, Nihilism and the New American 'Smart' Film," *Screen* 43, no. 4 (Winter 2002): 349–369.

4. By 1990, after the American Independent Cinema had begun to crossover into the mainstream with the huge success of *sex, lies and videotape* (Steven Soderbergh, 1989), *The King of Comedy* started to be reevaluated, often positioned with other contemporary films that had been overlooked including, for example, Stephen Mamber, "Parody, Intertextuality, Signature: Kubrick, DePalma, Scorsese," *Quarterly Review of Film Studies* 12, no. 1–2 (March 1990), 29–35, and Timothy Corrigan, "Spinning the Spectator: Fans and Terrorists in the Third Generation (*The King of Comedy, The Third Generation, My Beautiful Laundrette*)," in *A Cinema without Walls: Movies and Culture after Vietnam* (New Brunswick, NJ: Rutgers University Press, 1991), 197–227. Most recently, noted film critic Jonathan Rosenbaum included the film in his article, "A Dozen Undervalued Movie Satires," with the telling comment, "I didn't warm to Martin Scorsese's own poisoned valentine to the world of show biz the first time I saw it, but it's grown steadily in stature ever since." http://www.dvdbeaver.com/film/articles/dozen_undervalued_movie_satires.htm (assessed July 20, 2012)

5. "The late 1970s and start of the 1980s was a period in which the infrastructure [of American Independent Cinema] began to consolidate," Geoff King, *American Independent Cinema* (Bloomington: Indiana University Press, 2005), 20.

6. For example, see Amy Taubin, "Beyond the Sons of Scorsese," *Sight and Sound* 2, no. 9 (Sept. 1992): 37. Also reprinted in *American Independent Cinema: A Sight and Sound Reader*, ed. Jim Hillier (London: British Film Institute, 2001), 89–92.

7. King, 2005, defines independent cinema through five considerations, to which he devotes a chapter each: Industry, Narrative, Form, Genre, and Alternative

Visions. As he states: "Industrial factors are important, but do not provide the only grounds for definition of the particular varieties of filmmaking to which the label independent has most prominently been attached in recent decades" (9).

8. Sconce, 350.

9. One should note that none of the films Sconce mentions were big box-office successes. The difference is, however, is that they were made cheaply and aimed at this small demographic; thus they were not considered failures. *The King of Comedy*, however, was made as a studio film with big stars and was intended for a more general audience.

10. Les Keyser, *Martin Scorsese* (New York: Twayne Publishing, 1992), 137.

11. Sconce, 352.

12. For a detailed description of Scorsese as an auteur signature, see Patrick Phillips, "Genre, Star and Auteur—Critical Approaches to Hollywood Cinema," in *An Introduction to Film Studies*, ed. Jill Nelmes, 2nd ed. (London: Routledge, 1999), 202–203.

13. Roger Ebert, "The King of Comedy," *Chicago Sun–Times*, May 15, 1983; in *Scorsese* by Ebert: 68–70.

14. William Ian Miller, " 'I Can Take a Hint': Social Ineptitude, Embarrassment, and *The King of Comedy*," in *The Movies: Texts, Receptions, Exposures*, ed. Laurence Goldstein and Ira Konigsberg (Ann Arbor: University of Michigan Press, 1996), 76–97.

15. Robert B. Ray, *A Certain Tendency of the Hollywood Cinema, 1930–1980* (Princeton, NJ: Princeton University Press, 1985), 351.

16. Peter Biskind, *Down and Dirty Pictures: Miramax, Sundance, and the Rise of Independent Film* (New York: Simon and Schuster, 2004), 298.

17. King, 2005, 197.

18. Sconce, 352.

19. Ibid., 359.

10. Thompson and Christie, 88.

21. Sconce, 353.

22. Ibid., 354. With regard to *Seinfeld*, one of the show's stars, Jason Alexander, was very skeptical about the possibility for the program's success. In a retrospective documentary included on the DVD box set (*Seinfeld Vol. 1*), he recalls saying to the show's cocreator, Jerry Seinfeld, that the show will never work: "The only people who will like this show are people like me, and I don't watch television." In other words, Alexander felt that *Seinfeld* was "too smart" for television. However, one can explain its success in part to the growing popularity of independent cinema and the growing backlash against "dumb" movies and television. The same year *Seinfeld* premieres, independent cinema has its first major success: *sex, lies and videotape*.

23. Although this incident has become infamous, it is worth recounting briefly. Hinckley, a figure who clearly identified with the lead character of *Taxi Driver*, became obsessed with the film and its young costar, Jodie Foster. He then attempted to assassinate Reagan to gain her attention, not unlike the assassination attempt in *Taxi Driver*. As a result, Scorsese and his film came under a

certain amount of scrutiny and criticism for inciting violence. One should also note the then-recent assassination in New York City of John Lennon by Mark Chapman as a further context to the film.

24. Sconce, 364.

25. Wood, 269.

26. Andrew Britton, "Blissing Out: The Politics of Reaganite Entertainment," *Movie* 31-32 (Winter 1986): 2.

27. For example, see David A. Cook, "Auteur Cinema and the 'Film Generation' in 1970s Hollywood," in *The New American Cinema*, ed. Jon Lewis (Durham, NC: Duke University Press, 1998), 11–37. Cook writes, "Scorsese may be the only director of 'the film generation' who still passionately cares about the medium *as such*. This is evident in his own work as from his tireless efforts on behalf of film preservation and restoration, which extend from the resurrection of 70mm epics like *Lawrence of Arabia* (David Lean, 1962) and *El Cid* (Anthony Mann, 1961) to the reissue on videocassette of classics like Michael Powell's *Black Narcissus* (1947) or Nicholas Ray's *Johnny Guitar* (1954)" (28).

28. Gregory Solman, "Anamorphobia," in *Projections 4: Filmmakers on Filmmaking* (ed. John Boorman et al) (London: Faber and Faber, 1995), 29–39.

29. Steve Daly, "Technical Knockout," *Entertainment Weekly*, Feb. 15, 1991, 73.

30. Ibid., 43.

31. The Criterion Collection started making laser discs in 1984 with the release of a special edition of *Citizen Kane*. Their focus was mainly classical Hollywood films and art house staples, with a few rare contemporary films such as *Blade Runner* (Ridley Scott, 1982), *The Princess Bride* (Rob Reiner, 1987), and *Ghostbusters* (Ivan Reitman, 1984). None of these films had nearly the same level of critical prestige as Scorsese's films.

32. Daly, 74.

33. Klinger, 2006, 11.

34. Ibid., 20.

35. Mitsubishi advertisement, "Martin Scorsese on Television," *Video Review*, May 1988.

36. Martin Scorsese, "Letter from IFC," Apr. 1, 1997 (Scorsese File, Museum of Modern Art, New York).

37. Http://www.film-foundation.org/common/11004/aboutNewsStory.cfm?QID=8109&ClientID=11004&TopicID=0&sid=1&ssid=3 (assessed on July 20, 2012)"

38. Roger Ebert, "Guilty Pleasures," *Film Comment* 14, no. 4 (July-Aug. 1978): 49–51.

39. Martin Scorsese, "Martin Scorsese's Guilty Pleasures," *Film Comment* 14, no. 5 (Sept.-Oct. 1978): 63–66.

40. Ibid., 66.

41. Martin Scorsese, "Internal Metaphors, External Horror," in *David Cronenberg*, ed. Wayne Drew (London: British Film Institute, 1984), 54.

42. Ibid., 54.

43. Ibid., 54.

44. Martin Scorsese, "Martin Scorsese's Video Picks," *Premiere*, Oct. 1987, 91.

45. Martin Scorsese, "John Cassavetes, My Mentor," 1989; available in the booklet for DVD release of the Criterion Collection Cassavetes box set.

46. See chap. 1 in King, 2005, "Industry," 11–57.

47. Martin Scorsese, "Amid Clowns and Brutes Fellini Found the Divine," *New York Times* (Oct. 24, 1993), H21.

48. Martin Scorsese, "*Europa '51 (The Greatest Love)*," in *The Hidden God: Film and Faith*, ed. Mary Lea Bandy and Antonio Monda (New York: Museum of Modern Art, 2003), 76.

49 This tendency to stress the emotional impact of European cinema can be extended into Scorsese's treatment of Michael Powell, both through various audio commentaries as well as introductions to Powell's work. See Scorsese's forewords to Ian Christie, *Arrows of Desire: The Films of Michael Powell and Emeric Pressburger* (London: Faber and Faber, 1994), xv; and Michael Powell, *Million Dollar Movie* (New York: Random House, 1995), ix. Scorsese can be heard in the audio commentary for Powell and Pressburger's *The Life and Death of Colonel Blimp* (1943), *Black Narcissus* (1947), *The Red Shoes* (1948), and *The Tales of Hoffmann* (1951).

50. Martin Scorsese, "Ida Lupino: Behind the Camera, a Feminist," *New York Times Magazine*, Dec. 31, 1995, 43.

51. Martin Scorsese, "The Men Who Knew Too Much," *Premiere*, Sept. 1997), 70.

52. Potter, 374.

53. Jonathan Rosenbaum, "Scenes from an Overrated Career," *New York Times*, Aug. 4, 2007, http://www.nytimes.com/2007/08/04/opinion/04jrosenbaum.html?pagewanted=all (assessed July 20, 2012).

54. Martin Scorsese, "The Man Who Set Film Free," *New York Times*, Aug. 12, 2007, http://www.nytimes.com/2007/08/12/movies/12scor.html (assessed July 20, 2012); Woody Allen, "The Man Who Asked Hard Questions," *New York Times*, Aug. 12, 2007, http://www.nytimes.com/2007/08/12/movies/12alle.html (assessed July 20, 2012).

55. One example of this is Scorsese's introduction to the DVD release of the South Korean film *Woman Is the Future of Man* (Hong Sang–soo, 2004).

56. For an example of this perspective on Hollywood remakes as cultural imperialism, see Thomas Leitch, "Twice–Told Tales: Disavowal and the Rhetoric of the Remake," in *Dead Ringers: The Remake in Theory and Practice*, ed. Jennifer Forrest and Leonard R. Koos (Albany: SUNY Press, 2002), 37–62.

57. Steven E. Savern, "Robbie Robertson's Big Break: A Reevaluation of Martin Scorsese's *The Last Waltz*," *Film Quarterly* 56. no. 2 (Winter 2002-2003): 27.

58. Ibid., 27.

59. Ibid., 26.

60. See Levon Helm and Stephen Davis, *This Wheel's on Fire: Levon Helm and the Story of The Band* (Chicago: Chicago Review Press, 2000); Helm also appears on an audio commentary track on the DVD release of the film.

61. Bourdieu, 1984, 19.

62. Ibid., 19.

63. Charles Burnett, *"Warming by the Devil's Fire,"* in *Martin Scorsese Presents the Blues: A Musical Journey*, ed. Peter Guralnick, Robert Santelli, Holly George–Warren, and Christopher John Farley (New York: Harper–Collins, 2003), 100.

64. Martin Scorsese, *"Feel Like Going Home,"* in *Martin Scorsese Presents the Blues: A Musical Journey*, ed. Peter Guralnick, Robert Santelli, Holly George–Warren, and Christopher John Farley (New York: Harper–Collins, 2003), 64.

65. Andrew Ross, *No Respect: Intellectuals and Popular Culture* (New York: Routledge, 1989), 69.

66. Nelson W. Aldrich, "What's Wrong with Celebrity Guest Editors?" *Civilization*, Feb.-Mar. 1998, 11.

67. Martin Scorsese, "From Martin Scorsese," *Civilization*, Feb.–Mar. 1998, 55.

68. Ibid., 55.

69. Martin Scorsese, "Sacred Images," *Civilization*, Feb.–Mar. 1998, 68–75.

70. Garry Wills, "War Refugee," *Civilization*, Feb.–Mar. 1998, 65–67.

71. Terry Teachout, "The Genius of Pure Effect," *Civilization*, Feb.–Mar. 1998, 43–44.

72. Peter Biskind, "Slouching Towards Hollywood," in *Martin Scorsese: Interviews*, ed. Peter Brunette (Jackson: University of Mississippi Press, 1999), 196.

73. Dade Hayes, "Birth of a Nation," *Variety*, Dec. 9–15, 2002), A2.

74. A listing of the major reviews of the film can be found at: http://www.metacritic.com/movie/gangs-of-new-york (assessed July 20, 2012)

75. "Scorsese signs with Paramount," *The Guardian* (Nov. 8, 2006), http://www.guardian.co.uk/film/2006/nov/08/news.martinscorsese (assessed July 20, 2012)

76. Peter Biskind, *Down and Dirty Pictures: Miramax, Sundance, and the Rise of Independent Film* (New York: Simon and Schuster, 2004), 437–469.

77. For a summary of *Ray*'s reception, see: http://www.metacritic.com/movie/ray (assessed July 20, 2012). For a summary of *The Aviator*'s reception, see: http://www.metacritic.com/movie/the-aviator (assessed July 20, 2012)"

78. Chris Nashawaty, "Back on the Mean Streets," *Entertainment Weekly*, Sept. 22, 2006, http://www.ew.com/ew/article/0,,1537678,00.html (assessed July 20, 2012).

79. *The Departed* grossed $132 million domestically with a $90 million budget; http://www.imdb.com/title/tt0407887/business (assessed on July 20, 2012). It also received some of the best reviews of the year: http://www.metacritic.com/movie/the-departed (assessed on July 20, 2012).

80. David Bordwell analyzes the conventionality of *The Departed*'s style in his essay *"The Departed*: No Departure"*: available online at: change to "The Departed: No Departure," (October 10, 2006); http://www.davidbordwell.net/blog/2006/10/10/the-departed-no-departure/ (assessed July 20, 2012).

81. Scorsese and Wilson, 165–166.

82. One should note that Scorsese is not alone in seeing Kazan as an outsider despite his HUAC cooperation. See Brian Neve, *Elia Kazan: The Cinema of an American Outsider* (New York: Palgrave Macmillan, 2009). Neve devotes a chapter to Kazan's HUAC testimony, but underestimates the importance of

Kazan's testimony to his ability to be an "outsider" in his post–*On the Waterfront* work. He does acknowledge a certain irony in his very well–written concluding sentence, "For all his outsider's perspective, and his infamous 1952 testimony, Kazan's cinematic project would have been easier had the blacklist not disrupted the potential of others of his generation to join him in welding new cinematic forms and approaches to mainstream American practice" (196).

83. See Richard Schickel, *Elia Kazan: A Biography* (New York: HarperCollins, 2005), particularly chap. 12, "Testimonies," 251–272.

84. While the notion of judgment on Kazan is not a simple task, it is important not to apologize for or diminish his actions, however one may view him as a filmmaker. My own position is closest to Jeff Young, who published a book of interviews celebrating Kazan's artistry while making clear his negative view of Kazan's testimony, even challenging him directly toward the conclusion of their conversations. See Young, *Kazan: The Master Director Discusses His Films: Interviews with Elia Kazan* (New York: Newmarket Press, 2001), esp. p. 331.

85. Typical of the critical response (admittedly limited because it did not play theatrically), Rob Nelson calls the film "quite possibly the most tender documentary ever made about movies." See Nelson, "Martin Scorsese Finally Tells His Hero How He Feels," *Village Voice*, Sept. 22, 2010), http://www.villagevoice.com/2010-09-22/film/scorsese-letter-to-elia-kazan/ (assessed July 20, 2012).

Conclusion. The Next Scorsese (?), The Future of Artistic Reputations in American Cinema

1. Tom Carson, "The Next Scorsese," *Esquire*, March 2000, 217.

2. Andrew Sarris, "The Next Scorsese: Kevin Smith," *Esquire*, March 2000, 218.

3. Tom Carson, "The Next Scorsese: Alexander Payne," *Esquire*, March 2000, 223.

4. Todd McCarthy, "The Next Scorsese: Paul Thomas Anderson," *Esquire*, March 2000, 221.

5. Kenneth Turan, "The Next Scorsese: David O. Russell," *Esquire*, March 2000, 220.

6. Martin Scorsese, "The Next Scorsese: Wes Anderson," *Esquire*, March 2000, 225.

Sources

Author's Interviews

Bolles, Harry, Nov. 11, 2006.
Butman, John, Oct. 18, 2006.
Del Costello, Mark, Aug. 20, 2008.
Lenzer, Don, Dec. 15, 2006.
Rea, Peter, Sept. 10, 2004.
Summer, Ed, Aug. 2, 2009.
Tanis, Nick, Mar. 25, 2007.

Writings by Martin Scorsese (Listed Chronologically)

"Martin Scorsese's Guilty Pleasures." *Film Comment* 14, no. 5 (Sept.–Oct. 1978):
63–66.
"À mes amis et collègues: Au sujet de nos films." *Positif* no. 232–233 (July–
Aug. 1980): 126–127.
"Outline for a Preservation Strategy." 1980. Scorsese File, Museum of Modern
Art, New York.
"Confessions of a Movie Brat." In *Anatomy of the Movies*. Edited by David Pirie.
New York: Macmillan, 1981.
"Internal Metaphors, External Horror." In *David Cronenberg*. Edited by Wayne
Drew. London: British Film Institute, 1984.
"Martin Scorsese's Video Picks." *Premiere*, October 1987.
"John Cassavetes, My Mentor." 1989; available in the booklet for DVD release of
the Criterion Collection Cassavetes box set.
Acceptance Speech: American Cinematheque Award, The Moving Picture Ball.
March 22, 1991. Scorsese File, Museum of Modern Art, New York.
"Amid Clowns and Brutes Fellini Found the Divine." *New York Times*, Oct. 24,
1993, H21.
"Why Make Fellini the Scapegoat for New Cultural Intolerance?" *New York
Times*, Nov. 25, 1993, A26.

"Foreword." In *Arrows of Desire: The Films of Michael Powell and Emeric Pressburger*. Edited by Ian Christie. London: Faber and Faber, 1994.

"Foreword." In *Million Dollar Movie*. Edited by Michael Powell. New York: Random House, 1995.

"Ida Lupino: Behind the Camera, a Feminist," *New York Times Magazine*, Dec. 31, 1995, 43.

"Letter from IFC." April 1, 1997. Scorsese File, Museum of Modern Art, New York.

"The Men Who Knew Too Much." *Premiere*, Sept. 1997, 70.

"From Martin Scorsese." *Civilization*, Feb.–Mar. 1998, 55.

"Sacred Images," *Civilization*, Feb.–Mar. 1998, 68–75.

"The Next Scorsese: Wes Anderson," *Esquire*, March 2000, 225.

"*Europa '51 (The Greatest Love)*." In *The Hidden God: Film and Faith*. Edited by Mary Lea Bandy and Antonio Monda. New York: Museum of Modern Art, 2003.

"*Feel Like Going Home*." In *Martin Scorsese Presents the Blues: A Musical Journey*. Edited by Peter Guralnick, Robert Santelli, Holly George–Warren, and Christopher John Farley. New York: Harper–Collins, 2003.

"The Man Who Set Film Free." *New York Times*, Aug. 12, 2007).

Scorsese, Martin, and Michael Henry Wilson. *A Personal Journey with Martin Scorsese through American Movies*. New York: Hyperion, 1997.

Selected Bibliography

Arkush, Allan. "I Remember Film School." *Film Comment* 19, no. 11 (November 1983): 57–59.

Barthes, Roland. "The Death of the Author." In *Image–Music–Text*, edited and translated by Stephen Heath, 142–148. London: Fontana, 1977.

Becker, Howard S. *Art Worlds*. Berkeley: University of California Press, 1982.

Bickerton, Emile. "Adieu to Cahiers: Life Cycle of a Cinema Journal. *New Left Review* 42 (Nov.–Dec. 2006): 69–97.

Biskind, Peter. *Easy Riders, Raging Bulls: How the Sex–Drugs–and Rock n' Roll Generation Saved Hollywood*. New York: Simon and Schuster, 1998.

———. *Gods and Monsters: Thirty Years of Writing on Film and Culture from One of America's Most Incisive Writers*. New York: Nation Books, 2004.

Blake, Richard A. *Street Smart: The New York of Lumet, Allen, Scorsese, and Lee*. Lexington: University Press of Kentucky, 2005.

Bliss, Michael. *The Word Made Flesh: Catholicism and Conflict in the Films of Martin Scorsese*. Lanham, MD: Scarecrow Press, 1995.

Bordwell, David, Kristin Thompson, and Janet Staiger. *The Classical Hollywood Cinema: Film Style and Mode of Production to 1960*. New York: Columbia University Press, 1985.

Bourdieu, Pierre. *Distinction: A Social Critique of the Judgement of Taste*. Translated by Richard Nice. Cambridge, MA: Harvard University Press, 1984.

————. *The Field of Cultural Production*. Edited and intro by Randal Johnson. New York: Columbia University Press, 1993.

————. *Outline of a Theory of Practice*. Translated by Richard Nice. New York: Cambridge University Press, 1977.

————Braudy, Leo. "The Sacraments of Genre: Coppola, DePalma, Scorsese." *Film Quarterly* 39, no. 3 (1986): 17–28.

Britton, Andrew. "Blissing Out: The Politics of Reaganite Entertainment." *Movie* 31–32 (Winter 1986): 1–42.

————. "The Philosophy of the Pigeonhole: Wisconsin Formalism and 'The Classical Style.'" *CineAction!* 15 (1988): 47–63.

Bruce, Bryan. "Martin Scorsese: Five Films," *Movie* 31–32 (Winter 1986): 88–94.

Brunette, Peter, ed. *Martin Scorsese: Interviews*. Jackson: University of Mississippi Press, 1999.

Carney, Ray. *Cassavetes on Cassavetes*. New York: Faber and Faber, 2001.

Casillo, Robert. *Gangster Priest: The Italian American Cinema of Martin Scorsese*. Toronto: University of Toronto Press, 2006.

Caughie, John, ed. *Theories of Authorship*. London: Routledge, 1981.

Christie, Ian. *Arrows of Desire: The Films of Michael Powell and Emeric Pressburger*. London: Faber and Faber, 1994.

Christie, Ian. "The Rules of the Game." *Sight and Sound* 11, no. 9 (Sept. 2002): 24–27.

Comolli, Jean–Louis, and Jean Narboni. "Cinema/Ideology/Criticism." In *Movies and Methods*, ed. Bill Nichols, 22–30. Berkeley: University of California Press, 1976.

Connelly, Marie Katheryn. *Martin Scorsese: An Analysis of His Feature Films, with a Filmography of His Entire Directorial Career*. London: MacFarland, 1991.

Cook, David A. *Lost Illusions: American Cinema in the Shadow of Watergate and Vietnam, 1970–1979*. New York: Scribner's, 2000.

Cook, Pam. "Masculinity in Crisis?" *Screen* 23, no. 4 (Sept.–Oct. 1982): 39–46.

Corrigan, Timothy. *A Cinema without Walls: Movies and Culture after Vietnam*. New Brunswick, NJ: Rutgers University Press, 1991.

Daly, Steve. "Technical Knockout." *Entertainment Weekly*, Feb. 15, 1991, 73–74.

Dargis, Manohla. "'It Just Jumped Out of My Head Like an Animal': *Taxi Driver*, 20 Years Later." *Los Angeles Weekly*, Feb. 16–22, 1996, 31–32.

Decherney, Peter. *Hollywood and the Culture Elite: How the Movies became American*. New York: Columbia University Press, 2005.

Donato, Raffaele. "Docufictions: An Interview with Martin Scorsese on Documentary Film." *Film History* 19, no. 2 (2007): 199–207.

Dougan, Andy. *Martin Scorsese: The Making of His Movies*. London: Orion, 1997.

Ebert, Roger. "Guilty Pleasures." *Film Comment* 14, no. 4 (July–Aug. 1978): 49–51.

Ebert, Roger. *Scorsese by Ebert*. Chicago: University of Chicago Press, 2008.

Ehrenstein, David. *The Scorsese Picture: The Art and Life of Martin Scorsese*. New York: Birch Lane Press, 1992.

————. "Wise Guy," *Image*, Sept. 23, 1990, 8–13.

Enticknap, Leo. "Some Bald Assertion by an Ignorant and Badly Educated Frenchman: Technology, Film Criticism and the 'Restoration' of *Vertigo*." *Moving Image* 4, no. 1 (Spring 2004): 130–141.

Farber, Manny. *Negative Space: Manny Farber on the Movies*. New York: Praeger, 1971.

Farber, Stephen. "Has Martin Scorsese Gone Hollywood?" *New York Times*, Mar. 30, 1975, C1, C13.

Fensch, Thomas. *Films on the Campus*. New York: Barnes, 1970.

Fine, Marshall. *Accidental Genius: How John Cassavetes Invented the American Independent Film*. New York: Miramax Books, 2006.

Fish, Stanley. *Is There a Text in Tis Class? The Authority of Interpretive Communities*. Cambridge, MA: Harvard University Press, 1980.

Foucault, Michel. *Language, Counter–Memory, Practice*. In *Language, Counter–Memory, Practice: Selected Essays and Interviews*, ed. Donald F. Bouchard and trans. Donald F. Bouchard and Sherry Simon. Oxford: Blackwell, 1977.

Frick, Caroline. *Saving Cinema: The Politics of Preservation*. New York: Oxford University Press, 2011.

Friedman, Lawrence S. *The Cinema of Martin Scorsese*. New York: Continuum, 1997.

Gans, Herbert J. *Popular Culture and High Culture: An Analysis and Evaluation of Taste*. New York: Basic Books, 1974

Gracy, Karen Frances. *Film Preservation: Competing Definitions of Value, Use, and Practice*. Chicago, IL: Society of American Archivists, 2007.

Grist, Leighton. *The Films of Martin Scorsese 1963–1977: Authorship and Context*. Basingstoke, Eng.: St. Martin's Press, 2000.

Guralnick, Peter et al., eds. *Martin Scorsese Presents the Blues: A Musical Journey*. New York: Harper–Collins, 2003.

Haberski, Raymond. *It's Only a Movie: Films and Critics in American Culture*. Lexington: University Press of Kentucky, 2001.

Herrnstein–Smith, Barbara. "Contingencies of Value." *Critical Inquiry* 10 (Sept. 1983): 1–35.

Hess, John. "La Politique des Auteurs (Part One), Worldview as Aesthetic." *Jump Cut* no. 1 (May–June 1974): 19–22, and "La Politique des Auteurs (Part Two), Truffaut's Manifesto," *Jump Cut* no. 2 (July–Aug. 1974): 20–22.
———. "*Godfather II*: A Deal Coppola Couldn't Refuse." *Jump Cut* no. 7 (1975): 1, 10–11; reprinted in *Movies and Methods Volume I*, ed. Bill Nichols, 81–90. Berkeley: University of California Press, 1976.

Hirschberg, Lynn. "The Directors: Woody Allen and Martin Scorsese." *New York Times Magazine*, Nov. 16, 1997, 94.

Huyssen, Andreas. *After the Great Divide: Modernism, Mass Culture, Postmodernism*. Bloomington: Indiana University Press, 1986.

James, Nick. "Modern Times." *Sight and Sound* 11, no. 12 (Dec. 2002): 20–23.

Johnson, Ross. "The Next Scorsese." *Esquire* 133 (Mar. 2000): 216–225.

Jones, Kent. "Roughing Up the Surface: Simon Schama and Martin Scorsese Talk about How They Make History." *Civilization*, Feb.–Mar. 1998, 82–89.

Kael, Pauline. *For Keeps*. New York: Dutton, 1994.

Kaplan, James. "The Outsider." *New York*, Mar. 4, 1996, 32–40, 101.

Kapsis, Robert. *Hitchcock: The Making of a Reputation*. Chicago: University of Chicago Press, 1992.

Kellman, Steven G. *Perspectives on Raging Bull*. New York: G. K. Hall, 1994.

Kelly, Mary Pat. *Martin Scorsese: The First Decade*. Pleasantville, NY: Redgrave, 1980.

———. *Martin Scorsese: A Journey*. New York: Thunder's Mouth Press, 2004.

Keyser, Les. *Martin Scorsese*. New York: Twayne, 1992.

King, Geoff. *New Hollywood Cinema: An Introduction*. New York: Columbia University Press, 2002.

King, Geoff. *American Independent Cinema*. Bloomington: Indiana University Press, 2005.

Klinger, Barbara. *Beyond the Multiplex: Cinema, New Technology, and the Home*. Berkeley: University of California Press, 2006.

———. " 'Cinema/Ideology/Criticism' Revisited: The Progressive Genre." In *Film Genre Reader III*, ed. Barry Keith Grant, 75–91. Austin: University of Texas Press, 2003.

Kolker, Robert Philip. *A Cinema of Loneliness: Penn, Kubrick, Scorsese, Coppola, Altman*. New York: Oxford University Press, 1980.

———. *A Cinema of Loneliness: Penn, Kubrick, Scorsese, Spielberg, Altman*. 2nd ed. New York: Oxford University Press, 1988.

———. *A Cinema of Loneliness: Penn, Stone, Kubrick, Scorsese, Spielberg, Altman*. 3rd ed. New York: Oxford University Press, 2000.

Kouvaros, George. *Where Does It Happen? John Cassavetes and Cinema at the Breaking Point*. Minneapolis: University of Minnesota, 2004.

Levy, Emmanuel, ed. *Citizen Sarris, American Film Critic: Essays in Honor of Andrew Sarris*. Lanham, MD: Scarecrow Press, 2001.

Lewis, Jon. *Whom God Wishes to Destroy: Francis Coppola and the New Hollywood*. Durham, NC: Duke University Press, 1995.

Lewis, Jon, ed. *New American Cinema*. Durham, NC: Duke University Press, 1998.

Lippe, Richard. "*New York, New York* and the Hollywood Musical." *Movie* 31–32 (1986): 95–100.

LoBrutto, Vincent. *Martin Scorsese: A Biography*. Westport, CT: Praeger, 2008.

Lourdeaux, Lee. *Italian and Irish Filmmakers in America: Ford, Capra, Coppola, Scorsese*. Philadelphia: Temple University Press, 1990.

Lyons, Charles. *The New Censors: Movies and the Culture Wars*. Philadelphia: Temple University Press, 1997.

Mamber, Stephen. "Parody, Intertextuality, Signature: Kubrick, DePalma, Scorsese." *Quarterly Review of Film Studies* 12, no. 1–2 (1990): 29–35.

Mariani, John. "The Four Horsemen and the Apocalypse." *Attenzione* (July 1979): 40–44.

Menand, Louis. "Wise Guy: How Martin Scorsese Works the System." *New Yorker*, Dec. 8, 1997, 111–115.

Miller, William Ian. "'I Can Take a Hint': Social Ineptitude, Embarrassment, and *The King of Comedy*" In *The Movies: Texts, Receptions, Exposures*, ed. Laurence Goldstein and Ira Konigsberg, 76–97. Ann Arbor: University of Michigan Press, 1996.

Monaco, James. American Film Now. New York: Zoetrope, 1984.

Morrison, Susan. "An Interview with Martin Scorsese." *CineAction!* 6 (Fall 1986): 3–11.

Morrison, Susan. "Sirk, Scorsese and Hysteria: a Double(d) Reading." *CineAction!* 6 (Fall 1986): 17–25.

Morrison, Susan. "La Haine, Fallen Angels, and Some Thoughts on Scorsese's Children." *CineAction!* no. 39 (Dec. 1995): 44–50.

Murray, Edward. Nine American Film Critics: A Study of Theory and Practice. New York: Ungar, 1975.

Nair, Kartik. "Aura, Auteurism and the *Key to Reserva*," *Wide Screen*, 1, no. 2 (June 2010): 1–19.

Naremore, James. *More than Night: Film Noir and Its Contexts*. Berkeley: University of California Press, 1998.

Neale, Steve. "New Hollywood Cinema," *Screen* 17, no. 2 (Summer 1976): 117–122.

Neve, Brian. *Elia Kazan: The Cinema of an American Outsider*. New York: Palgrave Macmillan, 2009.

Newman, Michael Z. Indie: An American Film Culture. New York: Columbia University Press, 2011.

Nichols, Bill. *Representing Reality: Issues and Concepts in Documentary*. Bloomington: Indiana University Press, 1991.

Nicholls, Mark. *Scorsese's Men: Melancholia and the Mob*. Melbourne, Australia: Pluto Press, 2004.

Patterson, Patricia, and Manny Farber. "The Power and the Gory." *Film Comment* 12, no. 3 (May–June 1976): 26–32.

Perkins, V. F. *Film as Film: Understanding and Judging Movies*. Harmondsworth, Eng.: Penguin Books, 1972.

Pezzotta, Alberto. "A Journey through Italian Cinema." *Senses of Cinema* no. 26 (May–June 2003), http://sensesofcinema.com/2003/feature-articles/journey_italian/ (assessed July 20, 2012).

Phillips, Patrick. "Genre, Star and Auteur—Critical Approaches to Hollywood Cinema." In *An Introduction to Film Studies*, ed. Jill Nelmes, 2nd ed., 161–208. London: Routledge, 1999.

Potter, James Cole. "Martin Scorsese and the Poetics of Post–Classical Authorship." PhD Diss., Northwestern University, 1998.

Powell, Michael. *Million Dollar Movie*. New York: Random House, 1995.

Ray, Robert B. *A Certain Tendency of the Hollywood Cinema 1930–1980*. Princeton, NJ: Princeton University Press, 1985.

———. *How a Film Theory Got Lost (And Other Mysteries in Cultural Studies)*. Bloomington: Indiana University Press, 2001.

Raymond, Marc. "Politics, Authorship and History: The Production, Reception and Marginalization of Street Scenes 1970." *Film History* 22, no.2 (June 2010): 133–147.

———. "Too Smart, Too Soon: The King of Comedy and American Independent Cinema Sensibility." *Film Criticism* 34, no. 1 (Fall 2009): 17–35.

Riley, Robin. *Film, Faith, and Cultural Conflict: The Case of Martin Scorsese's* The Last Temptation of Christ. London: Praeger, 2003.

Rosen, Marjorie. "New Hollywood: Martin Scorsese Interviewed," *Film Comment* 11, no. 2 (Mar.–Apr. 1975): 42–46.

Rosenbaum, Jonathan. *Essential Cinema: On the Necessity of Film Canons.* Baltimore, MD: John Hopkins University Press, 2004.

———. "Hell on Wheels." *Chicago Reader*, Mar. 1, 1996, 37–39.

———. *Movie Wars: How Hollywood and the Media Conspire to Limit What Films We Can See.* Chicago: Chicago Review Press, 2000.

Ross, Andrew. *No Respect: Intellectuals and Popular Culture.* New York: Routledge, 1989.

Sarris, Andrew. *The American Cinema: Directors and Directions 1929–1968.* New York: Dutton, 1968.

———. "The Independent Cinema." In *The New American Cinema: A Critical Anthology*, ed. Gregory Battcock, 51–56. New York: Dutton, 1967.

———. "Notes on the Auteur Theory in 1962." In *The Primal Screen.* New York: Simon and Schuster, 1973; reprinted from *Film Culture*, no. 27 (Winter 1962–1963): 1–8.

———. *Politics and Cinema.* New York: Columbia University Press, 1978.

Savern, Stephen E. "Robbie Robertson's Big Break: A Reevaluation of Martin Scorsese's *The Last Waltz*," *Film Quarterly* 56, no. 2 (Winter 2002–2003): 25–31.

Schaefer, Eric. *'Bold! Daring! Shocking! True! A History of Exploitation Films, 1919–1959.* Durham, NC: Duke University Press, 1999.

Schickel, Richard. *Elia Kazan: A Biography.* New York: HarperCollins, 2005.

Schrader, Paul. "Notes on Film Noir." *Film Comment* 8, no. 1 (Spring 1972): 8–13.

———. *Transcendental Style in Film: Ozu, Bresson, Dreyer.* Berkeley: University of California Press, 1972.

Sconce, Jeffrey. "Irony, Nihilism and the New American 'Smart' Film." *Screen* 43, no. 4 (Winter 2002): 349–369.

Scorsese, Catherine. *Italianamerican: The Scorsese Family Cookbook.* New York: Random House, 1996.

Solman, Gregory. "Anamorphobia." In *Projections 4: Filmmakers on Filmmaking*, ed. John Boorman et al., 29–39. London: Faber and Faber, 1995.

Staiger, Janet. "The Politics of Film Canons." *Cinema Journal* 24, no. 3 (Spring 1985): 4–23.

Stern, Leslie. *The Scorsese Connection.* London: British Film Institute, 1995.

Taubin, Amy. "Beyond the Sons of Scorsese." *Sight and Sound* 2, no. 9 (Sept. 1992); reprinted in *American Independent Cinema: A Sight and Sound Reader*, ed. Jim Hillier, 89–92. London: British Film Institute, 2001.

———. "A Checkered Past." *Village Voice*, Feb. 20, 1996, 64.

———. "God's Lonely Man." *Sight and Sound* 9, no. 4 (April 1999): 16–19.

———. *Taxi Driver.* London: British Film Institute, 2000.

Taylor, Bella. "Martin Scorsese." In *Close-Up: The Contemporary Director*, ed. Jon Tuska, 293–368. Metuchen, NJ: Scarecrow Press, 1981.

Sources

Taylor, Greg. *Artists in the Audience: Cults, Camps, and American Film Criticism.* Princeton, NJ: Princeton University Press, 1999.

Thompson, David, and Ian Christie, eds. *Scorsese on Scorsese.* London: Faber and Faber, 1996.

Thompson, Richard. "Screen Writer: *Taxi Driver*'s Paul Schrader." *Film Comment* 12, no. 2 (Mar.–Apr. 1976): 7–19.

Tomasevskij, Boris. "Literature and Biography," In *Readings in Russian Poetics: Formalist and Structuralist Views,* ed. Ladislav Matejka and Krystyna Pomorska, 47–55. Ann Arbor: Michigan Slavic Publications, 1978.

Truffaut, François. "A Certain Tendency of the French Cinema." *Cahiers du Cinéma* no. 31 (Jan. 1954); reprinted in *Movies and Methods,* vol. 1, ed. Bill Nichols, 224–237. Berkeley: University of California Press, 1976.

Van Gunden, Kenneth. *Postmodern Auteurs: Coppola, Lucas, DePalma, Spielberg and Scorsese.* Jefferson, NC: McFarland, 1991.

Weiss, Marion. *Martin Scorsese: A Guide to References and Resources.* Boston: G. K. Hall, 1987.

White, Hayden. *The Content of the Form: Narrative Discourse and Historical Representation.* Baltimore, MD: John Hopkins University Press, 1978.

Wilinsky, Barbara. *Sure Seaters: The Emergence of Art House Cinema.* Minneapolis: University of Minnesota Press, 2001.

Wilson, Michael Henry. *Martin Scorsese: Entretiens avec Michael Henry Wilson.* Paris: Centre Pompidou/Cahiers du Cinéma, 2005.

Wood, Robin. *Hollywood from Vietnam to Reagan . . . and Beyond.* Rev. and exp. ed. New York: Columbia University Press, 2003.

Woods, Paul A., ed. *Scorsese: A Journey through the American Psyche.* London: Plexus, 2005.

Wyatt, Justin. *High Concept: Movies and Marketing in Hollywood.* Austin: University of Texas Press, 1994.

Index